BICKERSTAFF PAPERS

JONATHAN SWIFT

Jonathan Swift
An early portrait in the possession of C. Briscoe, Esq., Bellinter

JONATHAN SWIFT

BICKERSTAFF PAPERS

and Pamphlets on the Church

Edited by Herbert Davis

Oxford: Basil Blackwell: 1957

Printed in Great Britain
at the Shakespeare Head Press
Saint Aldates, Oxford.

Reprinted by photolithography 1957 by
The Compton Printing Works (London) Ltd.
and bound by
The Kemp Hall Bindery, Oxford.

The CONTENTS

C. CONTRIBUTIONS TO THE TATLER AND THE SPEC-
   TATOR ATTRIBUTED TO SWIFT OR CONTAINING
   HINTS FURNISHED BY HIM

ADDENDUM TO APPENDIX B

ILLUSTRATIONS

*Acknowledgement is gratefully made to C. Briscoe, Esq., of Bell-
inter, for permission to reproduce the frontispiece, and to Dr Francis
Bourke for the photographing of it; to Professor Nichol-Smith for per-
mission to reproduce the portrait of John Partridge from the rare copy of
'Merlinus Liberatus' in his possession; and to the Trustees of the British
Museum for that of Isaac Bickerstaff.*

FACSIMILES of TITLE PAGES, etc.

The INTRODUCTION

MOST of the works included in this volume were written in England, during a visit which lasted from November 29, 1707, until June 29, 1709. Swift accompanied[1] the Earl of Pembroke, the Lord-Lieutenant of Ireland, who had just been recalled from Dublin, and after visiting his mother for some weeks at Leicester, resumed his attendance upon the Lord-Lieutenant in London, staying at the house of their friend and companion in punning, Sir Andrew Fountaine.[2] He had come over to use the influence of his 'great friends' to obtain for the Irish Church the remission of the First-Fruits and the twentieth parts, such as had already been given to the English clergy. At the same time he hoped for some suitable preferment for himself. Within the first few weeks at London both these hopes were disappointed. On January 1, 1707-8, he warns Archbishop King that 'a new difficulty may arise in this matter, that it must perhaps be purchased by a compliance with what was undertaken and endeavoured in Ireland last sessions';[3] that is to say, that it would be granted only on condition that the Test Act should be repealed in Ireland. And not long afterwards, although he had been told that the Archbishop of Canterbury and the Court were strongly engaged on his behalf, he learned that the bishopric of Waterford had gone to another.[4]

Nevertheless he continued at once his campaign on behalf of the Church of England, which *A Tale of a Tub* had 'celebrated as the most perfect of all others in discipline and doctrine.'[5] He attacked its enemies, whether among the dissenters or free-thinkers, with all the power of his wit and humour; and he began

---

[1]See *Correspondence of Jonathan Swift*, ed. F. Elrington Ball, London, 1910-14, i, 60-63. [Afterwards referred to as *Corr.*]

[2]During this visit Sir Andrew Fountaine helped Swift to prepare illustrations for the fifth edition of *A Tale of a Tub*.

[3]*Corr.* i, 67.

[4]*Corr.* i, 69–70. See also C. H. Firth, *Dean Swift and Ecclesiastical Preferment*, R.E.S., ii, 2.

[5]See Vol. I of this edition, p. 2.

b

to make himself its apologist by setting forth clearly the sentiments of a moderate churchman with regard to politics and religion.

The first of these writings to appear was *Predictions for the Year* 1708[1] by Isaac Bickerstaff Esq, which was published before the end of January, 1708, and therefore must have been written and left with the printer before Swift went on a visit to the Berkeleys at Cranford on January 22.[2] It has not been sufficiently recognized hitherto that Swift's attack upon Partridge, the almanack-maker, was not merely a joke to amuse the town at the expense of a poor old quack, or even a superb finish to a campaign which had long been carried on by Tom Brown and Ned Ward and some of Partridge's rivals.[3] Swift attacked him also because of the violence with which he had abused the clergy of the Church of England. In his *Merlinus Liberatus* for 1706 there was enough to rouse Swift's anger; the opening verses in the Almanack were entitled *The Englishman's Humble Thanks to the Honourable Peers of England, both Temporal and Spiritual*, and this is the tone of them:

> Like Noble Patriots you our Chains have broke
> And bravely freed us from the *hated Yoak*.
> A Y O A K . . .
> By Papists forg'd, by Perkin's Friends fil'd o'er,
> By *High-Church* hugg'd, whose Seal & Stamp it bore.
> *High-Church!* the common Curse, the Nation's Shame.
> 'Tis only *Pop'ry* by another Name,
> The Shortest Way, Blood, Ruin to Excess,
> *Sa——ll's* Brimstone Church is nothing less.
> *Betray'd to France*, and had the Trick took place,

---

[1]See below, p. 139. It seemed better to arrange all the Partridge papers together, and to print them just before the *Tatlers*, at the end of this volume.

[2]John Forster, *Life of Jonathan Swift*, London, 1875, p. 213.

[3]W. A. Eddy, *Tom Brown and Partridge the Astrologer*, Mod. Phil. xxviii, 163. I am indebted to President Eddy for kindly allowing me to use photographs and materials on the Bickerstaff papers in his possession.

> They'd brought again their wish'd-for *Babe of Grace*,
> *Rome*'s little *Hobby-horse*, High Church's Heir;
> A special Bargain: Then we'd *Tack'd* it fair.

In George Parker's *Ephemeris* for 1707, Partridge is taunted for these verses, and exposed in every way for his false predictions and his swindling, but again in that year he prints verses addressed to the Peers, for 'sinking the Bill against Occasional Conformity':

> 'Twas such a Bill, it's like was never seen,
> To *Squeeze* the *Subjects*, and Embroil the *Queen*;
> To *Cramp* the *Nation*, clog the *Common Cause*,
> And set *High-Church* above the *Crown* and *Laws*:

There can be little doubt that Swift wished to put an end to this sort of popular propaganda against the Church; for this reason he chose Partridge as his butt rather than any of his rivals, though he speaks of them also with contempt.[1] The particular manner of attack was certainly suggested to him by Partridge's reiterated challenges to rival astrologers to compete with him in drawing nativities. In 1699, he had issued this challenge:

I do friendly and fairly Invite and Challenge my Adversaries and, in particular, *Gadbury* and *Coley*, who value themselves as Masters of the Art, to pitch upon five or ten Nativities, and like an Artist to tell the world in print which of them hath no *Hileg* who is *Giver of Life*, and who the Ananeta, who is the Poionosos, who the Poiothanatos; but above all, to tell us when they *will Dye*, with the Astrologic reasons thereof. And I will take the same Nativities, and treat of all those particulars according to my Method and Principles, and then every man may be judge who is true, and Master of his Trade, and who not.

In 1700, he had boasted of his skill in having foretold the death of Dr. *Francis Bernard*:

---

[1] See below, p. 142-3. Cf. also *The Account of Partridge's Death*, p. 153: 'On his "Death-Bed" he declared himself a Nonconformist, and had a fanatick Preacher to be his spiritual Guide.'

About four years before this Gentleman died, a Person of
Honour did request me to try my skill in this Nativity, and
tell him when he would dye; I did it, and gave it him under
my own hand fixed to the time he died, or near it, which he
hath by him to shew when he pleaseth;

Again in 1704 and in 1706 he had repeated this challenge; and
in 1707 Parker had exposed him for 'selling for £12 a Nativity
for a Gentlewoman, in which according to his Old Method,
there's all the promises of Felicity Imaginable in it. But she had
died the previous September at 42, the most loathsom Spectacle
of the Pox.'

Swift now accepted his challenge, and predicted that Partridge himself would die 'upon the 29th of March next, about
eleven at Night, of a raging Fever.' The joke took so well that all
sorts of pirated editions[1] of Swift's paper appeared within the
next few days. During February a reply appeared entitled *Mr.
Partridge's Answer etc.*[2] insinuating that Bickerstaff's *Predictions* were obviously the work of a 'Jacobite Shuffler' and boast-
ing that the end of March will plainly shew the Cheat. But the
best *Answer to Bickerstaff*[3] was written about February 5, though
it seems not to have been printed until it was included in Swift's
works among a collection of papers which had come into the
hands of Deane Swift, and first appeared in the eighth volume of
Hawkesworth's quarto edition in 1765. Whether it was written
by Swift himself or by one of his friends, it has a particular interest in that it contains an allusion which would identify Bickerstaff with the author of *A Tale of a Tub*, and may possibly for
that reason not have been printed.[4]

But there is no doubt about the authorship of the papers
which appeared at the end of March, announcing the death of
Partridge. The first was in the form of a *Letter to a Person of
Honour*,[5] giving an account of the accomplishment of the first of
Mr. Bickerstaff's *Predictions* within about four hours of his cal-
culations, and including an edifying paragraph giving Mr. Par-

[1]See facsimile of the t.p. of one of these pirated editions, p. xiii.
[2]See Appendix B, p. 201.   [4]See below, p. 199.
[3]See Appendix B, p. 195.   [5]See below, p. 151.

Esquire *Bickerstaff's*

Most strange and wonderful

PREDICTIONS

For the YEAR, 1708.

Wherein the Month and Day of the Month are set down, when several most surprizing Accidents shall certainly come to pass, as particularly that the present *French* King shall Die on the 29th of *July*. The Pope to Die the 11th of *September*. The *Dauphin* the *French* King's Son to dye on the 7th of *May*. That *Partridge* the famous Astrologer is to dye on the 29th of *March*. On the 23d of *May* a famous Actor of the Play-house will die a ridiculous death, suitable to his Vocation. Upon the 25th of *August*, will arrive from *Flanders* such a welcome Express of Victory, that a Thousand Bonfires will be made in London for Joy of the News, and in the same Month a Noble Admiral will gain immortal Honour, by obtaining a signal Victory at Sea On the 6th of *June* the City of *Paris* will be burnt down to the Ground. Towards the end of *August* will be great Mischief done in Bartholomew-Fair, by the tumbling down of a Booth; with several other strange Things too tedious here to be related.

Licensed according to Order.

Sold by *John Stiles*, 1708

tridge's confession and last words. The second was an elegy and epitaph in verse, first printed as a Broadside, elaborating brilliantly on Partridge's triple trade of 'Cobler, Starmonger, and Quack.'[1] Others now joined in the joke, and a very amusing paper appeared in April, entitled *Squire Bickerstaff Detected*.[2] Swift allowed it to appear in the *Miscellanies* of 1727, with a note that he had not written it; and in his own copy the words 'this piece' and 'not written' are underlined.[3] In Faulkner's edition of the *Works*, 1735, the note is altered and the author is said to have been 'that famous poet, Nicholas Row Esq.';[4] again, in 1755, this is contradicted by Hawkesworth who adds that 'the reverend Dr. Yalden, preacher of Bridewell, Mr Partridge's near neighbour, drew it up for him.'[5]

Meanwhile Swift was waiting for any opportunity to advance the business of the First-Fruits, and was becoming increasingly aware of the intentions of his friends among the Whigs to tamper with the Test clause. When later, in 1714, he discussed the change in the Queen's Ministry in 1710, he denied that he had been a favourer of the low party at this time: 'it hath been manifest to all men, that, during the highest dominion of that faction, I had published several tracts in opposition to the measures then taken.' He also claimed to have warned both Lord Somers and Lord Halifax against the danger of uniting the church, as one man, to oppose them; and boasted that they admitted afterwards when it was too late, that they had called to mind what he had said to them above five years before.[6]

Writing to Dean Sterne and to Archbishop King, in April,

---

[1]*Swift's Poems*, ed. H. Williams, Clarendon Press, 1937, p. 101. [Afterwards referred to as *Poems*.]

[2]See Appendix B, p. 217. It was attributed to Congreve by Addison, when he sent a copy to Lord Wharton two years later. See *Gent. Mag.* (Feb. 1786) LVI, 91.

[3]Copy of *Miscellanies*, 1727, in the possession of Lord Rothschild, I, 289.

[4]*Works*, Dublin, 1735, I, 167.

[5]*Works*, London, 1755, II, 161.

[6]*Memoirs Relating to that Change which happened in the Queen's Ministry in the Year* 1710.

1708, he refers to the activities of Broderick, the Irish Speaker, to get the Test clause repealed, and gives notice to the Archbishop of his intention to publish some paper in opposition to it.[1] Most likely he was already at work upon the tract in which he wished to clarify his own position and to state the point of view of the moderate churchmen, who distrusted the extremes of both parties.

It is clear that Swift was gathering materials for a volume, and that several of the pieces were written in the course of this summer. In a letter to Archbishop King, on June 10, he says: 'For myself, I have nothing to do here but to attend my Lord Lieutenant's motions, of whose return we are very uncertain, and to manage some personal affairs of my own.'[2] On September 14, in a letter to Ambrose Philips, he states more specifically what those affairs were, namely, 'every day writing by speculations in my chamber.'[3] And some time before the end of the year he made a list headed 'Subjects for a Volume', in which he included the first four tracts discussed below. It is impossible to say in what order they were written; they are printed in this edition as they were arranged by Swift in the *Miscellanies* and in the collected *Works*, 1735.

They all bear out his claim that already in 1708 he had taken up the position of a moderate churchman, opposed alike to the 'low party' of the Dissenters, the freethinkers and the moneyed men, and to the high Tories, who were either non-jurors or Jacobites. His views were in fact much nearer the views of Harley though he did not yet know him, than of his 'great friends' among the Whigs; like Harley, he refused to be driven into a purely partisan view, and to label himself Whig or Tory. His first tract is a plain statement of the *Sentiments of a Church of England Man with respect to Religion and Government*. 'I believe'— he says—'I am no bigot in Religion, and I am sure I am none in Government.' He maintains throughout an attitude of studied

---

[1] *Corr.* i, 82–9.   [2] *Corr.* i, 95.
[3] *Corr.* i, 111 and *note*. Perhaps Swift is using the phrase 'by speculations' in the sense indicated in the *Tatler*, No. 241: 'By-Words (as they call a Sentence a Man particularly affects).'

moderation, and hopes that if both parties cannot be persuaded to think him in the right, they may both equally decide to think him in the wrong; though he attempts to win the favour of some from both sides by stating simply and deliberately a preference, from which I believe he never swerved himself through the whole course of his life; 'I should think that, in order to preserve the Constitution entire in Church and State; whoever has a true value for both, would be sure to avoid the Extremes of Whig for the sake of the former, and the Extremes of Tory on account of the latter.'[1]

On the matter of Occasional Conformity he had been un-decided even at the time when, four years earlier, the Tory, High-Church party was in complete control of the House of Commons; finally, after being persuaded that the Whig Lords meant no harm to the Church, he had with some misgivings gone so far as to write against the Bill. But now that the Whigs were gaining power and influence, he is careful to explain that the opposition of Churchmen at that time was not because they did not recognize the practice of occasional conformity as an evil, but that the remedy seemed too violent. He then proceeds fur-ther to warn the Whigs that no Churchman will be found ready to give way on the Test Act, and recommends a definite policy for dealing with the dissenters: 'to preserve their Obedience upon all Emergencies, a Government cannot give them too much Ease, nor trust them with too little Power.'[2]

With regard to government his sentiments are equally moder-ate. He stresses the foolishness of party strife, and insists that in fundamentals there is much agreement. He maintains the same principles as he had set forth in the *Contests and Dissensions,* in 1701, admitting different forms of government, but not arbi-trary power; dictatorship whether of the One or the Many is worse than anarchy, 'as much as a Savage is in a happier State of Life than a Slave at the Oar.'[3] He draws a careful distinction be-tween the legislative and the administrative power, a distinction which had been overlooked by Hobbes and by the High-Church clergy, who had thus been misled into the doctrine of Non-

[1]See below, p. 25.   [2]See below, p. 12.   [3]See below, p. 15.

Resistance. As the sincerity of Swift's convictions are often doubted, it is well to remember his admiration for the pious and heroic members of the non-juring party. One of his earliest poems[1] had been written in honour of Archbishop Sancroft, who had been deprived for refusing the oath of allegiance to William and Mary; and here Swift refers to his acquaintance with the 'very pious, learned and worthy gentleman,'[2] Mr Robert Nelson, the author of *A Companion for the Feasts and Fasts of the Church of England; with Collects and Prayers for each Solemnity*, 1704, an extremely popular manual of devotion. But Jacobites like Charles Leslie,[3] who was constantly pouring out a torrent of extravagant abuse upon all the enemies of the Church and all the advocates of moderation, and who had in 1703 attacked Swift's *Contests and Dissensions*, seemed to him just as dangerous as the extremists of the low party.

Swift never wavered in accepting the Revolution settlement of 1688, and never doubted the wisdom of maintaining the Protestant succession after the death of Queen Anne. These Whig principles he approved because he thought they best promoted the good of Church and State; but he refused for that reason to call himself a Whig, or to promise any obedience to the leaders of that party. There was much that he disapproved of, especially their attitude of contempt for the clergy, their scandalous reflections upon the universities, and the liberty they allowed to freethinkers to attack the fundamental doctrines of Christianity.

Such a book, for instance, as Tindall's *Rights of the Christian Church asserted against the Romish and other Priests, who claim an independent Power over it; with a Preface concerning the Church of England, by law established* particularly roused Swift's anger. Tindall had boasted that it would 'make the clergy mad';[4] for it was a cleverly disguised attack upon the very idea of a national, state-supported Church.

---

[1] *Poems*, p. 33.
[2] See below, p. 21.
[3] See below, p. 13.
[4] See Dr George Hickes, *Preliminary Discourse to Spinoza Reviv'd*, 1709, p. 1.

Swift probably read it in 1707 (he possessed a copy of the third edition) and planned a detailed examination of particular passages of the book. He included these *Remarks* in his list of subjects for a Volume, but evidently abandoned the idea, as in a letter to Ford, dated March 8, 1709, he says: 'No, the Report of my Answering Tindall's Book is a Mistake; I had some thoughts that way, but they are long layd aside.'[1] He left Tindal to be answered by people like the Rev William Wotton and Dr Hickes; and to be dealt with later by the Grand Jury of Middlesex, who brought in a Presentment against the author, printer and publisher; and by the House of Commons, who in 1710 ordered the book to be publicly burned by the hangman.[2]

---

[1] *Letters to Ford*, ed. D. Nichol Smith, Clarendon Press, 1935, p. 5.

[2] The controversy was carried on with great violence for several years and Swift would have found himself in strange company among the crowd of Tindal's attackers. The first was the Rev. William Wotton, one of his victims in the *Battle of the Books*, who preached a sermon against Tindal's book on Sep. 2, 1706. Dr Potter, just before returning to Oxford as Regius Professor of Divinity, published his *Discourse of Church Government* against it in 1707; Dr Hickes, Dean of Worcester, who had been Tindal's tutor at Lincoln College, began a series of violent attacks in the same year with his *Two Treatises &c*, which reached a third, much enlarged edition in 1711. Dr Turner, the Rev. Samuel Hill, and Charles Leslie followed with a crowd of anonymous pamphleteers. To give the long unvaried titles of these tracts would not indicate the real grounds of the resentment of the clergy so well as the following remarks of Dr Hickes. He describes Tindal as an 'Author who hath licked up the Venom of *Hobbes*, *Selden*, *Spinoza* and *Marvel*, and disgorged it upon the Church:' as 'the Penman of the Deists'. His book is the 'One *Masterpiece* of their Antichristian Heresy, which before it was put to the Press passed through as many of their Hands to *patch* it up as neatly as they could, together, and give it all the Advantages, that Wit, and Malice could give it, to make it acceptable to a wicked World. In particular, it was perused by Mr *Lock* before he died, as the great Dispenser, and Preconizer of it at home and abroad.' For *Presentment of the Grand Jury*, see Appendix A. See also *House of Commons Journals*, March 25 & April 3, 1710.

He chose rather another method of attack, giving him more scope for his Bickerstaffian qualities, an attack upon the whole body of the deists and freethinkers, written in such a way that they themselves and their followers would be sure to read it. It was called *An Argument to prove that the Abolishing of Christianity in England may, as things now stand, be attended with some Inconveniences, and perhaps not produce those many good Effects proposed thereby*. This is, as Sir Walter Scott said, 'one of the most felicitous efforts in our language, to engage wit and humour on the side of religion;'[1] it is one of the best examples of that 'irony which Swift was born to introduce.'[2] It was, at that time, as Swift intended it to be, the best reply to 'the trumpery lately written by Asgil, Tindal, Toland, Coward, and forty more.'[3] But if I am not mistaken, it was also intended as an appeal by Swift to his great friends among the Whig leaders, in a manner and on a level which they would understand, to recognize the dangers which would result from any attack on the Church of England, as by Law established. With a scepticism rather like Mandeville's, he chose his ground in such a way that the most worldly-wise politician could not escape him; he was not so foolish as 'to stand up in the Defence of *real* Christianity. . . . To offer at the Restoring of that, would indeed be a wild Project; it would be to dig up Foundations; to destroy at one Blow *all* the Wit, and *half* the Learning of the Kingdom etc.'[4] He was only concerned with the advantages of preserving *Nominal* Christianity, and proving that that was preferable to open infidelity; just as in his *Project*, he insisted that though he did not hope for real virtue, even the appearance of virtue was better than open vice. On that firm foundation of scepticism and common sense, he could then indulge in Bickerstaffian gaiety and wit, rallying all the groups of the 'low party', and, almost without arousing any suspicions, pursue his main intention of meeting all criticisms put forward by those whose design was to destroy the power and influence of the Church by the repeal of the Test Act.

Swift intended to publish these papers in a volume which was

---

[1] *Swift's Works* ed. by Sir W. Scott (1814), VIII, 183.
[2] *Poems*, p. 555.   [3] See below, p. 29.   [4] See below, p. 27.

to have appeared in 1709, with a preface by Sir Richard Steele.[1] For some reason Swift or the printer delayed, and the volume did not appear until 1711. But, in the meantime, one of the papers was printed separately with a dedication to the Countess of Berkeley, and instead of a preface, Steele wrote a complimentary paragraph about it in the *Tatler*, April 20, 1709. It was entitled *A Project for the Advancement of Religion and the Reformation of Manners*, and was evidently a revision, with additions, of a paper included in Swift's list of October, 1708, called *A Project for the Reformation of Manners*. It seems to have been published about the beginning of April, and as usual Swift did not put his name to it, though he might well have done so, if he had written it primarily with a view to his own preferment. The author is described as 'a Person of Quality'. It is very significant also that in a hurried note sent to Swift by the Earl of Berkeley, recommending him to present a copy to the Queen, there is not the slightest hint that he had Swift's personal interests in view. He wrote: 'I earnestly entreat you, if you have not done it already, that you would not fail of having your bookseller enabling the Archbishop of York to give a book to the Queen; for, with Mr Nelson, I am entirely of opinion, that her Majesty's reading of that book of the project for the increase of morality and piety may be of very great use to that end.'[2] We do not know whether this was done, but it is unfair to assume that Swift must have neglected it, because we know that he got nothing out of it himself.

Among all the various attempts to improve the standard of public morals since the Revolution, Swift's proposal is at least dignified, sensible and practical. Like Defoe, he recognized the futility and the injustice of petty legislation against vices which were at the same time condoned by gentlemanly standards. He proposed, therefore, a perfectly logical scheme, which would enforce better standards among all those connected with the court and the government. As he was dealing with religious practices as well as with moral behaviour, his intention was here also to uphold the authority of the Established Church, and in

---

[1]*Corr.* i, 167 and 185.   [2]*Corr.* i, 152.

particular to appeal to the Queen to exert all the influence of the Court against its enemies—the men of pleasure, freethinkers, and despisers of religion among the 'low party', who 'rattle it out against Popery and Arbitrary Power, and Priestcraft and High Church.'[1]

Against all such, Swift's attitude had hardened since the moment when, owing to the death of the Prince on October 28, 1708, the Whig leaders had seized their opportunity to force certain changes upon the ministry, by making Pembroke, Lord High Admiral; Somers, Lord President of the Council; and Wharton, Lord Lieutenant of Ireland. Swift was then in close touch with Somers and Halifax, and naturally expected through their influence to obtain at last some satisfactory results both for the Irish Church and for himself. But he realized at the same time the danger that his Whig friends might now demand from him compromises that he would be unwilling to make. Writing to Archbishop King on November 9, he said: 'not knowing how far my friends may endeavour to engage me in the service of a new Government, I would beg your Grace to have favourable thoughts of me on such an occasion; and to assure you, that no prospect of making my fortune, shall ever prevail on me to go against what becometh a man of conscience and truth, and an entire friend to the Established Church.' And to Archdeacon Walls on the same day he wrote more bluntly: 'it is thought that most of those I have credit with will come into play. But yet, if they carry things too far, I shall go to Vienna, or even to Laracor, rather than fall in with them.'[2]

Before the end of the month Swift received a reply from Archbishop King, suggesting that his best way to preferment would be, if possible, to come over as chaplain to the new Lord Lieutenant. But Wharton had already appointed Dr Lambert, who had just made a bid for the favour of the Whigs by preaching the annual sermon to the Irish Protestants in London, urging a closer union between the Church and the Dissenters. Whereupon Swift, either out of revenge or to strengthen his own resolution, immediately wrote and published in December, 1708, *A*

---

[1] See below, p. 62.   [2] *Corr.* i, 117 and 120–1.

Letter from a Member of the House of Commons in Ireland to a Member of the House of Commons in England, Concerning the Sacramental Test. This was an emphatic challenge to the 'low party', and a warning to the Whig leaders not to attempt, even in Ireland, to tamper with the Test Act. Its tone is very different from the other papers we have been discussing. Swift appears as a champion both of Ireland and of the Established Church, and shows already the power that he was soon to put forth in support of Harley's government, and later on behalf of the rights of the Irish people. Here is his first cry of indignation against the attitude of the English government towards Ireland. 'If your little Finger be sore, and you think a Poultice made of our *Vitals* will give it any Ease, speak the Word and it shall be done.'[1] And then he proceeds to show the danger that it would bring to Ireland to repeal the Sacramental Test at that time.[2] It is still not exactly a party tract, nor written entirely from a Tory point of view. He is careful to point out that the lines are drawn very differently in Ireland, and that there are not six members of the Irish House of Commons who may not fairly be described as moderate Whigs, if that means supporting the present Crown and Establishment, and detesting Popery and the Pretender. He insists that the real danger in Ireland is not from the Papists, but from the Presbyterians and their abettors. And even for them a majority would readily admit such a Toleration by Law, as has been granted them in England; only, he adds with a grin, 'we make a mighty Difference here between suffering *Thistles* to grow among us, and wearing them for *Posies*.'[3]

This paper was written nearly two years before Swift began his campaign as a party writer for Harley, and at the time when

---

[1]See below, p. 114.

[2]Swift was not alone in this attitude. Cf. Letter from Addison to Lord Halifax, dated Dublin Castle, May 7, 1709: 'They (all parties) were under great apprehensions at his (Wharton's) first coming that He would drive directly at repealing the Test and had formed themselves into a strong Body for its defence, . . .' B. M. Add. MSS. 7121 (9).

[3]See below, p. 124.

his particular friends among the Whigs were at the height of their power. It shows Swift in an entirely independent and uncompromising position; and he included it more than twenty-five years later among his collected works, with a note indicating that it still expressed his views; indeed, 'the Author's Way of Reasoning seems at present to have more Weight, than it had in those Times, when the Discourse first appeared.'[1] Of course he had taken pains to disguise his hand. In its original form, it contained certain personal allusions which probably deceived its earliest readers in London, and convinced them that it was a genuine letter written by someone in Dublin. But it did not deceive the Archbishop of Dublin,[2] and therefore probably did not deceive Swift's friends in London, who must have enjoyed the fun of his oblique references to himself and to his rival, who had been appointed chaplain to Lord Wharton.

The supposed writer of the Letter from Dublin refers to gossip they had heard about two divines in London:

> I do not believe they are one degree greater Whigs than Five Hundred of their Brethren, and I have heard, that *one of them* (who is they say made chief Chaplain to our new Governour) has always declared against Repealing the *Test*; He is reckoned a worthy Person, and I know not how it can be consistent with that Character to employ his Pen either in a Public or Private manner against his Opinion, neither do I think he designs it. As for the *other Divine*, we all expected here that he was to be the Person his Excellency would bring over his Chaplain: But since that hath otherwise happened, it may not be altogether improbable that his great Friends have dropp'd him, which Disappointment, if he be a right Courtier may chance to cool his Zeal that way, if he had any before, of which I cannot accuse him. However that be, he will find it a difficult matter, with his Skill in Politicks, or Talent at Ridicule, backed by all the Wit he is said to be Master of, to Reason or laugh us out of the *Sacramental Test*; and will find by the Event that my PREDICTIONS are truer than *His*.[3]

Swift must have sucked in his cheeks several times with pleasure

---

[1] See below, p. 110.   [2] *Corr.* i, 137.   [3] See below, p. 284.

as he wrote that, first of Lambert, this worthy person who had just changed his views on the Test in time to get his chaplaincy, and secondly of himself as he was in the very act of proving by this pamphlet how much his Whig zeal, if he had ever had any, had already cooled.

There was little bitterness in Swift at this time; he seems to have been almost content with the role of Isaac Bickerstaff, which he took up again at the beginning of 1709. When John Partridge ventured to publish his Almanack again, and even to attack Bickerstaff with some violence, Swift replied at once in a triumphant paper, entitled *The Vindication of Isaac Bickerstaff Esq.* and had no trouble in finding further evidence in this new Almanack to prove that John Partridge was certainly dead.[1] And soon after followed *A Famous Prediction of Merlin*, in which Swift parodied the political prophecy, giving it the very appearance of a sixteenth century translation by printing the verses in black-letter, and adding explanatory notes. To complete the verisimilitude, he refers to a volume printed by Johan Haukyns in 1530, and promises 'to have the very Book sent to the Printer of this Paper, with Directions to let any Body see it that pleases; because, I believe, it is pretty scarce.'[2]

----

[1] Further proofs of Partridge's death appeared in *Bickerstaff's Almanack for the Year* 1710. For facsimile of the t.p and an extract, see Appendix B, pp. 229 and 231.

The next year appeared *The British Visions: or, Isaac Bickerstaff's Twelve Prophecies for the Year* 1711. . . . Printed first in the North, and now Reprinted at London. A closer imitation of the *Predictions* was shown to me by Mr D. Nichol Smith, who has a copy in his possession—*Predictions For the Year*, 1712. *By Isaac Bickerstaff, Esq; In a Letter to the Author of the Oxford Almanack*. Printed in the Year, 1712. An academic paper, with satirical references to Bentley's edition of Horace, and to Toland's conversion to Christianity.

[2] It has caused some amusement that Dr Johnson really believed that Swift was annotating a sixteenth century Prophecy of Merlin. It would not be surprising to find that he was parodying an actual prophecy, though I have not succeeded in discovering it. It has not been pointed out that he was at least referring to an actual printer, Johan Haukyns, who was in London in 1530, when he completed the printing of Palsgrave's *Lesclarcissement de la Langue Francoyse*.

Before he left London on May 5, 1709, he was probably engaged in launching Isaac Bickerstaff on the most famous part of his career; for, although I shall have to show that Swift may have contributed less to the *Tatler* than has been generally supposed, I shall suggest that he had more to do with it at the start than is implied by his lending Steele the pseudonym Bickerstaff.

We know that Swift was constantly in Steele's company during the greater part of this visit to England, when he was in London, for he refers to their regular meetings in several letters; and one such reference in particular gives us a glimpse of him towards the end of August, 1708, in the Gazeteer's office, behaving in a manner which suggests that he had made himself at home there:

> In the last Gazette it was certainly affirmed that there would be a battle: but the copy coming to the office to be corrected I prevailed with them to let me soften the phrase a little, so as to leave some room for possibilities;[1]

In a letter of March 22, 1709, to Colonel Hunter, who was still a prisoner in Paris, he requests 'that you will henceforward address your letter for me at Mr. Steele's office at the Cockpit, who has promised his care in conveying them.'[2] And in the same letter there is a remark which might possibly be taken as a hint of the project which, at this time, three weeks before the appearance of the first *Tatler*, must have been already planned:

> The vogue of operas holds up wonderfully, though we have had them a year; but I design to set up a party among the wits to run them down by next winter, if true English caprice does not interpose to save us the labour.

Addison had probably been too busy to come into any such scheme; he was 'in amphibious circumstances'—preparing to go

---

[1] *Corr*. i, 106.

N.B. When Swift returned to England in 1710, he arranged for his letters from Ireland to be sent to him under cover to the Gazeteer's office.

[2] *Corr*. i, 145.

[3] *Corr*. i, 142.

over with Lord Wharton as Secretary of State for Ireland, yet still attached to Lord Sunderland's office. But as the first *Tatler* appeared just a few days after he had left London, it is strange that it was launched without his knowledge.[1] He did not begin to contribute regularly until his return to London at the end of the summer. But Swift, having just printed his *Project for the Advancement of Religion etc.* and completed his edition of the *Memoirs, Part III*, of Sir William Temple, was free to help Steele in the new venture.

In the Preface to the Fourth Volume of the *Tatler*, Steele begins his account of the assistance he had had in that perform-mance with acknowledgments to Dr Swift,

> whose pleasant Writings, in the Name of Bickerstaff, created an Inclination in the Town towards any Thing that could appear in the same Disguise. I must acknowledge also, that at my first entring upon this Work, a certain uncommon Way of Thinking, and a Turn in Conversation peculiar to that agreeable Gentleman, rendered his Company very advan-tageous to one whose Imagination was to be continually em-ployed upon obvious and common Subjects, though at the same Time obliged to treat of them in a new and unbeaten Method. His Verses on the *Shower in Town*, and the *Description of the Morning*, are Instances of the Happiness of that Genius, which could raise such pleasing Ideas upon Occasions so barren to an ordinary Invention.[2]

This must mean that Swift not only lent Steele the good will of Isaac Bickerstaff, which was of considerable value in starting a new paper, but also provided him with hints and suggestions for the earliest papers. Bickerstaff's Vindication of himself against Partridge is referred to in the first *Tatler*, and the argu-ment repeated and carried further, thus:

---

[1] This may be assumed from Tickell's statement; see Addison, *Works*, 1720, I, xii: 'He was in that Kingdom [Ireland], when he first discovered Sir *Richard Steele* to be Author of *The Tatler*, by an observation upon *Virgil*, which had been by him communicated to his friend.'

[2] *Tatler* (1710) IV, A5a.

I have in another Place, and in a Paper by it self, sufficiently convinc'd this Man that he is dead, and if he has any Shame, I don't doubt but that by this Time he owns it to all his Acquaintance: For tho' the Legs and Arms, and whole Body of that Man may still appear and perform their animal Functions; yet since, as I have elsewhere observ'd, his Art is gone, the Man is gone. I am, as I said, concern'd, that this little Matter should make so much Noise; but since I am engag'd, I take myself oblig'd in Honour to go on in my Lucubrations, and by the Help of these Arts of which I am Master, as well as my Skill in Astrological Speculations, I shall, as I see Occasion, proceed to confute other dead Men, who pretend to be in Being, that they are actually deceased.[1]

Here, I suggest, we may catch a glimpse of the soul of Bickerstaff in actual process of transmigration.[2] I shall make no claim that Swift actually wrote any of the papers that appeared during April, before No. 9, which contained his *Description of the Morning*; but I think there can be little doubt that these early papers contain many hints and suggestions given by Swift to Steele, or directly worked up from Swift's conversation. I shall instance only one, in No. 4, dated from Will's Coffee House, April 18, on the subject of Italian opera, which we know, from the letter quoted above, Swift was eager to attack. I do not think it was Swift who 'fell into fits in the Gallery, at seeing, not only Time and Place, but Languages and Nations confus'd in the most incorrigible Manner;' but I am sure that it was Swift who promised to publish a treatise against operas, with 'a very elaborate Digression upon the *London Cries*, wherein he has shown from Reason and Philosophy, why Oysters are cried, Cardmatches sung, and Turneps and all other Vegetables neither cried, sung, nor said, but sold with an Accent and Tone neither natural to Man or Beast.'[3]

Two days later, from Will's Coffee-House, Steele reports in his best manner of happy compliment the impression made by a little Treatise, called *A Project for the Advancement of Religion; Dedicated to the Countess of Berkeley*, concluding with a sentence

---

[1] *Tatler* (1710) I, 8–9.   [2] See below, p. 257.   [3] *Ibid.*, I, 29.

of which the very tone is carefully chosen to suit the temper of Swift: 'It was said by one of this Company, alluding to that Knowledge of the World the Author seems to have, the Man writes much like a Gentleman, and goes to Heaven with a very good Mien.'[1] Later in 1714, when they had become bitter political opponents, Steele refers to this compliment, as a proof of his feelings towards Swift then: 'The Gentleman I here intended was Dr Swift; this kind of Man I thought him at that time: We have not met of late, but I hope he deserves the Character still.'[2]

In the *Tatler*, No. 7, there is a further reminder of the Partridge connection, and Mr Bickerstaff's last will and testament is given with a wealth of detail, which may quite probably include some hints from Swift, such as the following:

Item, I give my Wit, (as Rich Men give to the Rich) among such as think they have enough already. And in case they shall not accept of the Legacy, I give it to Bentivolio, to defend his Works from Time to Time, as he shall think fit to publish 'em.

Item, I bestow my Learning upon the Honourary Members of the Royal Society.[3]

No. 10 is the first of the papers by Mrs Jenny Distaff, Half-sister to Mr Bickerstaff, all of which were once attributed to Swift.[4] But there is definite evidence against his authorship; Steele himself later states that some of them were written by Addison.

After Swift's departure Steele may well have felt despondent before the task of carrying on his venture alone, as he indicates in the paper, *From my own Apartment, May* 10. But he says he had been ordered to go on in his design of observing upon things, and forbearing persons; and perhaps he had been promised further assistance. As Dr Elrington Ball pointed out, Swift wrote to Steele three times from Leicester, on May 11 and 26,

---

[1] *Tatler* (1710), I, 37.
[2] *Mr Steele's Apology for Himself and his Writings; Occasioned by his Expulsion from the House of Commons*, London, 1714, p. 49.
[3] *Tatler* (1710) I, 57.
[4] *Tatler*, ed. by John Nichols, London, 1786, II, 447.

and on June 13, and then no more until October 30, 1709, in reply to a letter from Steele complaining that he had never heard from him since his return to Ireland.

'In face of these facts,' says Dr Ball, 'the only conclusion which seems to me possible is that the contributions to the "Tatler" during the year 1709, hitherto attributed to Swift ("Prose Works," ix, 5-37), did not come from his pen, however much they may owe to his influence—a view in which I feel greatly strengthened by the opinion of Sir Henry Craik ("Life," i, 255 note) that in several cases the style is unlike that of Swift. As regards the contents of the three letters which Swift sent to Steele from Leicester, I venture to suggest contributions to the "Tatler" which have been never before assigned to Swift.'[1]

The first of these suggestions, a letter dated from Bath on May 11, hardly sounds like Swift, and has little to recommend it but the date. It is not included here; but the other two are reprinted in the *Appendix* as probably Swift's work. The second, from *Tatler* No. 21, is a letter from York dated May 16. There is some evidence to show that Swift may have made a visit to York at this time.[2] The letter itself is not convincing, but the reference in the Postscript to the Advertisements[3] suggests the hand of Swift, as we know that he disapproved of their increasing prominence in the paper. The third, the letter from *Tatler* No. 31, bears so obvious a resemblance to Swift's *Polite Conversation* that it might well be accepted as indubitably his contribution.

The first contribution in prose which has usually been attributed to Swift is part of the *Tatler*, No. 32, from White's Chocolate-house, June 22. This was a satire upon Mary Astell's *A Serious Proposal to the Ladies* (1694) 'to erect a monastery or religious retirement, being not only a retreat from the world for

---

[1]*Corr.* i, 166 *n.*

[2]See *Journal to Stella*, Feb. 21, 1712–13, where Swift refers to a letter from Mrs Davis, a schoolmaster's widow, at York. 'She reproaches me for not writing to her these four years.' This might mean that Swift had been in York in May, 1709.

[3]See below, p. 236–7.

those who desire that advantage, but likewise, an institution and previous discipline, to fit us to do the greatest good in it.' Nichols says[1] it was sent in by Addison, although he was little more than the amanuensis for Swift; but this is impossible as Swift did not arrive back in Ireland in time to have collaborated with Addison. It was an immediate reply to *Bart'lemy Fair: Or, An Enquiry after Wit; In which due Respect is had to a Letter concerning Enthusiasm, To my Lord XXX. By M. Wotton.* And this theme may have been suggested to Steele by Swift. This was, at any rate, the view put forward by the author, Mary Astell, in her *Advertisement* to the second edition, published in 1722:

This Treatise though it appear'd at first under a borrow'd Name, happen'd to be ascrib'd to one who sees nothing in it to be asham'd of. It drew upon her indeed the Resentments of that sort of Men of Wit who are here expos'd, and was the true Cause, of a Fable which the worthy *Tatler* was pleased to invent and publish a little after the Enquiry appear'd; though he thought fit to give another Reason when he was charg'd with doing what was so contrary to his Professions in many of his *Tatlers*, where he wou'd seem to pay Respect to Religion and Vertue.

. . . But tho' the *Enquirer* had offended the *Tatler*, and his great Friends, on whom he so liberally bestows his Panegyrics, by turning their Ridicule very justly upon themselves; what had any of her Acquaintance done to provoke him? Who does he point at? For she knows of none who ever attempted to *erect a Nunnery*, or declar'd, *That Virginity was to be their State of Life*. . . .

The *Tatler* tells a Tale very agreeably, when he pleases, but he has scatter'd none of his *Attic* salt on this. One cannot help pitying him to see how he writes against the Grain, and labours under the Task his noble Benefactors impos'd. The harmless Satyr does not bite; and tho' it shew'd its teeth against the *Proposal to the Ladies*, our honest *Compilator* has made an honourable Amends to the Author, (I know not what he has to the Bookseller) by transcribing above an hun-

---

[1]*Tatler*, 1786, II, 449 ff.

dred Pages into his *Ladies Library, verbatim*; except in a few Places, which if the Reader takes the Trouble to compare, perhaps he will find improv'd.[1]

It is difficult to believe that Swift had anything to do with the writing of this harmless satire that does not bite; it is therefore not reprinted here.

After his return to Ireland Swift was in touch with Addison, whose first contribution had been printed as early as May 20; and together they may have been responsible for hints. But Swift, as we have noticed already, sent nothing himself, and Steele complained of this early in October, 1709: 'I wonder you do not write sometimes to me.'[2] Dr Ball concludes therefore that Swift cannot have contributed any of the *Tatlers* published in August and September, 1709, which have been generally attributed to him.

But the very next sentence in Steele's letter has been, and may well be, taken as an indication that Swift had had something to do with Nos. 67 and 68, which contained proposals for an election of candidates for the tables of Fame: 'The town is in great expectation from Bickerstaff; what passed at the election for his first table being to be published this day sevennight.' This continuation (No. 81) was duly published on October 15. Nichols has a long note[3] in which he suggests that Addison had brought over from Ireland some contributions from Swift, including 67 and 68, but that the promised sequel had not followed. And he

---

[1] *An Enquiry after Wit* etc., London, 1722, p. A2a.
N.B. It is possible that Swift may have felt himself attacked by her in the following passages, and that he may have prompted Steele to write this satire.
'those who write Letters to Ladys, who *creep into Houses*, and with their *Tales of a Tub lead captive silly Women*.' p. 82.
'Now for a Man to live by Religion, to get Wealth, Honor and Reputation by it, and to treat it as *Judas* did its Divine Author, Hail and Betray it, is so Detestable, that he must be lost to all Sense of Honour and Common Honesty, who can be guilty of so base a Practice.' p.110.
[2] *Corr*. i, 166 and *note*.
[3] *Tatler*, 1786, III, 57 ff.

develops a laboured case to prove that Swift could not possibly have written Nos. 74 and 81, attributed to him by Hawkesworth. His argument is convincing; but he seems to have forgotten it, when later he revised Sheridan's edition of Swift in 1801, and included both these *Tatlers* among Swift's work.

I have printed in the Appendix the parts of Nos. 67 and 68 which are concerned with the Tables of Fame, mainly because Swift allowed it to be stated in 1735 that he had furnished hints for them, as well as for *Tatler*, No. 249, and *Spectator*, No. 50:

> It is well known that the Author writ several Tatlers, and some Spectators; and furnished Hints for many more. Particularly, *The Tables of Fame, The Life and Adventures of a Shilling, The Account of* England *by an* Indian *King*, and some others. But, as we are informed, he would never tell his best Friends the particular Papers.[1]

Swift remained in Ireland until the end of August, 1710, when he returned to London with the Lord Lieutenant in the midst of the fresh political excitement brought about by the removal of Godolphin from office.[2] During this time Swift had written his first tract connected with Irish politics, entitled *A Letter to a Member of Parliament in Ireland Upon Chusing a new Speaker there*. The Irish House of Commons had been prorogued in the summer of 1709 until March, 1710, and as Lord Middleton had retired from the Speaker's Chair, a new Speaker had to be elected before the next meeting. It seems most probable, therefore, that the *Letter* was written early in 1710, certainly before May 19, when the House actually met.[3] It is unlikely that it was published then, as no printed copy is known.

It contains further evidence of Swift's persistent opposition to the 'High-flying Whigs' and their endeavours to repeal the Test clause. For he urges one thing only: to choose a Speaker, whose opinion on the Test clause is known to be in accord with

---

[1] Reprinted below, p. 173 *n*.

[2] See Swift's letter to Archbishop King, from Lincoln, Sept. 9, 1710. *Corr*. i, 192 ff.

[3] The Journals of the House of Commons of the Kingdom of Ireland 1692–1713. *Memorandum*, p. 638.

the majority of the House, the moderate men who think it 'beneath the Policy of common Gardners to cutt down the only hedge that shelters from the North.' His position is unaltered; he is among the moderate men and 'far from an inclination to multiply Party Causes'; but he is a Church of England man, who is genuinely disturbed by the number of those 'who would talk at the same Rate if the Question were, not only about abolishing the Sacramental Test, but the Sacrament itself.'[1]

When Swift returned to England again in September, 1710, his mission was the same as it had been three years before. He was furnished on this occasion with a definite commission from the Bishops of Ireland about the First-Fruits, dated August 31, 1710.[2] And for himself he now had the advantage, if his old friends would not, or could not, give him preferment, of seeking others in the 'new world', where he would 'have the merit of suffering by not complying with the old.' His first letter to Archbishop King, on September 9, contains an account of the situation upon his arrival: 'I found myself equally caressed by both parties, by one as a sort of bough for drowning men to lay hold of; and by the other as one discontented with the late men in power, for not being thorough in their designs, and therefore ready to approve present things.'[3] He decided, therefore, to approach Mr. Harley who had formerly made some advances towards him and would be likely to use him well.

Nevertheless he continued to enjoy the company of his old friends, and constantly dined or spent the evening with Addison and Steele. Finding Steele weary of his task, Swift immediately set to work to provide him with some *Tatlers*.

In the *Journal to Stella* Swift writes on September 29: 'I made a *Tatler* since I came: guess which it is, and whether the bishop of Clogher smoaks it.' This was No. 230, which had appeared the day before; it was reprinted by Faulkner in 1735. It could not have been difficult for Stella to recognize, for it contained remarks about style and propriety in language which her master in these matters must have frequently talked over with her. Swift repeated them later in his *Proposal for Correcting, Improving,*

---

[1] See below, pp. 131-2.   [2] *Corr.* i, 191-2.   [3] *Corr.* i, 193.

and Ascertaining the English Tongue, and in his *Letter to a Young Clergyman*; and when he came to prepare a collected edition of his works, he insisted on the removal of abbreviations and elisions[1] which had almost become a convention in English printing, and even reintroduced into his own text the forms of the Prayer-Book which he here blames the younger clergy for modernizing.   He maintained, unlike some of his contemporaries, that the English language reached its perfection in the early part of the seventeenth century; and he was intentionally a little old-fashioned, both in his orthography and his usage. Above all, he disliked 'affected Modes of Speech', and in accordance with his own practice, approved only 'that Simplicity which is the best and the truest Ornament of most Things in human Life.'[2] This is the only contribution to the *Tatler* that we definitely know to be Swift's work, except the verses, which he also claimed. His *Shower* appeared on October 17. But in the *Journal to Stella* he certainly gives the impression that he wrote also at least two more *Tatlers* in prose; and it is evident that his friends in Ireland tried to guess which they were, and did not succeed. It is therefore perhaps futile to try guessing now.

On October 4, he speaks of going to work at another *Tatler* and on the 7th, of 'going in charity to send Steele a *Tatler*, who is very low of late.' This may, or may not,[3] be the *Shower*, which is first referred to by name on October 10; on the 12th, Swift seems to have two pieces in hand: 'I have finished my poem on the *Shower*, all but the beginning, and am going on with my *Tatler*.' The latter is again mentioned on the following day as not yet written: 'I fancy you'll smoak me in the *Tatler* I am going to write; for I believe I have told you the hint.'

But it may never have been completed. It is not mentioned

---

[1] See below, p. 275.   [2] See below, p. 177.
[3] If Swift is not referring to the *Shower*, he may possibly mean a part of *Tatler*, No. 236 (IV, 264–7), concerning the importation of frogs into Ireland, which he mentions in a letter to John Temple June 15, 1706 (*Corr.* i, 58), and again in *Considerations about maintaining the Poor in Ireland*. I owe this suggestion to an unpublished paper kindly lent me by Mr P. V. Thompson. But I agree with him that the style does not seem like Swift.

again, and on November 3 Swift warns them instead: 'We have
scurvy *Tatlers* of late: so pray do not suspect me. I have one or
two hints I design to send him, and never any more; he does not
deserve it.' Swift had just taken over the *Examiner*, and it is unlikely that he contributed anything more than hints after this
date. At the end of November he says: 'The bishop is out entirely in his conjectures of my share in the *Tatlers*. I have other
things to mind.' And on November 30: 'I have just given him
one or two hints, and you have heard me talk about the *Shilling*.'
This is further explained on December 14: 'No, the *Tatler* of the
Shilling was not mine, more than the hint, and two or three
general heads for it. . . . and besides, the ministry hate to think
that I should help him, and have made reproaches on it; and I
frankly told them I would do it no more.' At the end of the year
Steele tired of it himself, and brought the *Tatler* to an end.

    Within ten days Swift set up a new Tatler, little Harrison,
whom he had described as 'a young poet, whose fortune I am
making.' The scheme, he says, was Mr Secretary St John's and
mine, and would have done well enough in good hands. But he
evidently had not much hope that Harrison would be successful.[1] However, he gave him a good deal of help to start it, and
Faulkner included No. 5 for January 27, and No. 20 for March 6,
1711, in Swift's *Works*, 1735. I have added in the Appendix Nos.
1 and 2, for January 13 and 16, and Nos. 302 and 306 for March
15 and March 24; because there is evidence in the *Journal to Stella*
to show that they were either suggested by Swift or revised by
him. Of the first he says: 'he was with me this morning and
evening, showing me his first, which comes out on Saturday.
. . . I recommended him to a printer, whom I sent for, and
settled the matter between them this evening. Harrison has just
left me, and I am tired with correcting his trash.' Of No. 2 he
says: 'I have given Harrison hints for another Tatler tomorrow.
The jackanapes wants a right taste: I doubt he won't do.' Of
No. 302 he says, on March 14: 'little Harrison the Tatler came
to me, and begged me to dictate a paper to him, which I was
forced in charity to do.'

---

[1] See *Journal to Stella*, Jan. 11, 1710–11.

The next day he reports that he has succeeded in getting 'the prettiest employment in Europe' for young Harrison; he is to go as secretary to the Ambassador Extraordinary at the Hague; 'so we shall lose the Tatlers in a fortnight.' No. 306 for March 24 describes the different forms Bickerstaff has assumed, and must have been at least suggested by Swift. The manner in which it is written is very like him; but he makes no reference to it at the time, and he did not recall it later to include it in his *Works*.

In the meantime Steele had started the *Spectator*; but it seems clear from Swift's reference to it that he was in no way concerned with this new venture. On March 16 he writes in the *Journal to Stella*:

> Have you seen the Spectator yet, a paper that comes out every day? 'Tis written by Mr Steele, who seems to have gathered new life, and have a new fund of wit; it is in the same nature as his Tatlers, and they have all of them had something pretty. I believe Addison and he club. I never see them; and I plainly told Mr Harley and Mr St. John, ten days ago, before my Lord-Keeper and Lord Rivers, that I had been foolish enough to spend my credit with them in favour of Addison and Steele; but that I would engage and promise never to say one word in their behalf, having been used so ill for what I had already done.

Nearly two years later, however, writing again on December 27, 1712, he claims that in spite of their coldness to him, he had continued to take more pains to recommend the Whig wits to the favour and mercy of the ministers than any other people:

> Steele I have kept in his place. Congreve I have got to be used kindly, and secured. Rowe I have recommended, and got a promise of a place. Philips I could certainly have provided for, if he had not run party mad, and made me withdraw my recommendation; and I set Addison so right at first, that he might have been employed, and have partly secured him the place he has; yet I am worse used by that faction than any man.

In view of these comments, and Swift's many activities during this period, it is unlikely that he made any contributions to the

Spectator, except indirectly, when Steele used up the hints Swift had formerly given him for the *Tatler*, as shown by the following statement in the *Journal to Stella*, on April 28, 1711:

> The Spectator is written by Steele with Addison's help: 'tis often very pretty. Yesterday it was made of a noble hint I gave him long ago for his Tatlers, about an Indian supposed to write his travels into England. I repent he ever had it. I intended to have written a book on that subject. I believe he has spent it all in one paper, and all the under hints there are mine too; but I never see him or Addison.

For the moment Mr Spectator was able to borrow a few of Isaac Bickerstaff's old jokes at the expense of the Whigs and the Tories; but 'the curse of party' had driven them apart. Nevertheless, even as 'Examiner', Swift continued to scoff at the use of these old party-labels,[1] and seems to have hoped, like Harley, to draw to the support of the new ministry the more moderate from both sides. He tried to prevent Steele and Addison and their friends from going into opposition; and when he did not succeed, he felt that he had been deceived by them, and that his genuine friendship for them had been slighted on account of party differences.[2]

As for his own attitude, he was clearly unconscious of any inconsistency or change of opinion. For in 1710, he had republished his *Tale of a Tub*, with its Dedication to Lord Somers, adding an *Apology* to show that, like the rest of his works, he had written it to support the Church of England against its enemies. At the same time he had left with Tooke, his printer, the rest of his miscellaneous pieces enough to make a volume, and now that it was no longer convenient to have them introduced by Steele, had promised him some hints for a preface, which he might 'get some friend to dress up'.[3] Tooke reminded him that he had promised some other pieces which were in Ireland; and as late as October 17, 1710, Swift was still attempting

---

[1] See *Examiner*, Vol. III, of this edition, p. 15.
[2] See *Journal to Stella*, March 16, 1710–11.
[3] *Corr.* i, 185–6.

to procure a copy of his letter to the Bishop of Killaloe with the help of Stella:

> 'I'd give a penny the letter to the bishop of Kilaloe was in it: 'twould do him honour. Could not you contrive to say you hear they are printing my Things together; and that you wish the bookseller had that letter among the rest: but don't say any thing of it as from me. I forgot whether it was good or no; but only having heard it much commended, perhaps it may deserve it.'

When the *Miscellanies* appeared, Swift remarks characteristically to Stella on February 28:

> Some bookseller has raked up everything I writ, and published it t'other day in one volume; but I know nothing of it, 'twas without my knowledge or consent: it makes a four shilling book, and is called Miscellanies in Prose and Verse. Tooke pretends he knows nothing of it, but I doubt he is at the bottom. One must have patience with these things; the best of it is, I shall be plagued no more. However, I'll bring a couple of them over with me for MD, perhaps you may desire to see them. I hear they sell mightily.

This manner of denying all responsibility for the publication of books, which his friends knew perfectly well had been planned and prepared by him with considerable care, became a habit of playful irony by which later biographers and editors have sometimes been and may still be deceived. Beneath this irony we can see here the satisfaction and pleasure Swift took in the publication of all the things the bookseller had raked together and associated with the well-known successes of Isaac Bickerstaff. And three months later, when Curll put out a pirated edition, he was probably not much perturbed, though the name of Dr Swift appeared on the title-page. For although the genuine and pirated editions contained a medley of pieces, written between 1701 and 1710, there was nothing among them to cause Swift embarrassment. Indeed, he probably arranged for the publication of the *Miscellanies* in order to vindicate himself from any charge of treachery, by revealing his views on matters concerning Church and State, as he had written them down as early as 1708.

If he had changed his opinion of certain persons, like Godolphin, the Lord Treasurer, whom he had praised in his Preface[1] to Sir William Temple's *Memoirs, Part III*, in 1709, and had now lampooned in *The Virtues of Sid Hamet the Magician's Rod*,[2] and if further he had now chosen new friends after the late Ministry had fallen because they had refused to listen to his warnings, that is sufficiently explained in a short note, obviously provided by Swift himself to serve as Advertisement to the *Letter concerning the Sacramental Test*:

> The following Letter is supposed by some judicious Persons to be of the same Author, and if their Conjectures be right, it will be no disadvantage to him to have it here revived, considering the Time when it was Writ, the Persons then at the Helm, and the Designs in Agitation, against which this Paper so boldly appeared. I have been assured that the Suspicion which the supposed Author lay under for Writing this Letter, absolutely ruined him with the late M(ini)stry. I have taken leave to omit about a Page which was purely Personal, and of no use to the Subject.[3]

The omission, which as we have seen above referred to Swift's own hopes of preferment and the possible cooling of his zeal for some of his great friends, would obviously be out of place in this volume; but the rest of this pamphlet, giving his astonishingly rigorous and unchanging views on the Sacramental Test, is the real clue to all his actions during these difficult years. This piece above all he was anxious to revive, and with it the letter to the Bishop of Killaloe, which he failed to obtain. The latter is one of the lost writings of Swift, and I do not remember that anyone has suggested what the subject of that letter is likely to have been. It is, I think, a probable conjecture that it was about the same topic, the attack on the Test; and that Swift addressed

---

[1] See Vol. I of this edition, p. 268.
[2] See *Poems*, pp. 131 ff.
[3] *Miscellanies in Prose and Verse*, 1711, p. 314.

it to the Bishop of Killaloe because some years before he had been assaulted by Thomas Broderick, who shook him by his lawn sleeve, and told him in a very threatening manner 'that he hoped to live to see the day when there should not be one of his order in the kingdom'.[1]

But the contents of the *Miscellanies* were not wholly political; they showed the variety of Swift's talents in both verse and prose. They showed him as the leading wit of the age, with a gift of fun and humour, by which he had achieved immense popularity, and with a gift for invective and ridicule, by which he could become a terror to his enemies. They were the trophies of his achievement in winning access, by his own efforts alone, to the centre of power, and in gaining the friendship and admiration of the great men among both parties; they were at the same time a promise, which both his old and his new friends would do well to regard, of what might be expected from him in the future.

---

[1] See below, p. 117. Mr Harold Williams suggests however that 'Killaloe' may be a mistake for 'Killala'. Wm. Lloyd, bishop of Killala, was on very friendly terms with Swift and Stella; but, at this time, Swift was not well disposed to Thomas Lyndsay, bishop of Killaloe, one of the two Irish bishops to whom his commission was addressed. See *Corr.* i, 193: *Journal to Stella*, March 28, 1713.
There is a MS of 5 quarto leaves among the Swift MSS in the Forster Collection, which is I believe unprinted, which seemed at first sight to be possibly the missing letter. It is endorsed in a contemporary hand *Letter of Sacramental Test*, and is addressed 'My Lord', presumably to a Bishop, who has asked the writer to reply to *A Letter from a Gentleman in Scotland to his Friend in England against the Sacramental Test*, which had been published in Oct. 1708, and condemned by the House of Commons in Jan. 1709–10. It is catalogued as in the hand of Swift or Dr Lyon, but is in Mr Williams' opinion certainly not the hand of either. It is a well-written, careful answer, but contains some statements which could hardly have been made by Swift. I find no reference to the MS by Forster, nor any indication where he obtained it.

THE

SENTIMENTS

OF A

Church-of-England MAN,

With Respect to

RELIGION *and* GOVERNMENT.

Written in the YEAR 1708.

WHOEVER hath examined the Conduct and Proceedings of both *Parties* for some Years past, whether in or out of Power, cannot well conceive it possible to go far towards the Extreams of either, without offering some Violence to his Integrity or Understanding. A wise and a good Man may indeed be sometimes induced to comply with a Number, whose Opinion he generally approves, although it be perhaps against his own. But this Liberty should be made use of upon very few Occasions, and those of small Importance, and then only with a View of bringing over his own Side another Time to something of greater and more publick Moment. But, to sacrifice the Innocency of a Friend, the Good of our Country, or our own Conscience, to the Humour, or Passion, or Interest, of a Party; plainly shews that either our Heads or our Hearts are not as they should be: Yet this very Practice is the fundamental Law of each Faction among us; as may be obvious to any who will impartially, and without Engagement, be at the Pains to examine their Actions; which, however, is not so easy a Task: For, it seems a Principle in human Nature, to incline one Way more than another, even in Matters where we are wholly unconcerned. And it is a common Observation, that in reading a History of Facts done a Thousand Years ago; or standing by a Play among those

11 b

who are perfect Strangers to us; we are apt to find our Hopes and Wishes engaged on a sudden in favour of one Side more than another. No Wonder then, that we are all so ready to interest our selves in the Course of publick Affairs; where the most inconsiderable have some *real* Share, and by the wonderful Importance which every Man is of to himself, a very great *imaginary* one.

AND indeed when the two Parties that divide the whole Commonwealth, come once to a Rupture, without any Hopes left of forming a Third with better Principles, to ballance the others; it seems every Man's Duty to chuse one of the two Sides, although he cannot entirely approve of either; and all Pretences to Neutrality are justly exploded by both; being too stale and obvious; only intending the Safety and Ease of a few Individuals, while the Publick is embroiled. This was the Opinion and Practice of the latter *Cato*, whom I esteem to have been the wisest and best of all the *Romans*. But before Things proceed to open Violence, the truest Service a private Man may hope to do his Country, is by unbiassing his Mind as much as possible, and then endeavouring to moderate between the Rival Powers; which must needs be owned a fair Proceeding with the World: Because, it is of all others the least consistent with the common Design of making a Fortune by the *Merit* of an *Opinion*.

I HAVE gone as far as I am able in qualifying my self to be such a Moderator: I believe, I am no *Bigot* in Religion; and I am sure, I am none in Government. I converse in full Freedom with many considerable Men of both Parties; and if not in equal Number, it is purely accidental and personal, as happening to be near the Court, and to have made Acquaintance there, more under one Ministry than another. Then, I am not under the Necessity of declaring my self by the Prospect of an Employment. And lastly, if all this be not sufficient, I industriously conceal my Name; which wholly exempts me from any Hopes and Fears in delivering my Opinion.

IN consequence of this free Use of my Reason, I cannot possibly think so well or so ill of either Party, as they would endeavour to persuade the World of each other, and of themselves. For Instance; I do not charge it upon the Body of the *Whigs*, or the *Tories*, that their several Principles lead them to introduce Presbytery, and the Religion of the Church of *Rome*, or a Commonwealth and arbitrary Power. For, why should any Party be accused of a Principle which they solemnly disown and protest against? But, to this they have a mutual Answer ready; they both assure us, that their Adversaries are not to be believed; that they disown their Principles out of Fear; which are manifest enough when we examine their Practices. To prove this, they will produce Instances, on one Side, either of avowed Presbyterians, or Persons of libertine and atheistical Tenets; and on the other, of professed Papists, or such as are openly in the Interest of the abdicated Family. Now, it is very natural for all subordinate Sects and Denominations in a State, to side with some general Party, and to chuse that which they find to agree with themselves in some general Principle. Thus at the *Restoration*, the Presbyterians, Anabaptists, Independants, and other Sects, did all with very good Reason unite and solder up their several Schemes to join against the *Church*; who, without regard to their Distinctions, treated them all as equal Adversaries. Thus, our present Dissenters do very naturally close in with the Whigs, who profess *Moderation*, declare they abhor all Thoughts of *Persecution*, and think it hard, that those who differ only in a few *Ceremonies* and *Speculations*, should be denied the Privilege and Profit of Serving their Country in the highest Employments of State. Thus, the Atheists, Libertines, Despisers of Religion and Revelation in general; that is to say, all those who usually pass under the Name of *Free-Thinkers*, do properly joyn with the same Body; because they likewise preach up *Moderation*, and are not so over nice to distinguish between an unlimited Liberty of Conscience, and an unlimited Freedom of Opinion. Then, on the other Side, the profest Firmness of the *Tories* for Episcopacy, as an Apostolical Institution: Their Aversion from those Sects who lie under the Reproach of having once destroyed their Constitution, and who they imagine, by too indiscreet a Zeal for Reformation, have defaced the primitive Model of the Church: Next, their Veneration for Monarchical Government in the common Course of Succession, and their Hatred to Republican Schemes. These, I say, are Principles which not only the nonjuring Zealots profess, but even Papists themselves fall readily in with. And every Extreme here mentioned, flings a general Scandal upon the whole Body it pretends to adhere to.

But surely no Man whatsoever ought in Justice or good Manners to be charged with Principles he actually disowns, unless his Practices do openly, and without the least Room for Doubt, contradict his Profession: Not upon small Surmises, or because he has the Misfortune to have ill Men sometimes agree with him in a few general Sentiments. However, although the Extreams of *Whig* and *Tory* seem with little Justice to have drawn Religion into their Controversies, wherein they have small Concern; yet they both have borrowed one leading Principle from the Abuse of it; which is, to have built their several Systems of political Faith, not upon Enquiries after Truth, but upon Opposition to each other, upon injurious Appellations, charging their Adversaries with horrid Opinions, and then reproaching them for the want of Charity; *Et neuter falso.*

In order to remove these Prejudices, I have thought nothing could be more effectual than to describe the Sentiments of a *Church-of-*England *Man* with respect to *Religion* and *Government*. This I shall endeavour to do in such a Manner as may be liable to the least Objection from either Party; and which I am confident would be assented to by great Numbers in both, if they were not misled to those mutual Misrepresentations, by such Motives as they would be ashamed to own.

I shall begin with *Religion*.

And here, although it makes an odd Sound, yet it is necessary to say, that whoever professeth himself a Member of the Church of *England*, ought to believe a God, and his Providence, together with revealed Religion, and the Divinity of *Christ*. For beside those many Thousands, who (to speak in the Phrase of Divines) do practically deny all this by the Immorality of their Lives; there is no small Number, who in their Conversation and Writings directly or by consequence endeavour to overthrow it: Yet all these place themselves in the List of the National Church; although at the same Time (as it is highly reasonable) they are great Sticklers for Liberty of Conscience.

To enter upon Particulars: A *Church-of-*England *Man* hath a true Veneration for the Scheme established among us of Ecclesiastical Government; and although he will not determine whether Episcopacy be of Divine Right, he is sure it is most agreeable to primitive Institution; fittest, of all others for preserving Order and Purity, and under its present Regulations, best calculated for our Civil State: He should therefore think the Abolishment of that Order among us, would prove a mighty Scandal, and Corruption to our Faith, and manifestly dangerous to our Monarchy; nay, he would defend it by Arms against all the Powers on Earth, except our own Legislature; in which Case, he would submit as to a general Calamity, a Dearth, or a Pestilence.

As to Rites and Ceremonies, and Forms of Prayer, he allows there might be some useful Alterations; and more, which in the Prospect of uniting Christians might be very supportable, as Things declared in their own Nature indifferent; to which he therefore would readily comply, if the *Clergy*, or, (although this be not so fair a Method) if the *Legislature* should direct: Yet, at the same Time, he cannot altogether blame the former for their Unwillingness to consent to any Alteration; which, beside the Trouble, and perhaps Disgrace, would certainly never produce the good Effects intended by it. The only Condition that could make it prudent, and just for the Clergy to comply in altering the Ceremonial, or any other indifferent Part, would be a firm Resolution in the Legislature, to interpose by some strict and effectual Laws, to prevent the rising and spreading of new Sects, how plausible soever, for the future; else there must never be an End: And it would be to act like a Man, who should pull down and change the Ornaments of his House, in Compliance to every one who was disposed to find fault as he passed by; which, besides the perpetual Trouble and Expence, would very much damage, and perhaps in Time destroy the Building. Sects, in a State, seem only tolerated, with any Reason, because they are already spread; and because it would not be agreeable with so mild a Government, or so pure a Religion as ours, to use violent Methods against great Numbers of *mistaken* People, while they do not manifestly endanger the Constitution of either. But the greatest Advocates for general Liberty of Conscience, will allow that they ought to be checked in their Beginnings, if they will allow them to be an Evil at all; or, which is the same Thing, if they will only grant, it were better for the Peace of the State, that there should be none. But, while the Clergy consider the natural Temper of Mankind in general, or of our own Country in particular; what Assurances can they have, that any Compliances they shall make, will remove the Evil of Dissention, while the Liberty still continues of professing whatever new Opinions we please? Or, how can it be imagined, that the Body of Dissenting Teachers, who must be all undone by such a Revolution, will not cast about for some new Objections to with-hold their Flocks, and draw in fresh Proselytes by some further Innovations or Refinements?

UPON these Reasons, He is for tolerating such different Forms in religious Worship, as are already admitted; but, by no Means, for leaving it in the Power of those who are tolerated, to advance their own Models upon the Ruin of what is already established; which it is natural for all Sects to desire, and which they cannot justify by any consistent Principles, if they do not endeavour; and yet, which they cannot succeed in, without the utmost Danger to the publick Peace.

To prevent these Inconveniences, He thinks it highly just, that all Rewards of Trust, Profit, or Dignity, which the State leaves in the Disposal of the Administration, should be given only to those, whose Principles direct them to preserve the Constitution in all its Parts. In the late Affair of *Occasional Conformity*, the general Argument of those who were against it, was not, to deny it an Evil in it self, but that the Remedy proposed was violent, untimely, and improper; which is the Bishop of * *Salisbury*'s Opinion, in the Speech he made and published against the Bill: But, however just their Fears, or Complaints might have been upon that Score, he thinks it a little too gross and precipitate to employ their Writers already, in Arguments for repealing the *Sacramental Test*, upon no wiser a Maxim, than that no Man should, on the Account of Conscience, be deprived the Liberty of serving his Country; a Topick, which may be

---

* *Dr.* Burnet.

equally applied to admit *Papists*, *Atheists*, *Mahometans*, *Heathens*, and *Jews*. If the Church wants Members of its own, to employ in the Service of the Publick; or be so unhappily contrived, as to exclude from its Communion, such Persons who are likeliest to have great Abilities; it is time it should be altered, and reduced into some more perfect, or, at least, more popular Form: But, in the mean while, it is not altogether improbable, that when those, who dislike the Constitution, are so very zealous in their Offers for the Service of their Country, they are not wholly unmindful of their Party, or of themselves.

THE *Dutch*, whose Practice is so often quoted to prove and celebrate the great Advantages of a general Liberty of Conscience, have yet a National Religion, professed by all who bear Office among them: But why should they be a Precedent for us, either in Religion or Government? Our Country differs from theirs, as well in Situation, Soil, and Productions of Nature, as in the Genius and Complexion of Inhabitants. They are a Commonwealth, founded on a sudden, by a desperate Attempt in a desperate Condition, not formed or digested into a regular System, by mature Thought and Reason, but huddled up under the Pressure of sudden Exigences; calculated for no long Duration, and hitherto subsisting by Accident in the Midst of contending Powers, who cannot *yet* agree about sharing it amongst them. These Difficulties do, indeed, preserve them from any great Corruptions, which their crazy Constitution would extreamly subject them to in a long Peace. That Confluence of People, in a persecuting Age, to a Place of Refuge nearest at Hand, put them upon the Necessity of Trade, to which they wisely gave all Ease and Encouragement: And, if we could think fit to imitate them in this last Particular, there would need no more to invite Foreigners among us; who seem to think no farther, than how to secure their Property and Conscience, without projecting any Share in that Government which gives them Protection; or calling it *Persecution*, if it be denied them. But I speak it for the Honour of our Administration; that although our Sects are not so numerous as those in *Holland*; which I presume is not our *Fault*; and I wish may not be our *Misfortune*; we much excel them, and all *Christendom* besides, in our Indulgence to tender Consciences. * One single Compliance with the National Form of receiving the Sacrament, is all we require to qualify any Sectary among us for the greatest Employments in the State; after which, he is at Liberty to rejoin his own Assemblies for the rest of his Life. Besides, I will suppose any of the numerous Sects in *Holland*, to have so far prevailed as to have raised a Civil War, destroyed their Government and Religion, and put their *Administrators* to Death; after which, I will suppose the People to have recovered all again, and to have settled on their old Foundation: Then I would put a Query; whether that Sect, which was the unhappy Instrument of all this Confusion, could reasonably expect to be entrusted for the future with the greatest Employments; or, indeed, to be hardly tolerated among them?

To go on with the Sentiments of a *Church-of-*England *Man*: He does not see how that mighty Passion for the Church, which some Men pretend, can well consist with those Indignities, and that Contempt they bestow on the Persons of the Clergy. It is a strange Mark whereby to distinguish *High-Church* Men, that they are such, who imagine the Clergy can never be too *low*. He thinks the Maxim these Gentlemen are so fond of; that they are for an *humble* Clergy, is a very good one: And so is He; and for an humble Laity too; since Humility is a Virtue that perhaps equally befits and adorns every Station of Life.

BUT then, if the Scribblers on the other Side freely speak the Sentiments of their Party; a Divine of the Church of *England* cannot look for much better Quarter from thence. You shall observe nothing more frequent in their weekly Papers, than a way of affecting to confound the Terms of *Clergy* and *High-Church*; of applying both indifferently, and then loading the latter with all the Calumny they can invent. They will tell you they honour a Clergyman; but talk, at the same Time, as if there were not Three in the Kingdom, who could fall in with their Definition. After the like Manner, they insult the *Universities*, as poisoned Fountains, and Corrupters of Youth.

Now, it seems clear to me, that the *Whigs* might easily have pro-

---

* *When this was written, there was no Law against Occasional Conformity.*

cured, and maintained a Majority among the Clergy, and perhaps in the Universities, if they had not too much encouraged, or connived at this Intemperance of Speech, and Virulence of Pen, in the worst and most prostitute of their Party: Among whom there hath been, for some Years past, such a perpetual Clamour against the Ambition, the implacable Temper, and the Covetousness of the *Priesthood*: Such a Cant of *High-Church*, and *Persecution*, and being *Priest-ridden*; so many Reproaches about *narrow Principles*, or *Terms of Communion*: Then such scandalous Reflections on the Universities, for infecting the Youth of the Nation with arbitrary and *Jacobite* Principles; that it was natural for those, who had the Care of Religion and Education, to apprehend some general Design of altering the Constitution of both. And all this was the more extraordinary, because it could not easily be forgot, that whatever Opposition was made to the Usurpations of King *James*, proceeded altogether from the Church of *England*, and chiefly from the *Clergy*, and one of the Universities. For, if it were of any Use to recall Matters of Fact, what is more notorious than that Prince's applying himself first to the Church of *England*; and upon their Refusal to fall in with his Measures, making the like Advances to the *Dissenters* of all Kinds, who readily and almost universally complied with him; affecting, in their numerous Addresses and Pamphlets, the Style of *Our Brethren the Roman Catholicks*; whose Interests they put on the same Foot with their own: And some of *Cromwell*'s Officers took Posts in the Army raised against the Prince of *Orange*. These Proceedings of theirs, they can only extenuate by urging the Provocations they had met from the Church in King *Charles*'s Reign; which, although perhaps excuseable upon the Score of human Infirmity, are not, by any Means, a Plea of Merit, equal to the Constancy and Sufferings of the Bishops and Clergy; or of the Head and Fellows of *Magdalen* College; that furnished the Prince of *Orange*'s Declaration with such powerful Arguments, to justify and promote the Revolution.

THEREFORE a *Church-of*-England *Man* abhors the Humour of the Age, in delighting to fling Scandals upon the Clergy in general; which, besides the Disgrace to the Reformation, and to Religion it self, casts an Ignominy upon the Kingdom, that it doth not deserve. We have no better Materials to compound the Priesthood of, than the Mass of Mankind, which, corrupted as it is, those who receive Orders, must have some Vices to leave behind them, when they enter into the Church; and if a few do still adhere, it is no wonder, but rather a great one that they are no worse. Therefore He cannot think *Ambition*, or *Love of Power*, more justly laid to their Charge, than to other Men; because, that would be to make Religion it self, or at least the best Constitution of Church-Government, answerable for the Errors and Depravity of human Nature.

WITHIN these last two Hundred Years, all Sorts of Temporal Power have been wrested from the Clergy, and much of their Ecclesiastick: The Reason, or Justice of which Proceeding, I shall not examine; but that the Remedies were a little too violent, with respect to their *Possessions*, the Legislature hath lately confessed, by the Remission of their *first Fruits*. Neither do the common Libellers deny this; who in their Invectives only tax the Church with an unsatiable Desire of Power and Wealth, (equally common to all Bodies of Men as well as Individuals) but thank God, that the Laws have deprived them of both. However, it is worth observing the Justice of Parties: The Sects among us are apt to complain, and think it hard Usage to be reproached now, after Fifty Years, for overturning the State, for the Murder of a King, and the Indignity of an Usurpation; yet these very Men, and their Partisans, are continually reproaching the Clergy, and laying to their Charge the Pride, the Avarice, the Luxury, the Ignorance, and Superstition of *Popish* Times, for a Thousand Years past.

HE thinks it a Scandal to Government, that such an unlimited Liberty should be allowed of publishing Books against those Doctrines in Religion, wherein all Christians have agreed; much more to connive at such Tracts as reject all Revelation, and, by their Consequences, often deny the very Being of a God. Surely it is not a sufficient Atonement for the Writers, that they profess much Loyalty to the present Government, and sprinkle, up and down, some Arguments in Favour of the *Dissenters*; that they dispute, as strenuously as they can, for Liberty of Conscience, and inveigh largely against all Ecclesiasticks, under the

Name of *High-Church*; and, in short, under the Shelter of some popular Principles in Politicks and Religion, undermine the Foundations of all Piety and Virtue.

As He doth not reckon every *Schism* of that damnable Nature, which some would represent; so He is very far from closing with the new Opinion of those, who would make it no Crime at all; and argue at a wild Rate, that God Almighty is delighted with the Variety of Faith and Worship, as he is with the Varieties of Nature. To such Absurdities are Men carried by the Affectation of *Free-thinking*, and *removing the Prejudices of Education*; under which Head, they have, for some Time, begun to list *Morality* and *Religion*. It is certain, that before the *Rebellion* in 1642, although the Number of *Puritans* (as they were then called) were as great as it is with us; and although they affected to follow Pastors of that Denomination, yet those Pastors had Episcopal Ordination, possessed Preferments in the Church, and were sometimes promoted to Bishopricks themselves. But a Breach, in the general Form of Worship, was, in those Days, reckoned so dangerous and sinful in it self, and so offensive to *Roman Catholicks* at home and abroad; that it was too unpopular to be attempted: Neither, I believe, was the Expedient then found out, of maintaining separate Pastors out of private Purses.

When a *Schism* is once spread in a Nation, there grows, at length, a Dispute which are the Schismaticks. Without entering on the Arguments, used by both Sides among us, to fix the Guilt on each other; it is certain, that in the Sense of the Law, the *Schism* lies on that Side which opposeth it self to the Religion of the State. I leave it among *Divines* to dilate upon the Danger of *Schism*, as a Spiritual Evil; but I would consider it only as a Temporal one. And I think it clear, that any great Separation from the established Worship, although to a new one that is more pure and perfect, may be an Occasion of endangering the publick Peace; because, it will compose a Body always in Reserve, prepared to follow any discontented Heads, upon the plausible Pretexts of advancing *true Religion*, and opposing Error, Superstition, or Idolatry. For this Reason, *Plato* lays it down as a Maxim, that *Men ought to worship the Gods, according to* *the Laws of the Country*; and he introduceth *Socrates*, in his last Discourse, utterly disowning the Crime laid to his Charge, of *teaching new Divinities*, or Methods of Worship. Thus the poor *Hugonots* of *France*, were engaged in a Civil War, by the specious Pretences of some who, under the Guise of Religion, sacrificed so many Thousand Lives to their own Ambition, and Revenge. Thus was the whole Body of *Puritans* in *England*, drawn to be the Instruments, or Abettors of all Manner of Villany, by the Artifices of a *few Men*, whose * Designs, from the first, were levelled to destroy the Constitution, both of Religion and Government. And thus, even in *Holland* it self, where it is pretended that the Variety of Sects live so amicably together, and in such perfect Obedience to the Magistrate; it is notorious, how a turbulent Party joining with the *Arminians*, did, in the Memory of our Fathers, attempt to destroy the Liberty of that Republick. So that, upon the whole, where *Sects* are tolerated in a State, it is fit they should enjoy a full Liberty of Conscience, and every other Privilege of free-born Subjects, *to which no Power is annexed*. And to preserve their Obedience upon all Emergencies, a Government cannot give them too much Ease, nor trust them with too little *Power*.

*Lord Clarendon's Hist.

THE *Clergy* are usually charged with a *persecuting Spirit*, which they are said to discover by an implacable Hatred against all *Dissenters*; and this appears to be more unreasonable, because they suffer less in their Interests by a *Toleration*, than any of the *Conforming Laity*: For, while the *Church* remains in its present Form, no *Dissenter* can possibly have any Share in its Dignities, Revenues, or Power; whereas, by once receiving the Sacrament, he is rendered capable of the highest Employments in the State. And it is very possible, that a narrow Education, together with a Mixture of human Infirmity, may help to beget, among some of the *Clergy in Possession*, such an Aversion and Contempt for all *Innovators*, as *Physicians* are apt to have for *Empiricks*, or *Lawyers* for *Pettifoggers*, or *Merchants* for *Pedlars*. But, since the Number of Sectaries doth not concern the Clergy, either in Point of Interest, or Conscience, (it being an Evil not in their Power to remedy) it is more fair and reasonable to suppose, their Dislike proceeds from the Dangers they apprehend to the Peace of the Commonwealth; in the Ruin whereof, they must expect to be the first and greatest Sufferers.

To conclude this Section; it must be observed, that there is a very good Word, which hath of late suffered much by both Parties; I mean MODERATION; which the one Side very justly disowns, and the other as unjustly pretends to. Beside what passeth every Day in Conversation; any Man who reads the Papers published by Mr. *Lesly*, and others of his Stamp, must needs conclude, that if this Author could make the Nation see his Adversaries, under the Colours he paints them in; we had nothing else to do, but rise as one Man, and destroy such Wretches from the Face of the Earth. On the other Side, how shall we excuse the Advocates for *Moderation*; among whom, I could appeal to an Hundred Papers of universal Approbation, by the Cause they were writ for, which lay such Principles to the whole Body of the *Tories*, as, if they were true, and believed; our next Business should, in Prudence, be to erect Gibbets in every Parish, and hang them out of the Way. But, I suppose it is presumed, the common People understand *Raillery*, or at least *Rhetorick*; and will not take *Hyperboles* in too literal a Sense; which, however, in some Junctures might prove a desperate Experiment. And this is *Moderation*, in the *modern* Sense of the Word; to which, speaking impartially, the Bigots of both Parties are *equally* entituled.

SECT. II.

The Sentiments of a Church-of-*England* Man, *with respect to* Government.

WE look upon it as a very just Reproach, although we cannot agree where to fix it; that there should be so much Violence and Hatred in religious Matters, among Men who agree in all Fundamentals, and only differ in some Ceremonies; or, at most, meer speculative Points. Yet is not this frequently the Case between contending Parties in a State? For Instance; do not the Generality of *Whigs* and *Tories* among us, profess to agree in the same *Fundamentals*; their Loyalty to the Queen, their Abjuration of the *Pretender*, the Settlement of the

Crown in the *Protestant* Line; and a *Revolution Principle*? Their
Affection to the Church Established, with Toleration of *Dissenters*? Nay, sometimes they go farther, and pass over into each
other's Principles; the *Whigs* become great Asserters of the Prerogative; and the *Tories*, of the People's Liberty; these crying
down almost the whole Set of Bishops, and those defending
them; so that the Differences fairly stated, would be much of a
Sort with those in Religion among us; and amount to little
more than, *who should take Place*, or *go in and out first*, or *kiss the
Queen's Hand*; and what are these but a few *Court Ceremonies*? or
who should be in the Ministry? And what is that to the Body of the
Nation, but a meer *speculative Point*? Yet I think it must be allowed, that no religious Sects ever carried their mutual Aver-
sions to greater Heights, than our State Parties have done; who,
the more to enflame their Passions, have mixed Religious and
Civil Animosities together; borrowing one of their Appellations from the Church, with the Addition of *High* and *Low*; how
little soever their Disputes relate to the Term, as it is generally
understood.

I NOW proceed to deliver the Sentiments of a *Church-of-
England Man*, with respect to Government.

HE doth not think the Church of *England* so narrowly calculated, that it cannot fall in with any regular Species of Government; nor does he think any one regular Species of Government, more acceptable to God than another. The three generally
received in the *Schools*, have all of them their several Perfections,
and are subject to their several Depravations: However, few
States are ruined by any Defect in their Institution, but generally
by the Corruption of Manners; against which, the best Institution is no long Security, and without which, a very ill one may
subsist and flourish: Whereof there are two pregnant Instances
now in *Europe*. The first is the *Aristocracy* of *Venice*; which,
founded upon the wisest Maxims, and digested by a great
Length of Time, hath, in our Age, admitted so many Abuses,
through the Degeneracy of the Nobles, that the Period of its
Duration seems to approach. The other is the United Republicks of the *States General*; where a Vein of Temperance, Industry, Parsimony, and a publick Spirit, running through the whole

Body of the People, hath preserved an infant Commonwealth of an untimely Birth and sickly Constitution, for above an Hundred Years, through so many Dangers and Difficulties, as a much more healthy one could never have struggled against, without those Advantages.

WHERE Security of Person and Property are preserved by Laws, which none but the *Whole* can repeal, there the great Ends of Government are provided for, whether the Administration be in the Hands of *One*, or of *Many*. Where any one *Person*, or *Body* of Men, who do not represent the *Whole*, seize into their Hands the Power in the last Resort; there is properly no longer a Government, but what *Aristotle*, and his Followers, call the *Abuse* and *Corruption* of one. This Distinction excludes arbitrary Power, in whatever Numbers; which, notwithstanding all that *Hobbes*, *Filmer*, and others have said to its Advantage, I look upon as a greater Evil than *Anarchy* it self; as much as a *Savage* is in a happier State of Life, than a *Slave* at the Oar.

IT is reckoned ill Manners, as well as unreasonable, for Men to quarrel upon Difference in Opinion; because, that is usually supposed to be a Thing, which no Man can help in himself: But this I do not conceive to be an universal infallible Maxim, except in those Cases where the Question is pretty equally disputed among the Learned and the Wise: Where it is otherwise, a Man of tolerable Reason, some Experience, and willing to be instructed, may apprehend he is got into a wrong Opinion, although the whole Course of his Mind, and Inclination, would persuade him to believe it true: He may be convinced that he is in an Error, although he doth not see where it lies; by the bad Effects of it in the common Conduct of his Life; and by observing those Persons, for whose Wisdom, and Goodness he hath the greatest Deference, to be of a contrary Sentiment. According to *Hobbes*'s Comparison of *Reasoning* with *casting up Accounts*; whoever finds a Mistake in the *Sum total*, must allow himself out; although, after repeated Tryals, he may not see in which Article he hath misreckoned. I will instance, in one Opinion, which I look upon every Man obliged in Conscience to quit, or in Prudence to conceal; I mean, that whoever argues in Defence of absolute Power in a single Person, although he offers the old

Plausible Plea, that *it is his Opinion, which he cannot help, unless he be convinced*, ought, in all free States, to be treated as the common Enemy of Mankind. Yet this is laid as a heavy Charge upon the *Clergy* of the two Reigns before the *Revolution*; who, under the Terms of *Passive Obedience*, and *Non-Resistance*, are said to have preached up the unlimited Power of the Prince, because they found it a Doctrine that pleased the Court, and made Way for their Preferment. And I believe, there may be Truth enough in this Accusation, to convince us, that human Frailty will too often interpose it self among Persons of the holiest Function. However, it may be offered in Excuse for the Clergy, that in the best Societies there are some ill Members, which a corrupted Court and Ministry will industriously find out, and introduce. Besides, it is manifest that the greater Number of those, who held and preached this Doctrine, were misguided by equivocal Terms, and by perfect Ignorance in the Principles of Government, which they had not made any Part of their Study. The Question originally put, and as I remember to have heard it disputed in publick Schools, was this; *Whether under any Pretence whatsoever, it may be lawful to resist the supreme Magistrate*, which was held in the Negative; and this is certainly the right Opinion. But many of the Clergy and other learned Men, deceived by a dubious Expression, mistook the *Object* to which *Passive Obedience* was due. By the *Supreme Magistrate* is properly understood the Legislative Power, which in all Government must be absolute and unlimited. But the Word *Magistrate* seeming to denote a *single Person*, and to express the *Executive* Power; it came to pass, that the Obedience due to the *Legislature* was, for want of knowing or considering this easy Distinction, misapplied to the *Administration*. Neither is it any Wonder, that the Clergy, or other well-meaning People should often fall into this Error, which deceived *Hobbes* himself so far, as to be the Foundation of all the political Mistakes in his Book; where he perpetually confounds the *Executive* with the *Legislative* Power; though all well-instituted States have ever placed them in different Hands; as may be obvious to those who know any thing of *Athens*, *Sparta*, *Thebes*, and other Republicks of *Greece*; as well as the greater ones of *Carthage* and *Rome*.

BESIDES, it is to be considered, that when these **Doctrines** began to be preached among us, the Kingdom had not quite worn out the Memory of that horrid *Rebellion,* under the Consequences of which it had groaned almost twenty Years. And a *weak Prince,* in Conjunction with a Succession of most prostitute Ministers, began again to dispose the People to new Attempts; which it was, no doubt, the Clergy's Duty to endeavour to prevent; if some of them had not for want of Knowledge in Temporal Affairs; and others perhaps from a worse Principle, proceeded upon a Topick, that strictly followed, would enslave all Mankind.

AMONG other Theological Arguments made use of in those Times, in praise of Monarchy, and Justification of absolute Obedience to a Prince, there seemed to be one of a singular Nature: It was urged, that *Heaven* was governed by a *Monarch,* who had none to controul his Power, but was absolutely obeyed: Then it followed, That earthly Governments were the more perfect, the nearer they imitated the Government in Heaven. All which I look upon as the strongest Argument against *despotick* Power that ever was offered; since no Reason can possibly be assigned, why it is best for the World that God Almighty hath such a Power, which doth not directly prove that no Mortal Man should ever have the like.

BUT although a *Church-of*-England *Man* thinks every Species of Government equally *lawful*; he doth not think them equally *expedient*; or for every Country indifferently. There may be something in the Climate, naturally disposing Men towards one Sort of Obedience; as it is manifest all over *Asia,* where we never read of any Commonwealth, except some small ones on the *Western* Coasts, established by the *Greeks.* There may be a great deal in the Situation of a Country, and in the present *Genius* of the People. It hath been observed, that the temperate Climates usually run into moderate Governments, and the Extreames into despotick Power. It is a Remark of *Hobbes,* that the Youth of *England* are corrupted in their Principles of Government, by reading the Authors of *Greece* and *Rome,* who writ under Commonwealths. But it might have been more fairly offered for the Honour of Liberty, that while the rest of the known World was over-run with the Arbitrary Government of single Persons; *Arts* and *Sciences* took their Rise, and flourished only in those few small Territories where the People were *free*. And although *Learning* may continue after *Liberty* is lost, as it did in *Rome*, for a while upon the Foundations laid under the Commonwealth, and the particular Patronage of some Emperors; yet it hardly ever began under a *Tyranny* in any Nation: Because *Slavery* is of all Things the greatest Clog and Obstacle to *Speculation*. And indeed, Arbitrary Power is but the first natural Step from *Anarchy* or the *Savage Life*; the adjusting *Power* and *Freedom* being an Effect and Consequence of maturer Thinking: And this is no where so duly regulated as in a limited Monarchy: Because I believe it may pass for a Maxim in State, that *the Administration cannot be placed in too* few *Hands*, nor the *Legislature in too* many. Now in this material Point, the Constitution of the *English* Government far exceeds all others at this Time on the Earth; to which the present Establishment of the *Church* doth so happily agree, that I think, whoever is an Enemy to *either*, must of necessity be so to *both*.

He thinks, as our Monarchy is constituted, an Hereditary Right is much to be preferred before *Election*. Because, the Government here, especially by some late Amendments, is so regularly disposed in all its Parts, that it almost executes it self. And therefore, upon the Death of a Prince among us, the Administration goes on without any Rub, or Interruption. For the same Reasons, we have less to apprehend from the *Weakness*, or *Fury* of our Monarchs, who have such wise Councils to guide the first, and Laws to restrain the other. And therefore, this Hereditary Right should be kept so sacred, as never to break the Succession, unless where the preserving it may endanger the Constitution; which is not from any intrinsick Merit, or unalienable Right in a *particular Family*; but to avoid the Consequences that usually attend the Ambition of Competitors, to which elective Kingdoms are exposed; and which is the only Obstacle to hinder them from arriving at the greatest Perfection that Government can possibly reach. Hence appears the Absurdity of that Distinction between a King *de facto*, and one *de jure*, with respect to us: For every *limited* Monarch is a King *de jure*, because he governs by the Consent of the *Whole*; which is Authority sufficient to abolish all precedent Right. If a King come in by *Conquest*, he is no longer a *limited* Monarch: If he afterwards consent to Limitations, he becomes immediately King *de jure*, for the same Reason.

THE great Advocates for *Succession*, who affirm it ought not to be violated upon any Regard, or Consideration whatsoever, do insist much upon one Argument, that seems to carry but little Weight. They would have it, that a *Crown* is a Prince's Birthright, and ought, at least, to be as well secured to him, and his Posterity, as the Inheritance of any private Man: In short, that he has the same Title to his Kingdom, which every Individual hath to his Property. Now, the Consequence of this Doctrine must be, that as a Man may find several Ways to waste, mispend, or abuse his Patrimony, without being answerable to the Laws; so a King may, in like Manner, do what he will with *his own*; that is, he may squander and misapply his Revenues, and even alienate the Crown, without being called to an Account by his Subjects. They allow such a Prince to be guilty, indeed, of much Folly and Wickedness; but for these he is *answerable to God*, as every private Man must be, who is guilty of Mismanagement in his own Concerns. Now, the Folly of this Reasoning will best appear, by applying it in a parallel Case: Should any Man argue, that a Physician is supposed to understand his own Art best; that the Law protects and encourages his Profession: And therefore, although he should manifestly prescribe *Poison* to all his Patients, whereof they must immediately die; he cannot be justly punished, but is answerable only to God. Or, should the same be offered in Behalf of a Divine, who would preach against Religion, and moral Duties: In either of these two Cases, every Body would find out the Sophistry; and presently answer, that, although common Men are not exactly skilled in the Composition, or Application of Medicines, or in prescribing the Limits of Duty; yet the Difference between *Poisons* and *Remedies*, is easily known by their Effects, and common Reason soon distinguishes between *Virtue* and *Vice*: And it must be necessary to forbid both these the further Practice of their Professions; because, their Crimes are not purely personal to the Physician, or the Divine, but destructive to the Publick. All which is infinitely stronger, in respect to a Prince; in whose good, or ill Conduct, the Happiness, or Misery of a whole Nation is included; whereas, it is of small Consequence to the Publick, farther than Example, how any private Person manageth his Property.

BUT, granting that the Right of a lineal Successor to a Crown, were upon the same Foot with the Property of a Subject; still it may, at any Time, be transferred by the legislative Power, as other Properties frequently are. The supreme Power in a State can *do no Wrong*; because, whatever that doth, is the Action of all: And when the *Lawyers* apply this Maxim to the *King*, they must understand it only in that Sense, as he is Administrator of the supreme Power; otherwise, it is not universally true, but may be controuled in several Instances easy to produce.

AND these are the Topicks we must proceed upon, to justify our Exclusion of the young *Pretender* in *France*: That of his suspected Birth, being meerly popular, and therefore not made use of, as I remember, since the Revolution, in any Speech, Vote, or Proclamation, where there was Occasion to mention him.

As to the *Abdication* of King *James*, which the Advocates on that Side look upon to have been forcible and unjust, and consequently void in it self; I think a Man may observe every Article of the *English* Church, without being in much Pain about it. It is not unlikely that all Doors were laid open for his Departure, and perhaps not without the Privity of the Prince of *Orange*; as reasonably concluding, that the Kingdom might better be settled in his Absence: But, to affirm, he had any Cause to apprehend the same Treatment with his *Father*, is an improbable Scandal flung upon the Nation by a few biggotted *French* Scribblers, or the invidious Assertion of a ruined Party at home, in the Bitterness of their Souls: Not one material Circumstance agreeing with those in 1648; and the greatest Part of the Nation having preserved the utmost Horror for that ignominious *Murder*. But whether his Removal were caused by his own *Fears*, or other Mens *Artifices*, it is manifest to me, that supposing the Throne to be vacant, which was the Foot the Nation went upon; the Body of the People was thereupon left at Liberty, to chuse what Form of Government they pleased, by themselves, or their Representatives.

THE only Difficulty of any Weight against the Proceedings at the Revolution, is an obvious Objection, to which the Writers upon that Subject have not yet given a direct, or sufficient Answer; as if they were in Pain at some Consequences, which they apprehended those of the contrary Opinion might draw from it. I will repeat this Objection, as it was offered me some Time ago, with all its Advantages, by a very pious, learned, and worthy * Gentleman of the Non-juring Party.

THE Force of his Argument turned upon this; that the Laws made by the supreme Power, cannot otherwise than by the supreme Power be annulled: That this consisting in *England* of a King, Lords, and Commons, whereof each have a negative Voice, no Two of them can repeal, or enact a Law without Consent of the Third; much less, may any one of them be entirely excluded from its Part of the Legislature, by a *Vote* of the other Two. That all these Maxims were openly violated at the Revolution; where an Assembly of the *Nobles* and *People*, not summoned by the King's Writ, (which was an essential Part of the Constitution,) and consequently no lawful Meeting; did, meerly upon their own Authority, declare the King to have abdicated, the Throne vacant; and gave the Crown, by a Vote, to a *Nephew*, when there were three Children to inherit; although by the fundamental Laws of the Realm, the next Heir is immediately to succeed. Neither doth it appear, how a Prince's *Abdication* can make any other Sort of Vacancy in the Throne, than would be caused by his Death; since he cannot abdicate for his Children, (who claim their Right of Succession by Act of Parliament,) otherwise than by his own Consent, in Form, to a Bill from the two Houses.

AND this is the Difficulty that seems chiefly to stick with the most reasonable of those, who, from a meer Scruple of Conscience, refuse to join with us upon the Revolution Principle; but for the rest, are, I believe, as far from loving arbitrary Government, as any others can be, who are born under a free

* *Mr.* Nelson, *Author of the Feasts and Fasts, &c.*

Constitution, and are allowed to have the least Share of common good Sense.

IN this Objection, there are two Questions included: First, Whether upon the Foot of our Constitution, as it stood in the Reign of the late King *James*; a King of *England* may be deposed? The second is, Whether the People of *England*, convened by their own Authority, after the King had withdrawn himself in the Manner he did, had Power to alter the Succession?

As for the first; it is a Point I shall not presume to determine; and shall therefore only say, that to any Man who holds the Negative, I would demand the Liberty of putting the Case as strongly as I please. I will suppose a Prince limited by Laws like ours, yet running into a Thousand Caprices of Cruelty, like *Nero* or *Caligula*. I will suppose him to murder his Mother and his Wife, to commit Incest, to ravish Matrons, to blow up the Senate, and burn his Metropolis; openly to renounce God and Christ, and worship the Devil: These, and the like Exorbitances are in the Power of a single Person to commit without the Advice of a Ministry, or Assistance of an Army. And if such a King, as I have described, cannot be deposed but by his own Consent in Parliament, I do not well see how he can be *resisted*; or what can be meant by a *limited* Monarchy; or what signifies the People's Consent, in making and repealing Laws, if the Person who administers hath no Tie but Conscience, and is answerable to none but God. I desire no stronger Proof that an Opinion must be false, than to find very great Absurdities annexed to it; and there cannot be greater than in the present Case: For it is not a bare Speculation, that Kings may run into such Enormities as are above-mentioned; the Practice may be proved by Examples, not only drawn from the first *Cæsars*, or later Emperors, but many modern Princes of *Europe*; such as *Peter* the Cruel, *Philip* the Second of *Spain*, *John Basilovits* of *Muscovy*; and in our own Nation, King *John*, *Richard* the Third, and *Henry* the Eighth. But there cannot be equal Absurdities supposed in maintaining the contrary Opinion; because it is certain, that Princes have it in their Power to keep a Majority on their Side by any tolerable Administration; till provoked by continual Oppressions, no Man indeed can then answer where the Madness of the People will stop.

As to the second Part of the Objection; whether the People of *England* convened by their own Authority, upon King *James*'s precipitate Departure, had Power to alter the Succession?

In answer to this, I think it is manifest from the Practice of the wisest Nations, and who seem to have had the truest Notions of Freedom; that when a Prince was laid aside for Male-Administration, the *Nobles* and *People*, if they thought it necessary for the Publick Weal, did resume the Administration of the supreme Power, (the Power it self having been always in them) and did not only alter the Succession, but often the very Form of Government too; because they believed there was no natural Right in one Man to govern another; but that all was by Institution, Force, or Consent. Thus, the Cities of *Greece*, when they drove out their tyrannical Kings, either chose others from a new Family, or abolished the kingly Government, and became free States. Thus the *Romans*, upon the Expulsion of *Tarquin*, found it inconvenient for them to be subject any longer to the Pride, the Lust, the Cruelty, and arbitrary Will of single Persons; and therefore by general Consent, entirely altered the whole Frame of their Government. Nor do I find the Proceedings of either, in this Point, to have been condemned by any Historian of the succeeding Ages.

But a great deal hath been already said by other Writers, upon this invidious and beaten Subject; therefore I shall let it fall; although the Point be commonly mistaken, especially by the *Lawyers*; who of all other Professions seem least to understand the Nature of Government in general; like Underworkmen, who are expert enough at making a single Wheel in a Clock, but are utterly ignorant how to adjust the several Parts, or to regulate the Movement.

To return therefore from this Digression: It is a *Church-of-*England *Man*'s Opinion, that the Freedom of a Nation consists in an absolute *unlimited legislative* Power, wherein the whole Body of the People are *fairly* represented; and in an *executive* duly *limited*: Because on this Side likewise, there may be dangerous Degrees, and a very ill Extream. For when two Parties in a State are pretty equal in *Power*, *Pretensions*, *Merit*, and *Virtue*, (for these two last are, with relation to Parties and a Court, quite different Things,) it hath been the Opinion of the best Writers upon Government, that a Prince ought not in any sort to be under the Guidance, or Influence of either; because he declines, by this Means, from his Office of presiding over the *Whole*, to be the Head of a *Party*; which, besides the Indignity, renders him answerable for all publick Mismanagements, and the Consequences of them: And in whatever State this happens, there must either be a Weakness in the Prince or Ministry, or else the former is too much restrained by the Nobles, or those who represent the People.

To conclude: A *Church-of*-England *Man* may with Prudence and a good Conscience approve the professed Principles of one Party more than the other, according as he thinks they best promote the Good of Church and State; but he will never be swayed by Passion or Interest to advance an Opinion meerly because it is *That* of the Party he most approves; which one single Principle he looks upon as the Root of all our civil Animosities. To enter into a *Party* as into an Order of *Fryars*, with so resigned an Obedience to Superiors, is very unsuitable both with the civil and religious Liberties, we so zealously assert. Thus the Understandings of a whole Senate are often enslaved by three or four Leaders on each Side; who instead of intending the publick Weal, have their Hearts wholly set upon *Ways and Means* how to get, or to keep Employments. But to speak more at large; how has this Spirit of Faction mingled it self with the Mass of the People, changed their Nature and Manners, and the very Genius of the Nation? Broke all the Laws of Charity, Neighbourhood, Alliance and Hospitality; destroyed all Ties of Friendship, and divided Families against themselves? And no Wonder it should be so, when in order to find out the Character of a Person; instead of enquiring whether he be a Man of Virtue, Honour, Piety, Wit, good Sense, or Learning; the modern Question is only, Whether he be a *Whig* or a *Tory*; under which Terms all good and ill Qualities are included.

Now, because it is a Point of Difficulty to chuse an exact Middle between two ill Extreams; it may be worth enquiring in the present Case, which of these a wise and good Man would rather seem to avoid: Taking therefore their own good and ill

Characters with due Abatements and Allowances for Partiality and Passion; I should think that, in order to preserve the Constitution entire in Church and State; whoever hath a true Value for both, would be sure to avoid the Extreams of *Whig* for the Sake of the former, and the Extreams of *Tory* on Account of the latter.

I HAVE now said all that I could think convenient upon so nice a Subject; and find, I have the Ambition common with other Reasoners, to wish at least, that both Parties may think me *in the right*, which would be of some Use to those who have any Virtue left, but are blindly drawn into the Extravagancies of either, upon false Representations, to serve the Ambition or Malice of designing Men, without any Prospect of their own. But if that may not be hoped for; my next Wish should be, that both might think me *in the wrong*; which I would understand, as an ample Justification of my self, and a sure Ground to believe, that I have proceeded at least with Impartiality, and perhaps with Truth.

AN
ARGUMENT

To prove, That the

Abolishing of CHRISTIANITY

IN

ENGLAND,

May, as Things now Stand, be attended with some
Inconveniencies, and perhaps, not produce
those many good Effects proposed thereby.

Written in the YEAR 1708.

I AM very sensible what a Weakness and Presumption it is,
to reason against the general Humour and Disposition of the
World. I remember it was with great Justice, and a due
Regard to the Freedom both of the Publick and the Press, forbidden upon severe Penalties to write or discourse, or lay Wagers
against the *Union*, even before it was confirmed by Parliament:
Because that was looked upon as a Design to oppose the Current
of the People; which besides the Folly of it, is a manifest Breach
of the Fundamental Law, that makes this Majority of Opinion
the Voice of God. In like Manner, and for the very same Reasons, it may perhaps be neither safe nor prudent to argue against
the Abolishing of Christianity, at a Juncture when all Parties
appear so unanimously determined upon the Point; as we cannot
but allow from their Actions, their Discourses, and their Writings.
However, I know not how, whether from the Affectation of
Singularity, or the Perverseness of human Nature; but so it
unhappily falls out, that I cannot be entirely of this Opinion.

Nay, although I were sure an Order were issued out for my immediate Prosecution by the Attorney-General; I should still confess, that in the present Posture of our Affairs at home or abroad, I do not yet see the absolute Necessity of extirpating the Christian Religion from among us.

THIS perhaps may appear too great a Paradox, even for our wise and paradoxical Age to endure: Therefore I shall handle it with all Tenderness, and with the utmost Deference to that great and profound Majority, which is of another Sentiment.

AND yet the Curious may please to observe, how much the Genius of a Nation is liable to alter in half an Age: I have heard it affirmed for certain by some very old People, that the contrary Opinion was even in their Memories as much in Vogue as the other is now; and, that a Project for the Abolishing of Christianity would then have appeared as singular, and been thought as absurd, as it would be at this Time to write or discourse in its Defence.

THEREFORE I freely own, that all Appearances are against me. The System of the Gospel, after the Fate of other Systems is generally antiquated and exploded; and the Mass or Body of the common People, among whom it seems to have had its latest Credit, are now grown as much ashamed of it as their Betters: Opinions, like Fashions always descending from those of Quality to the middle Sort, and thence to the Vulgar, where at length they are dropt and vanish.

BUT here I would not be mistaken; and must therefore be so bold as to borrow a Distinction from the Writers on the other Side, when they make a Difference between nominal and real *Trinitarians*. I hope, no Reader imagines me so weak to stand up in the Defence of *real* Christianity; such as used in primitive Times (if we may believe the Authors of those Ages) to have an Influence upon Mens Belief and Actions: To offer at the Restoring of that, would indeed be a wild Project; it would be to dig up Foundations; to destroy at one Blow *all* the Wit, and *half* the Learning of the Kingdom; to break the entire Frame and Constitution of Things; to ruin Trade, extinguish Arts and Sciences with the Professors of them; in short, to turn our Courts, Exchanges and Shops into Desarts: And would be full as absurd as the Proposal of *Horace*, where he advises the *Romans*, all in a Body, to leave their City, and seek a new Seat in some remote Part of the World, by Way of Cure for the Corruption of their Manners.

THEREFORE, I think this Caution was in it self altogether unnecessary, (which I have inserted only to prevent all Possibility of cavilling) since every candid Reader will easily understand my Discourse to be intended only in Defence of *nominal* Christianity; the other having been for some Time wholly laid aside by general Consent, as utterly inconsistent with our present Schemes of Wealth and Power.

BUT why we should therefore cast off the Name and Title of Christians, although the general Opinion and Resolution be so violent for it; I confess I cannot (with Submission) apprehend the Consequence necessary. However, since the Undertakers propose such wonderful Advantages to the Nation by this Project; and advance many plausible Objections against the System of Christianity; I shall briefly consider the Strength of both; fairly allow them their greatest Weight, and offer such Answers as I think most reasonable. After which I will beg leave to shew what Inconveniencies may possibly happen by such an Innovation, in the present Posture of our Affairs.

First, ONE great Advantage proposed by the Abolishing of Christianity is, That it would very much enlarge and establish Liberty of Conscience, that great Bulwark of our Nation, and of the *Protestant* Religion, which is still too much limited by *Priest-Craft*, notwithstanding all the good Intentions of the Legislature; as we have lately found by a severe Instance. For it is confidently reported, that two young Gentlemen of great Hopes, bright Wit, and profound Judgment, who upon a thorough Examination of Causes and Effects, and by the meer Force of natural Abilities, without the least Tincture of Learning; having made a Discovery, that there was no God, and generously communicating their Thoughts for the Good of the Publick; were some Time ago, by an unparalleled Severity, and upon I know not what *obsolete* Law, broke *only* for *Blasphemy*. And as it hath been wisely observed; if Persecution once begins, no Man alive knows how far it may reach, or where it will end.

IN Answer to all which, with Deference to wiser Judgments; I think this rather shews the Necessity of a *nominal* Religion among us. Great Wits love to be free with the highest Objects; and if they cannot be allowed a *God* to revile or renounce; they will *speak Evil of Dignities*, abuse the Government, and reflect upon the Ministry; which I am sure, few will deny to be of much more pernicious Consequence; according to the Saying of *Tiberius*; *Deorum offensa Diis curæ.* As to the particular Fact related, I think it is not fair to argue from one Instance; perhaps another cannot be produced; yet (to the Comfort of all those, who may be apprehensive of Persecution) Blasphemy we know is freely spoke a Million of Times in every Coffee-House and Tavern, or where-ever else *good Company* meet. It must be allowed indeed, that to break an *English Free-born* Officer only for Blasphemy, was, to speak the gentlest of such an Action, a very high Strain of absolute Power. Little can be said in Excuse for the General; perhaps he was afraid it might give Offence to the Allies, among whom, for ought I know, it may be the Custom of the Country to believe a God. But if he argued, as some have done, upon a mistaken Principle, that an Officer who is guilty of speaking Blasphemy, may, some Time or other, proceed so far as to raise a Mutiny; the Consequence is, by no Means, to be admitted: For, surely the Commander of an *English* Army is like to be but ill obeyed, whose Soldiers fear and reverence him as little as they do a Deity.

IT is further objected against the Gospel System, that it obliges Men to the Belief of Things too difficult for Free-Thinkers, and such who have shaken off the Prejudices that usually cling to a confined Education. To which I answer, that Men should be cautious how they raise Objections, which reflect upon the Wisdom of the Nation. Is not every Body freely allowed to believe whatever he pleaseth; and to publish his Belief to the World whenever he thinks fit; especially if it serve to strengthen the Party which is in the Right? Would any indifferent Foreigner, who should read the Trumpery lately written by *Asgill*, *Tindall*, *Toland*, *Coward*, and Forty more, imagine the Gospel to be our Rule of Faith, and confirmed by Parliaments? Does any Man either believe, or say he believes, or desire to have it thought that he says he believes one Syllable of the Matter? And is any Man worse received upon that Score; or does he find his Want of *Nominal* Faith a Disadvantage to him, in the Pursuit of any Civil, or Military Employment? What if there be an old dormant Statute or two against him? Are they not now obsolete, to a Degree, that *Empson* and *Dudley* themselves, if they were now alive, would find it impossible to put them in Execution?

It is likewise urged, that there are, by Computation, in this Kingdom, above ten Thousand Parsons; whose Revenues added to those of my Lords the Bishops, would suffice to maintain, at least, two Hundred young Gentlemen of Wit and Pleasure, and Free-thinking; Enemies to Priest-craft, narrow Principles, Pedantry, and Prejudices; who might be an Ornament to the Court and Town: And then again, so great a Number of able (bodied) Divines might be a Recruit to our Fleet and Armies. This, indeed, appears to be a Consideration of some Weight: But then, on the other Side, several Things deserve to be considered likewise: As, First, Whether it may not be thought necessary, that in certain Tracts of Country, like what we call Parishes, there should be *one* Man at least, of Abilities to read and write. Then, it seems a wrong Computation, that the Revenues of the Church throughout this Island, would be large enough to maintain two Hundred young Gentlemen, or even Half that Number, after the present refined Way of Living; that is, to allow each of them such a Rent, as, in the modern Form of Speech, would make them *easy*. But still, there is in this Project a greater Mischief behind; and we ought to beware of the Woman's Folly, who killed the Hen, that every Morning laid her a Golden Egg. For, pray, what would become of the Race of Men in the next Age, if we had nothing to trust to, besides the scrophulous consumptive Productions furnished by our Men of Wit and Pleasure; when having squandered away their Vigour, Health, and Estates; they are forced, by some disagreeable Marriage, to piece up their broken Fortunes, and entail Rottenness and Politeness on their Posterity? Now, here are ten Thousand Persons reduced by the wise Regulations of *Henry* the Eighth, to the Necessity of a low Diet, and moderate Exercise, who are the only great Restorers of our Breed; without which, the Nation would, in an Age or two, become but one great Hospital.

ANOTHER Advantage proposed by the abolishing of Christianity, is, the clear Gain of one Day in Seven, which is now entirely lost, and consequently the Kingdom one Seventh less considerable in Trade, Business, and Pleasure; beside the Loss to the Publick of so many stately Structures now in the Hands of the Clergy; which might be converted into Theatres, Exchanges, Market-houses, common Dormitories, and other publick Edifices.

I HOPE I shall be forgiven a hard Word, if I call this a perfect Cavil. I readily own there hath been an old Custom, Time out of Mind, for People to assemble in the Churches every *Sunday*, and that Shops are still frequently shut; in order, as it is conceived, to preserve the Memory of that antient Practice; but how this can prove a Hindrance to Business, or Pleasure, is hard to imagine. What if the Men of Pleasure are forced, one Day in the Week, to game at home, instead of the *Chocolate-House*? Are not the *Taverns* and *Coffee-Houses* open? Can there be a more convenient Season for taking a Dose of Physick? Are fewer Claps got upon *Sundays* than other Days? Is not that the chief Day for Traders to sum up the Accounts of the Week; and for Lawyers to prepare their Briefs? But I would fain know how it can be pretended, that the Churches are misapplied. Where are more Appointments and Rendezvouzes of Gallantry? Where more Care to appear in the foremost Box with greater Advantage of Dress? Where more Meetings for Business? Where more Bargains driven of all Sorts? And where so many Conveniences, or Incitements to sleep?

THERE is one Advantage, greater than any of the foregoing, proposed by the abolishing of Christianity; that it will utterly extinguish Parties among us, by removing those factious Distinctions of High and Low Church, of *Whig* and *Tory*, *Presbyterian* and *Church-of-England*; which are now so many grievous Clogs upon publick Proceedings, and dispose Men to prefer the gratifying themselves, or depressing their Adversaries, before the most important Interest of the State.

I CONFESS, if it were certain that so great an Advantage

would redound to the Nation by this Expedient, I would submit
and be silent: But, will any Man say, that if the Words *Whoring,
Drinking, Cheating, Lying, Stealing*, were, by Act of Parliament,
ejected out of the *English* Tongue and Dictionaries; we should
all awake next Morning chaste and temperate, honest and just,
and Lovers of Truth. Is this a fair Consequence? Or if the Physicians would forbid us to pronounce the Words *Pox*, *Gout*,
Rheumatism, and *Stone*; would that Expedient serve like so many
Talismans to destroy the Diseases themselves? Are Party and
Faction rooted in Mens Hearts no deeper than Phrases borrowed
from Religion; or founded upon no firmer Principles? And is
our Language so poor, that we cannot find other Terms to
express them? Are Envy, Pride, Avarice and Ambition, such ill
Nomenclators, that they cannot furnish Appellations for their
Owners? Will not *Heydukes* and *Mamalukes*, *Mandarins*, and
Potshaws, or any other Words formed at Pleasure, serve to distinguish those who are in the *Ministry* from others, who *would
be in* it *if they could*? What, for Instance, is easier than to vary the
Form of Speech; and instead of the Word *Church*, make it a
Question in Politicks, Whether the *Monument* be in Danger? Be-
cause Religion was nearest at Hand to furnish a few convenient
Phrases; is our Invention so barren, we can find no others? Suppose, for Argument Sake, that the *Tories* favoured * *Margarita*,
the *Whigs* Mrs. *Tofts*, and the *Trimmers Valentini*; would not
Margaritians, *Toftians*, and *Valentinians*, be very tolerable Marks
of Distinction? The *Prasini* and *Veneti*, two most virulent Factions in *Italy*, began (if I remember right) by a Distinction of
Colours in Ribbonds; which we might do, with as good a
Grace, about the Dignity of the *Blue* and the *Green*; and would
serve as properly to divide the Court, the Parliament, and the
Kingdom between them, as any Terms of Art whatsoever,
borrowed from Religion. Therefore, I think there is little Force
in this Objection against *Christianity*; or Prospect of so great an
Advantage as is proposed in the Abolishing of it.

IT is again objected, as a very absurd, ridiculous Custom, that
a Set of Men should be suffered, much less employed, and hired

---

* Italian *Singers then in Vogue.*

to bawl one Day in Seven, against the Lawfulness of those Methods most in Use towards the Pursuit of Greatness, Riches, and Pleasure; which are the constant Practice of all Men alive on the other Six. But this Objection is, I think, a little unworthy so refined an Age as ours. Let us argue this Matter calmly. I appeal to the Breast of any polite Free-Thinker, whether in the Pursuit of gratifying a predominant Passion, he hath not always felt a wonderful Incitement, by reflecting it was a Thing forbidden: And therefore we see, in order to cultivate this Taste, the Wisdom of the Nation hath taken special Care, that the Ladies should be furnished with prohibited Silks, and the Men with prohibited Wine: And, indeed, it were to be wished, that some other Prohibitions were promoted, in order to improve the Pleasures of the Town; which, for want of such Expedients, begin already, as I am told, to flag and grow languid; giving way daily to cruel Inroads from the Spleen.

It is likewise proposed, as a great Advantage to the Publick, that if we once discard the System of the Gospel, all Religion will, of Course, be banished for ever; and consequently along with it, those grievous Prejudices of Education; which, under the Names of Virtue, Conscience, Honour, Justice, and the like, are so apt to disturb the Peace of human Minds; and the Notions whereof are so hard to be eradicated by right Reason, or Free-thinking, sometimes during the whole Course of our Lives.

Here, first, I observe how difficult it is to get rid of a Phrase, which the World is once grown fond of, although the Occasion that first produced it, be entirely taken away. For several Years past, if a Man had but an ill-favoured Nose, the Deep-Thinkers of the Age would, some way or other, contrive to impute the Cause to the Prejudice of his Education. From this Fountain are said to be derived all our foolish Notions of Justice, Piety, Love of our Country; all our Opinions of God, or a future State, Heaven, Hell, and the like: And there might formerly, perhaps, have been some Pretence for this Charge. But so effectual Care hath been since taken, to remove those Prejudices by an entire Change in the Methods of Education; that (with Honour I mention it to our polite Innovators) the young Gentlemen, who

II d

are now on the Scene, seem to have not the least Tincture left of those Infusions, or String of those Weeds; and, by Consequence, the Reason for abolishing *Nominal* Christianity upon that Pretext, is wholly ceased.

FOR the rest, it may perhaps admit a Controversy, whether the Banishing all Notions of Religion whatsoever, would be convenient for the Vulgar. Not that I am in the least of Opinion with those, who hold Religion to have been the Invention of Politicians, to keep the lower Part of the World in Awe, by the Fear of invisible Powers; unless Mankind were then very different from what it is now: For I look upon the Mass, or Body of our People here in *England*, to be as Free-Thinkers, that is to say, as stanch Unbelievers, as any of the highest Rank. But I conceive some scattered Notions about a superior Power to be of singular Use for the common People, as furnishing excellent Materials to keep Children quiet, when they grow peevish; and providing Topicks of Amusement in a tedious Winter Night.

LASTLY, It is proposed as a singular Advantage, that the Abolishing of Christianity, will very much contribute to the uniting of *Protestants*, by enlarging the Terms of Communion, so as to take in all Sorts of *Dissenters*; who are now shut out of the Pale upon Account of a few Ceremonies, which all Sides confess to be Things indifferent: That this alone will effectually answer the great Ends of a Scheme for Comprehension, by opening a large noble Gate, at which all Bodies may enter; whereas the chaffering with *Dissenters*, and dodging about this or the other Ceremony, is but like opening a few Wickets, and leaving them at jar, by which no more than one can get in at a Time, and that not without stooping and sideling, and squeezing his Body.

To all this I answer, That there is one darling Inclination of Mankind, which usually affects to be a Retainer to Religion, although she be neither its Parent, its Godmother, or its Friend; I mean the Spirit of Opposition, that lived long before Christianity, and can easily subsist without it. Let us, for Instance, examine wherein the Opposition of Sectaries among us consists; we shall find Christianity to have no Share in it at all. Does the

Gospel any where prescribe a starched squeezed Countenance, a stiff formal Gait, a Singularity of Manners and Habit, or any affected Modes of Speech, different from the reasonable Part of Mankind? Yet, if Christianity did not lend its Name, to stand in the Gap, and to employ or divert these Humours, they must of Necessity be spent in Contraventions to the Laws of the Land, and Disturbance of the publick Peace. There is a Portion of Enthusiasm assigned to every Nation, which if it hath not proper Objects to work on, will burst out, and set all in a Flame. If the Quiet of a State can be bought by only flinging Men a few Ceremonies to devour, it is a Purchase no wise Man would refuse. Let the Mastiffs amuse themselves about a Sheep-skin stuffed with Hay, provided it will keep them from worrying the Flock. The Institution of Convents abroad, seems in one Point a Strain of great Wisdom; there being few Irregularities in human Passions, that may not have recourse to vent themselves in some of those Orders; which are so many Retreats for the Speculative, the Melancholy, the Proud, the Silent, the Politick and the Morose, to spend themselves, and evaporate the noxious Particles; for each of whom, we in this Island are forced to provide a several Sect of Religion, to keep them quiet. And whenever Christianity shall be abolished, the Legislature must find some other Expedient to employ and entertain them. For what imports it, how large a Gate you open, if there will be always left a Number, who place a Pride and a Merit in refusing to enter?

HAVING thus considered the most important Objections against Christianity, and the chief Advantages proposed by the Abolishing thereof; I shall now with equal Deference and Submission to wiser Judgments as before, proceed to mention a few Inconveniences that may happen, if the Gospel should be repealed; which perhaps the Projectors may not have sufficiently considered.

AND first, I am very sensible how much the Gentlemen of Wit and Pleasure are apt to murmur, and be choqued at the sight of so many daggled-tail Parsons, who happen to fall in their Way, and offend their Eyes: But at the same Time these wise Reformers do not consider what an Advantage and Felicity it is, for great Wits to be always provided with Objects of Scorn and Contempt, in order to exercise and improve their Talents, and divert their Spleen from falling on each other, or on themselves; especially when all this may be done without the least imaginable *Danger to their Persons*.

AND to urge another Argument of a parallel Nature: If Christianity were once abolished, how would the Free-Thinkers, the strong Reasoners, and the Men of profound Learning be able to find another Subject so calculated in all Points whereon to display their Abilities. What wonderful Productions of Wit should we be deprived of, from those whose Genius, by continual Practice hath been wholly turned upon Raillery and Invectives against Religion; and would therefore never be able to shine or distinguish themselves upon any other Subject. We are daily complaining of the great Decline of Wit among us; and would we take away the greatest, perhaps the only Topick we have left? Who would ever have suspected *Asgill* for a Wit, or *Toland* for a Philosopher, if the inexhaustible Stock of Christianity had not been at hand to provide them with Materials? What other Subject through all Art or Nature could have produced *Tindal* for a profound Author, or furnished him with Readers? It is the wise Choice of the Subject that alone adorns and distinguishes the Writer. For had an hundred such Pens as these been employed on the Side of Religion, they would have immediately sunk into Silence and Oblivion.

NOR do I think it wholly groundless, or my Fears altogether imaginary; that the Abolishing of Christianity may perhaps bring the Church in Danger; or at least put the Senate to the Trouble of another Securing Vote. I desire, I may not be mistaken; I am far from presuming to affirm or think, that the Church is in Danger at present, or as Things now stand; but we know not how soon it may be so, when the Christian Religion is repealed. As plausible as this Project seems, there may a dangerous Design lurk under it. Nothing can be more notorious, than that the *Atheists, Deists, Socinians, Anti-Trinitarians*, and other Subdivisions of Free-Thinkers, are Persons of little Zeal for the present Ecclesiastical Establishment: Their declared Opinion is for repealing the Sacramental Test; they are very indifferent with regard to Ceremonies; nor do they hold the *Jus Divinum* of Episcopacy. Therefore this may be intended as one politick Step towards altering the Constitution of the Church Established, and setting up *Presbytery* in the stead; which I leave to be further considered by those at the Helm.

IN the last Place, I think nothing can be more plain, than that by this Expedient, we shall run into the Evil we chiefly pretend to avoid; and that the Abolishment of the Christian Religion, will be the readiest Course we can take to introduce Popery. And I am the more inclined to this Opinion, because we know it hath been the constant Practice of the *Jesuits* to send over Emissaries, with Instructions to personate themselves Members of the several prevailing Sects amongst us. So it is recorded, that they have at sundry Times appeared in the Guise of *Presbyterians*, *Anabaptists*, *Independents*, and *Quakers*, according as any of these were most in Credit: So, since the Fashion hath been taken up of exploding Religion, the *Popish* Missionaries have not been wanting to mix with the Free-Thinkers; among whom, *Toland*, the great Oracle of the *Anti-Christians*, is an *Irish* Priest, the Son of an *Irish* Priest; and the most learned and ingenious Author of a Book, called the *Rights of the Christian Church*, was, in a proper Juncture, reconciled to the *Romish* Faith; whose true Son, as appears by an Hundred Passages in his Treatise, he still continues. Perhaps I could add some others to the Number; but the Fact is beyond Dispute; and the Reasoning they proceed by, is right: For, supposing Christianity to be extinguished, the People will never be at Ease, till they find out some other Method of Worship; which will as infallibly produce Superstition, as this will end in *Popery*.

AND therefore, if, notwithstanding all I have said, it shall still be thought necessary to have a Bill brought in for repealing Christianity; I would humbly offer an Amendment, that instead of the Word *Christianity*, may be put *Religion* in general; which I conceive, will much better answer all the good Ends proposed by the Projectors of it. For, as long as we leave in Being a God, and his Providence, with all the necessary Consequences, which curious and inquisitive Men will be apt to draw from such Premises; we do not strike at the Root of the Evil, although we should ever so effectually annihilate the present Scheme of the Gospel. For, of what Use is Freedom of Thought, if it will not produce Freedom of Action; which is the sole End, how remote soever, in Appearance, of all Objections against Christianity? And therefore, the Free-Thinkers consider it as a Sort of Edifice, wherein all the Parts have such a mutual Dependance on each other, that if you happen to pull out one single Nail, the whole Fabrick must fall to the Ground. This was happily expressed by him, who had heard of a Text brought for Proof of the Trinity, which in an antient Manuscript was differently read; he thereupon immediately took the Hint, and by a sudden Deduction of a long *Sorites*, most logically concluded; Why, if it be as you say, I may safely whore and drink on, and defy the Parson. From which, and many the like Instances easy to be produced, I think nothing can be more manifest, than that the Quarrel is not against any particular Points of hard Digestion in the Christian System; but against Religion in general; which, by laying Restraints on human Nature, is supposed the great Enemy to the Freedom of Thought and Action.

Upon the whole; if it shall still be thought for the Benefit of Church and State, that Christianity be abolished; I conceive, however, it may be more convenient to defer the Execution to a Time of Peace; and not venture in this Conjuncture to disoblige our Allies; who, as it falls out, are all Christians; and many of them, by the Prejudices of their Education, so bigotted, as to place a Sort of Pride in the Appellation. If, upon being rejected by them, we are to trust to an Alliance with the *Turk*, we shall find our selves much deceived: For, as he is too remote, and generally engaged in War with the *Persian* Emperor; so his People would be more scandalized at our Infidelity, than our Christian Neighbours. Because, the *Turks* are not only strict Observers of religious Worship; but, what is worse, believe a God; which is more than is required of us, even while we preserve the Name of Christians.

To conclude: Whatever some may think of the great Advantages to Trade, by this favourite Scheme; I do very much apprehend, that in six Months Time, after the Act is past for the Extirpation of the Gospel, the Bank and *East-India* Stock may fall, at least, One *per Cent*. And, since that is Fifty Times more than ever the Wisdom of our Age thought fit to venture for the *Preservation* of Christianity, there is no Reason we should be at so great a Loss, meerly for the Sake of *destroying* it.

A
PROJECT

FOR THE

Advancement of Religion,

AND THE

Reformation of Manners.

By a Person of QUALITY.

O quisquis volet impias
Cædes; & rabiem tollere civicam :
Si quæret pater urbium
Subscribi statuis, indomitam audeat
Refrænare licentiam.   Hor.

LONDON:

Printed for *Benj. Tooke,* at the *Middle-Temple-Gate* in *Fleet-street.* M. DCC. IX.

A

PROJECT

FOR THE
Advancement of RELIGION,
AND THE
Reformation of MANNERS.

Written in the Year 1709.

TO THE
Countess of *BERKELEY*.

MADAM,

MY Intention in prefixing your Ladyship's Name, is not after the common Form, to desire your Protection of the following Papers; which I take to be a very unreasonable Request; since by being inscribed to your Ladyship, although without your Knowledge, and from a concealed Hand, you cannot recommend them without some Suspicion of Partiality. My real Design is, I confess, the very same I have often detested in most Dedications; That of publishing your Praises to the World. Not upon the Subject of your noble Birth, for I know others as noble; or of the Greatness of your Fortune, for I know others far greater; or of that beautiful Race (the Images of their Parents) which calls you Mother: For even this may, perhaps, have been equalled in some other Age, or Country. Besides, none of these Advantages do derive any Accomplishments to the Owners; but serve, at best, only to adorn what they really possess. What I intend, is your Piety, Truth, good Sense, and good Nature, Affability and Charity; wherein I wish your Ladyship had many Equals, or any Superiors; and I wish I could say,

I knew them too; for then your Ladyship might have had a Chance to escape this Address. In the mean Time, I think it highly necessary for the Interest of Virtue and Religion, that the whole Kingdom should be informed in some Parts of your Character: For Instance: That the easiest and politest Conversation, joined with the truest Piety, may be observed in your Ladyship, in as great Perfection, as they were ever seen apart in any other Persons. That by your Prudence and Management under several Disadvantages, you have preserved the Lustre of that most noble Family, into which you are grafted, and which the unmeasurable Profusion of Ancestors, for many Generations, had too much eclipsed. Then, how happily you perform every Office of Life, to which Providence hath called you: In the Education of those two incomparable Daughters, whose Conduct is so universally admired; in every Duty of a prudent, complying, affectionate Wife; in that Care which descends to the meanest of your Domesticks; and lastly, in that endless Bounty to the Poor, and Discretion where to distribute it. I insist on my Opinion, that it is of Importance for the Publick to know this, and a great deal more of your Ladyship; yet whoever goes about to inform them, shall, instead of finding Credit, perhaps be censured for a Flatterer. To avoid so usual a Reproach, I declare this to be no Dedication; but meerly an Introduction to a Proposal for the Advancement of Religion and Morals; by tracing, however imperfectly, some few Lineaments in the Character of a Lady, who hath spent all her Life in the Practice and Promotion of both.

A M O N G all the Schemes offered to the Publick in this projecting Age, I have observed, with some Displeasure, that there have never been any for the Improvement of Religion and Morals: Which, besides the Piety of the Design from the Consequences of such a Reformation in a future Life, would be the best natural Means for advancing the publick Felicity of the State, as well as the present Happiness of every Individual. For, as much as Faith and Morality are declined among us, I am altogether confident, they might, in a short Time, and with no very great Trouble, be raised to as high a Perfection, as Numbers are capable of receiving. Indeed, the Method is so easy and obvious, and some present Opportunities so good; that, in order to have this Project reduced to Practice, there seems to want nothing more than to put those in mind, who by their Honour, Duty, and Interest are chiefly concerned.

But, because it is idle to propose Remedies before we are assured of the Disease, or to be in Fear, until we are convinced of the Danger; I shall first shew in general, that the Nation is extreamly corrupted in Religion and Morals; and then, I will offer a short Scheme for the Reformation of both.

As to the first; I know it is reckoned but a Form of Speech, when Divines complain of the Wickedness of the Age: However, I believe, upon a fair Comparison with other Times and Countries, it would be found an undoubted Truth.

For first, to deliver nothing but plain Matter of Fact, without Exaggeration or Satyr: I suppose it will be granted, that hardly One in a Hundred among our People of Quality, or Gentry, appears to act by any Principle of Religion.   That great Numbers of them do entirely discard it, and are ready to own their Disbelief of all Revelation in ordinary Discourse. Nor is the Case much better among the Vulgar, especially in great Towns; where the Prophaneness and Ignorance of Handicraftsmen, small Traders, Servants, and the like, are to a Degree very hard to be imagined greater. Then, it is observed abroad, that no Race of Mortals hath so little Sense of Religion as the *English* Soldiers: To confirm which, I have been often told by great Officers in the Army, that in the whole Compass of their Acquaintance, they could not recollect three of their Profession, who seemed to regard, or believe one Syllable of the Gospel: And the same, at least, may be affirmed of the Fleet. The Consequences of all which, upon the Actions of Men, are equally manifest. They never go about, as in former Times, to hide or palliate their Vices; but expose them freely to View, like any other common Occurrences of Life, without the least Reproach from the World, or themselves. For Instance, any Man will tell you, he intends to be drunk this Evening, or was so last Night, with as little Ceremony or Scruple, as he would tell you the Time of the Day. He will let you know he is going to a Wench, or that he has got a Clap; with as much Indifferency as he would a Piece of publick News. He will swear, curse, or blaspheme, without the least Passion or Provocation. And, although all Regard for Reputation be not quite laid aside in the other Sex; it is, however, at so low an Ebb, that very few among them, seem to think Virtue and Conduct of any Necessity for preserving it. If this be not so; how comes it to pass, that Women of tainted Reputations find the same Countenance and Reception in all publick Places, with those of the nicest Virtue, who pay, and receive Visits from them, without any Manner of Scruple? Which Proceeding, as it is not very old among us, so I take it to be of most pernicious Consequence.   It looks like a Sort of compounding between Virtue and Vice; as if a Woman were allowed to be vicious, provided she be not profligate: As if there were a certain Point where Gallantry ends, and Infamy begins; or that an Hundred criminal Amours were not as pardonable as Half a Score.

BESIDE those Corruptions already mentioned, it would be endless to ennumerate such as arise from the Excess of Play, or Gaming: The Cheats, the Quarrels, the Oaths and Blasphemies, among the Men: Among the Women, the Neglect of Household Affairs, the unlimited Freedoms, the undecent Passion; and lastly the known Inlet to all Lewdness, when after an ill Run, the *Person* must answer the Defects of the *Purse*: The Rule on such Occasions holding true in Play, as it doth in Law; *Quod non habet in Crumena, luat in Corpore.*

BUT all these are Trifles in Comparison, if we step into other Scenes, and consider the Fraud and Cozenage of trading Men and Shop-Keepers; that insatiable Gulph of Injustice and Oppression: The *Law*. The open Traffick of all Civil and Military Employments (I wish it rested there) without the least Regard to Merit or Qualifications: The corrupt Management of Men in Office: The many detestable Abuses in chusing those, who represent the People; with the Management of Interest and Factions among the Representatives: To which I must be bold to add the Ignorance among some of the lower Clergy; the mean servile Temper of others; the pert pragmatical Demeanour of several young Stagers in Divinity, upon their first producing themselves into the World. With many other Circumstances needless, or rather invidious to mention; which falling in with the Corruptions already related, have, however unjustly, almost rendered the whole Order contemptible.

THIS is a short View of the general Depravities among us, without entering into Particulars, which would be an endless Labour. Now, as universal and deep-rooted as these Corruptions appear to be, I am utterly deceived, if an effectual Remedy might not be applied to most of them; neither am I at present upon a wild speculative Project, but such a one, as may be easily put in Execution.

FOR, while the Prerogative of giving all Employments continues in the Crown, either immediately or by Subordination; it is in the Power of the *Prince* to make Piety and Virtue become the Fashion of the Age; if at the same Time he would make them necessary Qualifications for Favour and Preferment.

IT is clear from present Experience, that the bare Example of the best Prince, will not have any mighty Influence where the Age is very corrupt. For, when was there ever a better Prince on the Throne than the present Queen? I do not talk of her Talent for Government, her Love of the People, or any other Qualities that are purely regal; but her Piety, Charity, Temperance, conjugal Love, and whatever other Virtues do best adorn a private Life; wherein without Question or Flattery, she hath no Superior: Yet neither will it be Satyr or peevish Invective to affirm, that Infidelity and Vice are not much diminished since her coming to the Crown; nor will, in Probability, till more effectual Remedies be provided.

THUS human Nature seems to lie under this Disadvantage, that the Example alone of a vicious Prince, will in Time corrupt an Age; but the Example of a good one will not be sufficient to reform it without further Endeavours. Princes must therefore supply this Defect by a vigorous Exercise of that Authority, which the Law hath left them, by making it every Man's Interest and Honour to cultivate Religion and Virtue; by rendering Vice a Disgrace, and the certain Ruin to Preferment or Pretensions: All which they should first attempt in their own Courts and Families. For Instance, might not the Queen's Domesticks of the middle and lower Sort, be obliged upon Penalty of Suspension, or Loss of their Employments, to a constant weekly Attendance on the Service of the Church; to a decent Behaviour in it; to receive the Sacrament four times a Year; to avoid Swearing and irreligious profane Discourses; and to the Appearance at least, of Temperance and Chastity? Might not the Care of all this be committed to the strict Inspection of proper Officers? Might not those of higher Rank, and nearer Access to Her Majesty, receive her own Commands to the same Purpose, and be countenanced or disfavoured according as they obey? Might not the Queen lay her Injunctions on the Bishops and other great Men of undoubted Piety, to make diligent Enquiry, and give Her Notice, whether any Person about Her should happen to be of Libertine Principles or Morals? Might not all those who enter upon any Office in Her Majesty's Family, be obliged to take an Oath parallel with that against *Symony*, which is administred to the Clergy? It is not to be doubted, but that if these or the like Proceedings were duly observed, Morality and Religion would soon become fashionable Court-Virtues; and be taken up as the only Methods to get or keep Employments there; which alone would have a mighty Influence upon many of the Nobility, and principal Gentry.

But, if the like Methods were pursued as far as possible, with Regard to those who are in the great Employments of the State; it is hard to conceive how general a Reformation they might in Time produce among us. For if Piety and Virtue were once reckoned Qualifications necessary to Preferment; every Man thus endowed, when put into great Stations, would readily imitate the Queen's Example in the Distribution of all Offices in his Disposal; especially, if any apparent Transgression through Favour or Partiality, would be imputed to him for a Misdemeanour, by which he must certainly forfeit his Favour and Station: And there being such great Numbers in Employment, scattered through every Town and County in this Kingdom; if all these were exemplary in the Conduct of their Lives, Things would soon take a new Face, and Religion receive a mighty Encouragement: Nor would the publick Weal be less advanced; since of nine Offices in ten that are ill executed, the Defect is not in Capacity or Understanding, but in common Honesty. I know no Employment, for which Piety disqualifies any Man; and if it did, I doubt, the Objection would not be very seasonably offered at present: Because, it is perhaps too just a Reflection, that in the Disposal of Places, the Question whether a Person be *fit* for what he is recommended to, is generally the last that is thought on, or regarded.

I HAVE often imagined, that something parallel to the Office of Censors antiently in *Rome*, would be of mighty Use among us; and could be easily limited from running into any Exorbitances. The *Romans* understood Liberty at least as well as we; were as jealous of it, and upon every Occasion as bold Assertors: Yet I do not remember to have read any great Complaints of the Abuses in that Office among them; but many admirable Effects of it are left upon Record. There are several pernicious Vices frequent and notorious among us, that escape or elude the Punishment of any Law we have yet invented, or have had no Law at all against them; such as Atheism, Drunkenness, Fraud, Avarice, and several others; which by this Institution wisely regulated, might be much reformed. Suppose for Instance, that itinerary Commissioners were appointed to inspect every where throughout the Kingdom, into the Conduct (at least) of Men in Office, with respect to their Morals and Religion, as well as their Abilities ; to receive the Complaints and Informations that should be offered against them; and make their Report here upon Oath, to the Court or the Ministry; who should reward or punish accordingly. I avoid entering into the Particulars of this or any other Scheme, which coming from a private Hand, might be liable to many Defects, but would soon be digested by the Wisdom of the Nation: And surely, six thousand Pounds a Year would not be ill laid out among as many Commissioners duly qualified; who in three Divisions should be personally obliged to take their yearly Circuits for that Purpose.

BUT this is beside my present Design, which was only to shew what Degree of Reformation is in the Power of the Queen, without Interposition of the Legislature; and which Her Majesty is without Question obliged in Conscience to endeavour by Her Authority, as much as She doth by her Practice.

It will be easily granted, that the Example of this great Town hath a mighty Influence over the whole Kingdom; and it is as manifest, that the Town is equally influenced by the Court and the Ministry, and those, who by their Employments or their Hopes, depend upon them. Now, if under so excellent a Princess, as the present Queen, we would suppose a Family strictly regulated as I have above proposed; a Ministry, where every single Person was of distinguished Piety; if we should suppose all great Offices of State and Law filled after the same Manner, and with such as were equally diligent in chusing Persons, who in their several Subordinations would be obliged to follow the Examples of their Superiors, under the Penalty of Loss of Favour and Place; will not every Body grant, that the Empire of Vice and Irreligion would be soon destroyed in this great Metropolis, and receive a terrible Blow through the whole Island, which hath so great an Intercourse with it, and so much affects to follow its Fashions?

For, if Religion were once understood to be the necessary Step to Favour and Preferment; can it be imagined, that any Man would openly offend against it, who had the least Regard for his Reputation or his Fortune? There is no Quality so contrary to any Nature, which Men cannot affect, and put on upon Occasion, in order to serve an Interest, or gratify a prevailing Passion: The proudest Man will personate Humility, the morosest learn to flatter, the laziest will be sedulous and active, where he is in pursuit of what he hath much at Heart: How ready therefore would most Men be to step into the Paths of Virtue and Piety, if they infallibly led to Favour and Fortune?

If Swearing and Prophaneness, scandalous and avowed Lewdness, excessive Gaming and Intemperance were a little discountenanced in the Army, I cannot readily see what ill Consequences could be apprehended: If Gentlemen of that Profession were at least obliged to some external Decorum in their Conduct; or even if a profligate Life and Character were not a Means of Advancement, and the Appearance of Piety a most infallible Hindrance; it is impossible the Corruptions there should be so universal and exorbitant. I have been assured by several great

Officers, that no Troops abroad are so ill disciplined as the *English*; which cannot well be otherwise, while the common Soldiers have perpetually before their Eyes the vicious Example of their Leaders: And it is hardly possible for those to commit any Crime, whereof these are not infinitely more guilty, and with less Temptation.

IT is commonly charged upon the Gentlemen of the Army, that the beastly Vice of Drinking to Excess, hath been lately from their Example restored among us; which for some Years before was almost dropt in *England*. But whoever the Introducers were, they have succeeded to a Miracle; many of the young Nobility and Gentry are already become great Proficients, and are under no manner of Concern to hide their Talent; but are got beyond all Sense of Shame, or Fear of Reproach.

THIS might soon be remedied, if the Queen would think fit to declare, that no young Person of Quality whatsoever, who was notoriously addicted to that or any other Vice should be capable of Her Favour, or even admitted into her Presence; with positive Command to Her Ministers and others in great Office, to treat them in the same Manner; after which, all Men, who had any Regard for their Reputation, or any Prospect of Preferment, would avoid their Commerce. This would quickly make that Vice so scandalous, that those, who could not subdue, would at least endeavour to disguise it.

BY the like Methods, a Stop might be put to that ruinous Practice of deep Gaming: And the Reason why it prevails so much, is because a Treatment *directly opposite* in every Point is made use of to promote it; by which Means the Laws enacted against this Abuse are wholly eluded.

IT cannot be denied, that the want of strict Discipline in the Universities, hath been of pernicious Consequence to the Youth of this Nation, who are there almost left entirely to their own Management; especially those among them of better Quality and Fortune; who, because they are not under a Necessity of making Learning their Maintenance, are easily allowed to pass their Time, and take their Degrees with little or no Improvement: Than which there cannot well be a greater Absurdity. For if no Advancement of Knowledge can be had from those

Places, the Time there spent is at best utterly lost, because every ornamental Part of Education is better taught elsewhere: And as for keeping Youths out of Harm's Way, I doubt, where so many of them are got together, at full Liberty of doing what they please, it will not answer the End. But, whatever Abuses, Corruptions, or Deviations from Statutes have crept into the Universities, through Neglect, or Length of Time; they might in a great Degree be reformed by strict Injunctions from Court, (upon each Particular, to the Visitors and Heads of Houses;) besides the peculiar Authority the Queen may have in several Colleges, whereof her Predecessors were the Founders. And among other Regulations, it would be very convenient to prevent the Excess of Drinking, with that scurvy Custom among the Lads, and Parent of the former Vice, the taking of Tobacco, where it is not absolutely necessary in point of Health.

FROM the Universities, the young Nobility, and others of great Fortunes are sent for early up to Town, for fear of contracting any Airs of Pedantry by a College-Education. Many of the younger Gentry retire to the Inns of Court, where they are wholly left to their own Discretion. And the Consequence of this Remisness in Education appears by observing that nine in ten of those, who rise in the Church or the Court, the Law or the Army, are younger Brothers, or new Men, whose narrow Fortunes have forced them upon Industry and Application.

As for the Inns of Court; unless we suppose them to be much degenerated, they must needs be the worst instituted Seminaries in any Christian Country; but whether they may be corrected without Interposition of the Legislature, I have not Skill enough to determine. However it is certain, that all wise Nations have agreed in the Necessity of a strict Education; which consisted among other Things, in the Observance of moral Duties, especially Justice, Temperance, and Chastity, as well as the Knowledge of Arts, and bodily Exercises: But all these, among us, are laughed out of Doors.

WITHOUT the least Intention to offend the Clergy; I cannot but think, that through a mistaken Notion and Practice, they prevent themselves from doing much Service, which otherwise might lie in their Power, to Religion and Virtue: I mean, by affecting so much to converse with each other, and caring so little to mingle with the Laity. They have their particular Clubs, and particular Coffee-Houses, where they generally appear in Clusters: A single Divine dares hardly shew his Person among Numbers of fine Gentlemen; or if he happen to fall into such Company, he is silent and suspicious; in continual Apprehension, that some pert Man of Pleasure should break an unmannerly Jest, and render him ridiculous. Now, I take this Behaviour of the Clergy, to be just as reasonable, as if the Physicians should agree to spend their Time in visiting one another, or their several Apothecaries, and leave their Patients to shift for themselves. In my humble Opinion, the Clergy's Business lies entirely among the Laity; neither is there, perhaps, a more effectual Way to forward the Salvation of Mens Souls, than for spiritual Persons to make themselves as agreeable as they can, in the Conversations of the World; for which a learned Education gives them great Advantage, if they would please to improve and apply it. It so happens, that the *Men of Pleasure,* who never go to Church, nor amuse themselves to read Books of Devotion, form their Ideas of the Clergy, from a few poor Strolers they often observe in the Streets, or sneaking out of some Person of Quality's House, where they are hired by the Lady at Ten Shillings a Month; while those of better Figure and Parts do seldom appear to correct these Notions. And let some Reasoners think what they please; it is certain, that Men must be brought to esteem and love the Clergy, before they can be persuaded to be in love with Religion. No Man values the best Medicine, if administered by a Physician, whose Person he hates or despises. If the Clergy were as forward to appear in all Companies, as other Gentlemen, and would a little study the Arts of Conversation, to make themselves agreeable, they might be welcome at every Party, where there was the least Regard for Politeness, or good Sense; and consequently prevent a Thousand vicious or prophane Discourses, as well as Actions: Neither would Men of Understanding complain, that a Clergyman was a Constraint upon the Company; because they could not speak Blasphemy, or obscene Jests before him. While the People are so jealous of the Clergy's Ambition, as to abhor all Thoughts of the Return of Ecclesiastick Discipline among them; I do not see any other Method left for Men of that Function to take, in order to reform the World, than by using all honest Arts to make themselves acceptable to the Laity. This, no doubt, is Part of that Wisdom of the Serpent, which the Author of Christianity directs; and is the very Method used by St. *Paul*, who *became all Things to all Men, to the* Jews *a* Jew, *and a* Greek *to the* Greeks.

How to remedy these Inconveniences, may be a Matter of some Difficulty; since the Clergy seem to be of an Opinion, that this Humour of sequestring themselves is a Part of their Duty; nay, as I remember, they have been told so by some of their Bishops in their Pastoral Letters, particularly by * *one* among them; who yet, in his own Practice, hath all his Life-time taken a Course directly contrary. But I am deceived, if an awkard Shame, and fear of ill Usage from the Laity, have not a greater Share in this mistaken Conduct, than their own Inclinations: However, if the outward Profession of Religion and Virtue, were once in Practice and Countenance at Court, as well as among all Men in Office, or who have any Hopes or Dependance for Preferment; a good Treatment of the Clergy would be the necessary Consequence of such a Reformation; and they would soon be wise enough to see their own Duty and Interest, in qualifying themselves for Lay-Conversation, when once they were out of Fear of being choqued by Ribaldry, or Prophaneness.

There is one further Circumstance upon this Occasion, which I know not whether it will be very orthodox to mention: The Clergy are the only Set of Men among us, who constantly wear a distinct Habit from others: The Consequence of which (not in Reason, but in Fact) is this, that as long as any scandalous Persons appear in that Dress, it will continue, in some Degree, a general Mark of Contempt. Whoever happens to see a *Scoundrel in a Gown*, reeling home at Midnight, (a Sight neither *frequent* nor *miraculous*) is apt to entertain an ill Idea of the whole Order; and, at the same Time, to be extreamly comforted in his own Vices. Some Remedy might be put to this, if those straggling Gentlemen, who come up to Town to *seek their Fortunes,*

---

* *Supposed to be Dr.* Burnet, *Bishop of* Salisbury.

were fairly dismissed to the *West Indies*; where there is Work enough, and where some better Provision should be made for them, than I doubt there is at present. Or, what if no Person were allowed to wear the Habit, who had not some Preferment in the Church; or, at least, some temporal Fortune sufficient to keep him out of Contempt?

THERE is one Abuse in this Town, which wonderfully contributes to the Promotion of Vice; when such Men are often put into the Commission of the Peace, whose Interest it is, that Virtue should be utterly banished from among us; who maintain, or at least enrich themselves by encouraging the grossest Immoralities; to whom all the *Bawds* of the *Ward* pay Contribution for Shelter and Protection from the Laws. Thus these worthy Magistrates, instead of lessening Enormities, are the Occasion of just twice as much Debauchery as there would be without them. For those infamous Women are forced upon doubling their Work and Industry, to answer double Charges, of paying the Justice, and supporting themselves: Like Thieves who escape the Gallows, and are let out to steal, in order to discharge the Goaler's Fees.

IT is not to be questioned, but the Queen and Ministry might easily redress this abominable Grievance; by enlarging the Number of Justices of the Peace; by endeavouring to chuse Men of virtuous Principles; by admitting none, who have not considerable Fortunes; perhaps by receiving into the Number some of the most eminent Clergy: Then, by forcing all of them, upon severe Penalties, to act when there is Occasion; and not permitting any, who are offered, to refuse the Commission. But in these two last Cases, which are very material, I doubt there would be need of the Legislature.

THE Reformation of the Stage is entirely in the Power of the Queen; and in the Consequences it hath upon the Minds of younger People, doth very well deserve the strictest Care. Beside the undecent and prophane Passages; beside the perpetual turning into Ridicule the very Function of the Priesthood; with other Irregularities in most modern Comedies, which have been often objected to them; it is worth observing the distributive Justice of the Authors, which is constantly applied to the Punishment of Virtue, and the Reward of Vice; directly opposite to the Rules of their best Criticks, as well as to the Practice of Dramatick Poets in all other Ages and Countries. For Example; a Country 'Squire, who is represented with no other Vice but that of being a Clown, and having the provincial Accent upon his Tongue, which is neither a Fault, nor in his Power to remedy, must be condemned to marry a cast Wench, or a cracked Chamber Maid. On the other Side, a Rakehell of the Town, whose Character is set off with no other Accomplishments but excessive Prodigality, Prophaneness, Intemperance, and Lust; is rewarded with the Lady of great Fortune, to repair his own, which his Vices had almost ruined. And as in a Tragedy, the Hero is represented to have obtained many Victories, in order to raise his Character in the Minds of the Spectators; so the Hero of a Comedy is represented to have been victorious in all his Intrigues for the same Reason. I do not remember that our *English* Poets ever suffered a criminal Amour to succeed upon the Stage, until the Reign of King *Charles* the Second. Ever since that Time, the Alderman is made a Cuckold, the deluded Virgin is debauched; and Adultery and Fornication are supposed to be committed behind the Scenes, as Part of the Action. These and many more Corruptions of the Theatre, peculiar to our Age and Nation, need continue no longer than while the Court is content to connive at, or neglect them. Surely a Pension would not be ill employed on some Man of Wit, Learning, and Virtue, who might have Power to strike out every offensive, or unbecoming Passage from Plays already written, as well as those that may be offered to the Stage for the future. By which, and other wise Regulations, the Theatre might become a very innocent and useful Diversion, instead of being a Scandal and Reproach of our Religion and Country.

THE Proposals I have hitherto made, for the Advancement of Religion and Morality, are such, as come within the Reach of the Administration; such as a pious active Prince, with a steddy Resolution, might soon bring to Effect. Neither am I aware of any Objections to be raised against what I have advanced; unless it should be thought, that the making Religion a necessary Step to Interest and Favour, might encrease Hypocrisy among us:

And I readily believe it would. But if One in Twenty should be brought over to true Piety by this, or the like Methods, and the other Nineteen be only Hypocrites, the Advantage would still be great. Besides, Hypocrisy is much more eligible than open Infidelity and Vice: It wears the Livery of Religion, it acknowledgeth her Authority, and is cautious of giving Scandal. Nay, a long continued Disguise is too great a Constraint upon human Nature, especially an *English* Disposition. Men would leave off their Vices out of meer Weariness, rather than undergo the Toil and Hazard, and perhaps Expence of practising them perpetually in private. And, I believe, it is often with Religion as it is with Love; which, by much Dissembling, at last grows real.

ALL other Projects to this great End, have proved hitherto ineffectual. Laws against Immorality have not been executed; and Proclamations occasionally issued out to enforce them, are wholly unregarded as Things of Form. Religious Societies, although begun with excellent Intention, and by Persons of true Piety, are said, I know not whether truly or no, to have dwindled into factious Clubs, and grown a Trade to enrich little knavish Informers of the meanest Rank, such as common Constables, and broken Shop-keepers.

AND that some effectual Attempt should be made towards such a Reformation, is perhaps more necessary, than People commonly apprehend; because the Ruin of a State is generally preceded by an universal Degeneracy of Manners, and Contempt of Religion; which is entirely our Case at present.

Diis te minorem, quod geris, imperas.

NEITHER is this a Matter to be deferred till a more convenient Time of Peace and Leisure: A Reformation in Mens Faith and Morals, is the best natural, as well as religious Means to bring the War to a good Conclusion. Because, if Men in Trust performed their Duty for Conscience Sake, Affairs would not suffer through Fraud, Falshood, and Neglect, as they now perpetually do: And if they believed a God and his Providence, and acted accordingly, they might reasonably hope for his Divine Assistance in so just a Cause as ours.

NOR could the Majesty of the *English* Crown appear, upon

any Occasion, in a greater Lustre, either to Foreigners, or Subjects, than by an Administration, which producing such good Effects, would discover so much Power. And Power being the natural Appetite of Princes; a limited Monarch cannot so well gratify it in any Point, as a strict Execution of the Laws.

BESIDES; all Parties would be obliged to close with so good a Work as this, for their own Reputation: Neither is any Expedient more likely to unite them. For, the most violent Partymen I have ever observed, are such as in the Conduct of their Lives have discovered least Sense of Religion, or Morality; and when all such are laid aside, at least those among them who shall be found incorrigible, it will be a Matter, perhaps, of no great Difficulty to reconcile the rest.

THE many Corruptions, at present, in every Branch of Business, are almost inconceivable. I have heard it computed by skilful Persons, that of Six Millions, raised every Year for the Service of the Publick, one Third, at least, is sunk and intercepted through the several Classes and Subordinations of artful Men in Office, before the Remainder is applied to the proper Use. This is an accidental ill Effect of our Freedom: And while such Men are in Trust, who have no Check from within, nor any Views but towards their Interest; there is no other Fence against them, but the Certainty of being hanged upon the first Discovery, by the arbitrary Will of an unlimited Monarch, or his *Vizier*. Among Us, the only Danger to be apprehended, is the Loss of an Employment; and that Danger is to be eluded a Thousand Ways. Besides, when Fraud is great, it furnisheth Weapons to defend it self: And, at worst, if the Crimes be so flagrant, that a Man is laid aside out of perfect Shame, (which rarely happens) he retires loaded with the Spoils of the Nation; *Et fruitur Diis iratis*. I could name a Commission, where several Persons out of a Sallary of Five Hundred Pounds, without other visible Revenues, have always lived at the Rate of Two Thousand, and laid out Forty or Fifty Thousand upon Purchases of Land, or Annuities. An Hundred other Instances of the same Kind might easily be produced. What Remedy, therefore, can be found against such Grievances in a Constitution like ours, but to bring Religion into Countenance, and encourage those who, from the Hope of future Reward, and Dread of future Punishment, will be moved to act with Justice and Integrity?

THIS is not to be accomplished any other Way, than by introducing Religion, as much as possible, to be the Turn and Fashion of the Age; which only lies in the Power of the Administration; the Prince with utmost Strictness regulating the Court, the Ministry, and other Persons in great Employment; and these, by their Example and Authority, reforming all who have Dependance on them.

IT is certain, that a Reformation, successfully carried on in this great Town, would, in Time, spread it self over the whole Kingdom; since most of the considerable Youth pass here that Season of their Lives, wherein the strongest Impressions are made, in order to improve their Education, or advance their Fortune: And those among them who return into their several Countries, are sure to be followed and imitated, as the greatest Patterns of Wit and good Breeding.

AND if Things were once in this Train; that is, if Virtue and Religion were established as the necessary Titles to Reputation and Preferment; and if Vice and Infidelity were not only loaden with Infamy, but made the infallible Ruin of all Mens Pretensions; our Duty, by becoming our Interest, would take Root in our Natures, and mix with the very Genius of our People; so that it would not be easy for the Example of one wicked Prince, to bring us back to our former Corruptions.

I HAVE confined my self (as it is before observed) to those Methods for the Advancement of Piety, which are in the Power of a Prince limited like ours, by a strict Execution of the Laws already in Force. And this is enough for a Project that comes without any Name, or Recommendation: I doubt, a great deal more than will suddenly be reduced into Practice. Although, if any Disposition should appear towards so good a Work, it is certain, that the Assistance of the legislative Power would be necessary to make it more compleat. I will instance only in a few Particulars.

IN order to reform the Vices of this Town, which, as we have said, hath so mighty an Influence on the whole Kingdom; it would be very instrumental, to have a Law made, that all Taverns, or Ale-houses should be obliged to dismiss their Company by Twelve at Night, and shut up their Doors; and that no Woman should be suffered to enter any Tavern, or Ale-house upon any Pretence whatsoever. It is easy to conceive, what a Number of ill Consequences such a Law would prevent; the Mischiefs of Quarrels and Lewdness, and Thefts, and Midnight Brawls, the Diseases of Intemperance and Venery; and a Thousand other Evils needless to mention. Nor would it be amiss, if the Masters of those publick Houses were obliged, upon the severest Penalties, to give only a proportioned Quantity of Drink to every Company; and when he found his Guests disordered with Excess, to refuse them any more.

I BELIEVE there is hardly a Nation in *Christendom*, where all Kind of Fraud is practised in so unmeasurable a Degree as with us. The Lawyer, the Tradesman, the Mechanick, have found so many Arts to deceive in their several Callings, that they far outgrow the common Prudence of Mankind, which is in no Sort able to fence against them. Neither could the Legislature, in any Thing, more consult the publick Good, than by providing some effectual Remedy against this Evil; which, in several Cases, deserves greater Punishment than many Crimes that are capital among us. The Vintner, who, by mixing Poison with his Wines, destroys more Lives than any malignant Disease: The Lawyer, who persuades you to a Purchase, which he knows is mortgaged for more than the Worth, to the Ruin of you and your Family: The Banquier or Scrivener, who takes all your Fortune to dispose of, when he hath beforehand resolved to break the following Day; do surely deserve the Gallows much better than the Wretch, who is carried thither for stealing a Horse.

IT cannot easily be answered to God or Man, why a Law is not made for limiting the Press; at least so far as to prevent the publishing of such pernicious Books, as under Pretence of *Free-Thinking*, endeavour to overthrow those Tenets in Religion, which have been held inviolable almost in all Ages by every Sect that pretends to be Christian; and cannot therefore with any Colour of Reason be called *Points in Controversy*, or *Matters of Speculation*, as some would pretend. The Doctrine of the *Trinity*, the *Divinity of Christ*, the *Immortality of the Soul*, and even the Truth of all Revelation are daily exploded, and denied in Books openly printed; although it is to be supposed, that neither Party avow such Principles, or own the supporting of them to be any way necessary to their Service.

IT would be endless to set down every Corruption or Defect, which requires a Remedy from the legislative Power. Senates are like to have little Regard for any Proposals that come from *without Doors*: Although under a due Sense of my own Inabilities, I am fully convinced that the unbiassed Thoughts of an honest and wise Man, employed on the Good of his Country, may be better digested, than the Results of a Multitude, where Faction and Interest too often prevail: As a single Guide may direct the Way, better than five Hundred who *have contrary Views*, or *look asquint*, or *shut their Eyes*.

I SHALL mention but one more Particular, which I think a Parliament ought to take under Consideration: Whether it be not a Shame to our Country, and a Scandal to Christianity, that in many Towns, where there is a prodigious Increase in the Number of Houses and Inhabitants, so little Care should be taken for the Building of Churches, that five Parts in six of the People are absolutely hindered from hearing Divine Service? Particularly here in * *London*, where a single Minister with one or two sorry Curates, hath the Care sometimes of above twenty thousand Souls incumbent on him. A Neglect of Religion so ignominious in my Opinion, that it can hardly be equalled in any civilized Age or Country.

BUT, to leave these airy Imaginations of introducing new Laws for the Amendment of Mankind: What I principally insist on is the due Execution of the old, which lies wholly in the Crown, and in the Authority derived from thence: I return therefore to my former Assertion; that, if Stations of Power, Trust, Profit, and Honour were constantly made the Rewards of Virtue and Piety; such an Administration must needs have a

---

* *This Paragraph is known to have given the first Hint to certain Bishops, particularly to that most excellent Prelate Bishop Atterbury, in the Earl of Oxford's Ministry, to procure a Fund for building fifty new Churches in London.*

mighty Influence on the Faith and Morals of the whole Kingdom: And Men of great Abilities would *then* endeavour to excel in the Duties of a religious Life, in order to qualify themselves for publick Service. I may possibly be wrong in some of the Means I prescribe towards this End; but that is no material Objection against the Design it self. Let those, who are at the Helm contrive it better, which perhaps they may easily do. Every Body will agree, that the Disease is manifest, as well as dangerous; that some Remedy is necessary, and that none yet applied hath been effectual; which is a sufficient Excuse for any Man who wishes well to his Country, to offer his Thoughts, when he can have no other End in View but the publick Good. The present Queen is a Prince of as many and great Virtues as ever filled a Throne: How would it brighten Her Character to the present and after Ages, if she would exert Her utmost Authority to instil some Share of those Virtues into Her People, which they are too degenerate to learn only from Her Example. And, be it spoke with all the Veneration possible for so excellent a Sovereign; Her best Endeavours in this weighty Affair, are a most important Part of Her Duty, as well as of Her Interest, and Her Honour.

But, it must be confessed, That as Things are now, every Man thinks he hath laid in a sufficient Stock of Merit, and may pretend to any Employment, provided he hath been loud and frequent in declaring himself hearty for the Government. It is true he is a *Man of Pleasure*, and a *Free-Thinker*; that is, in other Words, he is profligate in his Morals, and a despiser of Religion; but in Point of Party, he is one to be *confided* in; he is an Asserter of Liberty and Property; he rattles it out against *Popery*, and *Arbitrary Power*, and *Priest Craft*, and *High-Church*. It is enough: He is a Person fully qualified for any Employment in the Court, or the Navy, the Law, or the Revenue; where he will be sure to leave no Arts untried of Bribery, Fraud, Injustice, Oppression, that he can practice with any Hope of Impunity. No Wonder such Men are true to a Government, where Liberty runs high, where Property, *however attained*, is so well secured, and where the Administration is at least so gentle: It is impossible they could chuse any other Constitution, without changing to their Loss.

FIDELITY, to a present Establishment, is indeed one principal Means to defend it from a foreign Enemy; but without other Qualifications will not prevent Corruptions from within: And States are more often ruined by these than the other.

To conclude: Whether the Proposals I have offered towards a Reformation, be such as are most prudent and convenient, may probably be a Question; but it is none at all, whether *some* Reformation be absolutely necessary; because the Nature of Things is such, that if Abuses be not remedied, they will certainly encrease, nor ever stop till they end in the Subversion of a Common-Wealth. As there must always of Necessity be some Corruptions; so in a well-instituted State, the executive Power will be always contending against them, by *reducing Things* (as *Machiavel* speaks) *to their first Principles*; never letting Abuses grow inveterate, or multiply so far that it will be hard to find Remedies, and perhaps impossible to apply them. As he that would keep his House in Repair, must attend every little Breach or Flaw, and supply it immediately, else Time alone will bring all to Ruin; how much more the common Accidents of Storms and Rain? He must live in perpetual Danger of his House falling about his Ears; and will find it cheaper to throw it quite down, and build it again from the Ground, perhaps upon a new Foundation, or at least in a new Form, which may neither be so safe nor so convenient as the old.

REMARKS

UPON A

BOOK,

INTITLED,

The RIGHTS of the CHRISTIAN CHURCH
asserted, against the *Romish*, and all other
Priests, who claim an Independent Power
over it.

WITH A

PREFACE,

CONCERNING THE

GOVERNMENT

OF THE

CHURCH of ENGLAND

AS BY

LAW ESTABLISHED

PART I.

II f

REMARKS upon a Book, intitled, the RIGHTS of the CHRISTIAN CHURCH, &c.

Written in the Year, 1708.

BEFORE I enter upon a particular Examination of this Treatise, it will be convenient to do two Things:

First, To give some Account of the Author, together with the Motives, that might probably engage him in such a Work. And,

Secondly, to discover the Nature and Tendency in general, of the Work itself.

THE First of these, although it hath been objected against, seems highly reasonable, especially in Books that instill pernicious Principles. For, although a Book is not intrinsically much better or worse, according to the Stature or Complexion of the Author, yet when it happens to make a Noise, we are apt and curious, as in other Noises, to look about from whence it cometh. But however, there is something more in the Matter.

IF a theological Subject be well handled by a Layman, it is better received than if it came from a Divine; and that for Reasons obvious enough, which, although of little Weight in themselves, will ever have a great deal with Mankind.

BUT, when Books are written with ill Intentions to advance dangerous Opinions, or destroy Foundations; it may be then of real Use to know from what Quarter they come, and go a good Way towards their Confutation. For Instance, if any Man should write a Book against the Lawfulness of punishing Felony with Death; and upon Enquiry the Author should be found in New-gate under Condemnation for robbing a House; his Arguments would not very unjustly lose much of their Force, from the Circumstances he lay under. So, when *Milton* writ his Book of Divorces, it was presently rejected as an occasional Treatise; because every Body knew, he had a Shrew for his Wife. Neither can there be any Reason imagined, why he might not, after he was blind, have writ another upon the Danger and Inconvenience of Eyes. But, it is a Piece of Logic which will hardly pass on the World; that because one Man hath a sore Nose, therefore all the Town should put Plaisters upon theirs. So, if this Treatise about the Rights of the Church, should prove to be the Work of a Man steady in his Principles, of exact Morals and profound Learning, a true Lover of his Country, and a Hater of Christianity, as what he really believes to be a Cheat upon Mankind, whom he would undeceive purely for their Good; it might be apt to check unwary Men, even of good Dispositions towards Religion. But, if it be found the Production of a Man sowered with Age and Misfortunes, together with the Consciousness of past Miscarriages; of one, who, in Hopes of Preferment was reconciled to the *Popish* Religion; of one wholely prostitute in Life and Principles, and only an Enemy to Religion, because it condemns them: In this Case, and this last I find is the universal Opinion, he is like to have few Proselytes, beside those, who from a Sense of their vicious Lives, require to be perpetually supplied by such Amusements as this; which serve to flatter their Wishes, and debase their Understandings.

I KNOW there are some who would fain have it, that this Discourse was written by a Club of Free-Thinkers, among whom the supposed Author only came in for a Share. But, sure, we cannot judge so meanly of any Party, without affronting the Dignity of Mankind. If this be so, and if here be the Product of all their Quotas and Contributions, we must needs allow, that Free-thinking is a most confined and limited Talent. It is true indeed, the whole Discourse seemeth to be a motly, inconsistent Composition, made up of various Shreds of equal Fineness, although of different Colours. It is a Bundle of incoherent Maxims and Assertions, that frequently destroy one another. But, still there is the same Flatness of Thought and Style; the same weak Advances towards Wit and Raillery; the same Petulancy and Pertness of Spirit; the same . . . superficial Reading; the same . . . thread-bare Quotations; the same Affectation of forming general Rules upon false and scanty Premisses. And lastly, the same rapid Venom sprinkled over the Whole; which, like the dying impotent Bite of a trodden benumbed Snake, may be nauseous and offensive, but cannot be very dangerous.

AND, indeed, I am so far from thinking this Libel to be born of several Fathers, that it hath been the Wonder of several others as well as myself, how it was possible for any Man, who appeareth to have gone the common Circle of academical Education, who hath taken so universal a Liberty, and hath so entirely laid aside all Regards, not only of Christianity, but common Truth and Justice; one who is dead to all Sense of Shame, and seemeth to be past the getting or losing a Reputation, should with so many Advantages, and upon so unlimited a Subject, come out with so poor, so jejune a Production. Should we pity or be amazed at so perverse a Talent, which instead of qualifying an Author to give a new Turn to old Matter, disposeth him quite contrary to talk in an old beaten trivial Manner upon Topicks wholly new. To make so many Sallies into Pedantry without a Call, upon a Subject the most alien, and in the very Moments he is declaiming against it, and in an Age too, where it is so violently exploded, especially among those Readers he proposeth to entertain.

I KNOW it will be said, that this is only to talk in the common Style of an Answerer; but I have not so little Policy. If there were any Hope of Reputation or Merit from such Victory, I should be apt, like others, to cry up the Courage and Conduct of an Enemy. Whereas to detect the Weakness, the Malice, the Sophistry, the Falshood, the Ignorance of such a Writer, requireth little more than to rank his Perfections in such an Order, and place them in such a Light, that the commonest Reader may form a Judgment of them.

IT may still be a Wonder how so heavy a Book, written upon a Subject in Appearance so little instructive or diverting, should survive to three Editions, and consequently find a better Reception than is usual with such bulky spiritless Volumes; and this, in an Age that pretendeth so soon to be nauseated with what is tedious and dull. To which I can only return, that as burning a Book by the common Hangman, is a known Expedient to make it sell: So, to write a Book that deserveth such Treatment, is another: And a third, perhaps, as effectual as either, is to ply an insipid, worthless Tract with grave and learned Answers, as Dr. *Hicks*, Dr. *Potter*, and Mr. *Wotton* have done. Design and Performances however commendable, have glanced a Reputation upon the Piece; which oweth its Life to the Strength of those

Hands and Weapons that were raised to destroy it; like flinging a Mountain upon a Worm, which, instead of being bruised, by the Advantage of its Littleness, lodgeth under it unhurt.

BUT neither is this all. For the Subject as unpromising as it seemeth at first View, is no less than that of *Lucretius*, to free Men's Minds from the Bondage of Religion; and this not by little Hints and by Piece-meal, after the Manner of those little atheistical Tracts that steal into the World, but in a thorough Wholesale Manner; by making Religion, Church, Christianity, with all their Concomitants, a perfect Contrivance of the Civil Power. It is an Imputation often charged on these Sort of Men, that by their Invectives against Religion, they can possibly propose no other End than that of fortifying themselves and others against the Reproaches of a vicious Life; it being necessary for Men of libertine Practices to embrace libertine Principles, or else they cannot act in Consistence with any Reason, or preserve any Peace of Mind. Whether such Authors have this Design, (whereof I think they have never gone about to acquit themselves) thus much is certain; that no other Use is made of such Writings: Neither did I ever hear this Author's Book justified by any Person, either Whig or Tory, except such who are of that profligate Character. And, I believe, whoever examineth it, will be of the same Opinion; although indeed such Wretches are so numerous, that it seemeth rather surprizing, why the Book hath had no more Editions, than why it should have so many.

HAVING thus endeavoured to satisfy the Curious with some Account of this Author's Character, let us examine what might probably be the Motives to engage him in such a Work. I shall say Nothing of the Principal, which is a Sum of Money; because that is not a Mark to distinguish him from any other Trader with the Press. I will say Nothing of Revenge and Malice from Resentment of the Indignities and Contempt he hath undergone for his Crime of Apostacy. To this Passion he has thought fit to sacrifice Order, Propriety, Discretion and Common-Sense, as may be seen in every Page of his Book: But, I am deceived, if there were not a third Motive as powerful as the other two; and that is, Vanity. About the latter End of King *James*'s Reign he had almost finished a learned Discourse in Defence of the Church of *Rome*, and to justify his Conversion: All which, upon the Revolution, was quite out of Season. Having thus prostituted his Reputation, and at once ruined his Hopes, he had no Course left, but to shew his Spite against Religion in general; the false Pretensions to which, had proved so destructive to his Credit and Fortune; And, at the same Time, loath to employ the Speculations of so many Years to no Purpose; by an easy Turn, the same Arguments he had made Use of to advance Popery, were full as properly levelled by him against Christianity itself; like the Image, which while it was new and handsome, was worshipped for a Saint, and when it came to be old and broken, was still good enough to make a tolerable Devil. And, therefore every Reader will observe, that the Arguments for *Popery* are much the strongest of any in his Book, as I shall further remark when I find them in my Way.

There is one Circumstance in his Title-Page, which I take to be not amiss, where he calleth his Book, *Part the First*. This is a Project to fright away Answerers, and make the poor Advocates for Religion believe, he still keepeth further Vengeance in *Petto*. It must be allowed, he hath not wholely lost Time, while he was of the *Romish* Communion. This very Trick he learned from his old Father, the *Pope*; whose Custom it is to lift up his Hand, and threaten to fulminate, when he never meant to shoot his Bolts; because the Princes of Christendom had learned the Secret to avoid or despise them. Dr. *Hicks* knew this very well, and therefore in his Answer to this *Book of the Rights*, where a *second Part* is threatened, like a rash Person he desperately crieth, *Let it come.* But I, who have not too much Fl[e]ame to provoke angry Wits of his Standard, must tell the Author, that the Doctor plays the Wag, as if he were sure, it were all Grimace. For my Part, I declare, if he writeth a second Part, I will not write another Answer; or, if I do, it shall be published, before the other Part cometh out.

There may have been another Motive, although it be hardly credible, both for publishing this Work, and threatening a *Second Part*: It is not soon conceived how far the Sense of a Man's Vanity will transport him. This Man must have somewhere heard, that dangerous Enemies have been often bribed to Silence with Money or Preferment: And therefore, to shew how formidable he is, he hath published his first Essay; and, in Hopes of Hire to be quiet, hath frighted us with his Design of another. What must the Clergy do in these unhappy Circumstances? If they should bestow this Man Bread enough to stop his Mouth, it will but open those of a hundred more, who are every whit as well qualified to rail as he. And truly when I compare the former Enemies to Christianity, such as *Socinus, Hobbes,* and *Spinosa*; with such of their Successors, as *Toland, Asgil, Coward, Gildon,* this Author of the *Rights,* and some others; the Church appeareth to me like the sick old Lion in the Fable, who, after having his Person outraged by the Bull, the Elephant, the Horse, and the Bear, took nothing so much to Heart, as to find himself at last insulted by the Spurn of an Ass.

I will now add a few Words to give the Reader some general Notion of the Nature and Tendency of the Work itself.

I think I may assert, without the least Partiality, that it is a Treatise wholly devoid of Wit or Learning, under the most violent and weak Endeavours and Pretences to both. That it is replenished throughout with bold, rude improbable Falshoods, and gross Misrepresentations; and supported by the most impudent Sophistry and false Logick I have any where observed. To this he hath added a paultry, traditional Cant of *Priest-rid* and *Priest-craft,* without Reason or Pretext as he applieth it. And when he raileth at those Doctrines in *Popery* (which no Protestant was ever supposed to believe) he leads the Reader, however, by the Hand to make Applications against the *English* Clergy, and then he never faileth to triumph, as if he had made a very shrewd and notable Stroke. And because the Court and Kingdom seemeth disposed to Moderation with Regard to Dissenters, more perhaps than is agreeable to the hot unreasonable Temper of some mistaken Men among us; therefore under the Shelter of that popular Opinion, he ridiculeth all that is sound in Religion, even Christianity itself, under the Names of *Jacobite, Tackers, High-Church,* and other *Terms* of *factious Jargon*: All which, if it were to be first rased from his Book (as just so much of nothing to the Purpose) how little would remain to give the Trouble of an Answer! To which let me add, that the Spirit or Genius which animates the whole, is plainly perceived to be nothing else but the abortive Malice of an old neglected Man, who hath long lain under the Extreams of Obloquy, Poverty and Contempt; that have soured his Temper, and made him fearless. But, where is the Merit of being bold, to a Man that is secure of Impunity to his Person, and is past Apprehension of any Thing else? He that has neither Reputation nor Bread, hath very little to lose, and has therefore as little to fear. And, as it is usually said; *Whoever values not his own Life, is Master of another Man's*; so there is something like it in Reputation: He that is wholly lost to all Regards of Truth or Modesty, may scatter so much Calumny and Scandal, that some Part may perhaps be taken up before it fall to the Ground; because the ill Talent of the World is such, that those who will be at Pains enough to inform themselves in a malicious Story, will take none at all to be undeceived, nay, will be apt with some Reluctance to admit a favourable Truth.

To expostulate, therefore, with this Author for doing Mischief to Religion, is to strew his Bed with Roses; he will reply in Triumph, that this was his Design; and I am loth to mortify him, by asserting he hath done none at all. For I never yet saw so poor an atheistical Scribble, which would not serve as a Twig for sinking Libertines to catch at. It must be allowed in their Behalf, that the Faith of Christians is not as a Grain of Mustard Seed in Comparison of theirs, which can remove such Mountains of Absurdities, and submit with so entire a Resignation to such Apostles. If these Men had any Share of that Reason they pretend to, they would retire into Christianity meerly to give it Ease. And therefore Men can never be confirmed in such Doctrines, until they are confirmed in their Vices; which last, as we have already observed, is the principal Design of this and all other Writers against Revealed Religion.

I am now opening the Book which I propose to examine. An Employment, as it is entirely new to me, so it is that to which, of all others, I have naturally the greatest Antipathy. And, indeed, who can dwell upon a tedious Piece of insipid Thinking, and false Reasoning, so long as I am likely to do, without sharing the Infection?

But before I plunge into the Depths of the Book itself, I must be forced to wade through the Shallows of a long Preface.

THIS Preface, large as we see it, is only made up of such supernumerary Arguments against an Independent Power in the Church, as he could not, without nauseous Repetition, scatter into the Body of his Book: And it is detached, like a Forlorn Hope, to blunt the Enemy's Sword that intendeth to attack him. Now, I think, it will be easy to prove, that the Opinion of *Imperium in Imperio*, in the Sense he chargeth it upon the Clergy of *England*, is what no one Divine of any Reputation, and very few at all, did ever maintain; and, that their universal Sentiment in this Matter is such as few Protestants did ever dispute. But, if the Author of the *Regale*, or two or three more obscure Writers, have carried any Points further than Scripture and Reason will allow, (which is more than I know, or shall trouble myself to enquire) the Clergy of *England* is no more answerable for those, than the Layety is for all the Folly and Impertinence of this Treatise. And, therefore, that People may not be amused, or think this Man is somewhat, that he hath advanced or defended any oppressed Truths, or overthrown any growing dangerous Errors, I will set in as clear a Light as I can, what I conceive to be held by the Established Clergy, and all reasonable Protestants in this Matter.

EVERY Body knoweth and allows, that in all Government there is an absolute, unlimited, legislative Power, which is originally in the Body of the People, although by Custom, Conquest, Usurpation, or other Accidents, sometimes fallen into the Hands of one or a few. This in *England* is placed in the Three Estates (otherwise called the Two Houses of Parliament) in Conjunction with the King: And whatever they please to enact or to repeal in the settled Forms, whether it be Ecclesiastical or Civil, immediately becometh Law or Nullity. Their Decrees may be against Equity, Truth, Reason and Religion, but they are not against Law; because Law is the Will of the supreme Legislature, and that is, themselves. And there is no Manner of Doubt, but the same Authority, whenever it pleaseth, may abolish Christianity, and set up the *Jewish*, *Mahometan*, or *Heathen* Religion. In short, they may do any Thing within the Compass of human Power. And, therefore, who will dispute that the same Law, which de-

prived the Church, not only of Lands, misapplied to superstitious Uses, but even the Tythes and Glebes, (the antient and
necessary Support of Parish Priests) may take away all the rest,
whenever the Lawgivers please, and make the Priesthood as
primitive, as this Writer, or others of his Stamp, can desire.

But, as the Supreme Power can certainly do ten thousand
Things more than it ought, so there are several Things which
some People may think it can do, although it really cannot. For,
it unfortunately happens, that Edicts which cannot be executed,
will not alter the Nature of Things. So, if a King and Parliament
should please to enact, that a Woman, who hath been a Month
married, is *Virgo intacta*, would that actually restore her to her
primitive State? If the Supreme Power should resolve a Corporal
of Dragoons to be a Doctor of Divinity, Law, or Physick, few,
I believe, would trust their Souls, Fortunes, or Bodies to his
Direction; because that Power is neither fit to judge or teach
those Qualifications which are absolutely necessary to the several
Professions. Put the Case, that walking on the slack Rope were
the only Talent required by Act of Parliament for making a Man
a Bishop; no Doubt, when a Man had done his Feat of Activity
in Form, he might sit in the House of Lords, put on his Robes
and his Rotchet, go down to his Palace, receive and spend his
Rents; but it requireth very little Christianity to believe this
Tumbler to be one whit more a Bishop than he was before; because the Law of God hath otherwise decreed; which Law,
although a Nation may refuse to receive it, cannot alter in its
own Nature.

And here lies the Mistake of this superficial Man, who is not
able to distinguish between what the Civil Power can hinder,
and what it can do. *If the Parliament can annul Ecclesiastical Laws,
they must be able to make them, since no greater Power is required for
one than the other.* See Pref. p. 8. This Consequence he repeateth
above Twenty Times, and always in the wrong. He affecteth to
form a few Words into the Shape and Size of a Maxim, then
trieth it by his Ear, and according as he likes the Sound or Cadence, pronounceth it true. Cannot I stand over a Man with a
great Pole, and hinder him from making a Watch, although I am
not able to make one myself. If I have Strength enough to knock

a Man on the Head, doth it follow I can raise him to Life again? The Parliament may condemn all the *Greek* and *Roman* Authors; can it therefore create new ones in their Stead? They may make Laws, indeed, and call them Canon and Ecclesiastical Laws, and oblige all Men to observe them under Pain of High Treason. And so may I, who love as well as any Man to have in my own Family the Power in the last Resort, take a Turnip, then tye a String to it, and call it a Watch, and turn away all my Servants, if they refuse to call it so too.

FOR my own Part, I must confess that this Opinion of the Independent Power of the Church, or *Imperium in Imperio,* wherewith this Writer raiseth such a Dust, is what I never imagined to be of any Consequence, never once heard disputed among Divines, nor remember to have read, otherwise than as a Scheme in one or two Authors of middle Rank, but with very little Weight laid on it. And, I dare believe, that there is hardly one Divine in ten that ever once thought of this Matter. Yet to see a large swelling Volume written only to encounter this Doctrine, what could one think less than that the whole Body of the Clergy were perpetually tiring the Press and the Pulpit with nothing else?

I REMEMBER some Years ago a Virtuoso writ a small Tract about Worms, proved them to be in more Places than was generally observed, and made some Discoveries by Glasses. This having met with some Reception, presently the poor Man's Head was full of nothing but Worms; all we eat and drink, all the whole Consistence of human Bodies, and those of every other Animal, the very Air we breathe; in short, all Nature throughout was nothing but Worms: And by that System, he solved all Difficulties, and from thence all Cases in Philosophy. Thus it hath fared with our Author and his Independent Power. The Tack against Occasional Conformity, the Scarcity of Coffee, the Invasion of *Scotland,* the Loss of Kerseys and narrow Cloths, the Death of King *William,* the Author's turning Papist for Preferment, the Loss of the Battle of *Almanza,* with ten thousand other Misfortunes, are all owing to this *Imperium in Imperio.*

IT will be therefore necessary to set this Matter in a clear Light; by enquiring whether the Clergy have any Power independent of the Civil, and of what Nature it is.

WHENEVER the Christian Religion was embraced by the Civil Power in any Nation, there is no Doubt but the Magistrates and Senates were fully instructed in the Rudiments of it. Besides, the Christians were so numerous, and their Worship so open before the Conversion of Princes, that their Discipline, as well as Doctrine, could not be a Secret: They saw plainly a Subordination of Ecclesiasticks; Bishops, Priests, and Deacons: That these had certain Powers and Employments different from the Laity: That the Bishops were consecrated, and set apart for that Office by those of their own Order: That the Presbyters and Deacons were differently set apart, always by the Bishops: That none but the Ecclesiasticks presumed to pray or Preach in Places set apart for God's Worship, or to administer the Lord's Supper: That all Questions, relating either to Discipline or Doctrine, were determined in Ecclesiastical Conventions. These and the like Doctrines and Practices, being most of them directly proved, and the rest by very fair Consequences deduced from the Words of our Saviour and his Apostles, were certainly received as a Divine Law by every Prince or State which admitted the Christian Religion; and consequently, what they could not justly alter afterwards, any more than the common Laws of Nature. And, therefore, although the Supreme Power can hinder the Clergy or Church from making any new Canons, or executing the old; from consecrating Bishops, or refusing those that they do consecrate; or, in short, from performing any Ecclesiastical Office, as they may from eating, drinking and sleeping; yet they cannot themselves perform those Offices, which are assigned to the Clergy by our Saviour and his Apostles; or, if they do, it is not according to the Divine Institution, and consequently null and void. Our Saviour telleth us, *His Kingdom is not of this World*; and therefore, to be sure, the World is not of his Kingdom, nor can ever please him by interfering in the Administration of it, since he hath appointed Ministers of his own, and hath empowered and instructed them for that Purpose: So, that I believe the Clergy, who, as he sayeth, *are good at distinguishing*, would think it reasonable to distinguish between their Power, and the Liberty of exercising this Power. The former they claim immediately from Christ, and the latter from the Permission, Connivance, or Authority of the Civil Government; with which the

Clergy's Power, according to the Solution I have given, cannot possibly interfere.

BUT this Writer, setting up to form a System upon stale, Scanty Topicks, and a narrow Circle of Thought, falleth into a thousand Absurdities. And for a further Help, he hath a Talent of rattling out Phrases, which seem to have Sense, but have none at all: The usual Fate of those who are ignorant of the Force and Compass of Words, without which it is impossible for a Man to write either pertinently or intelligibly upon the most obvious Subjects.

So, in the Beginning of his Preface, Page 4, he says, *The Church of* England *being established by Acts of Parliament, is a perfect Creature of the Civil Power; I mean the Polity and Discipline of it, and it is that which maketh all the Contention; for as to the Doctrines expressed in the Articles, I do not find High Church to be in any Manner of Pain; but they who lay Claim to most Orthodoxy can distinguish themselves out of them.* It is observable in this Author, that his Stile is naturally harsh and ungrateful to the Ear, and his Expressions mean and trivial; but whenever he goeth about to polish a Period, you may be certain of some gross Defect in Propriety or Meaning: So the Lines just quoted seem to run easily over the Tongue; and, upon Examination, they are perfect Nonsense and Blunder: To speak in his own borrowed Phrase, what is contained in the Idea of *Established*? Surely, not Existence. Doth *Establishment* give *Being* to a Thing? He might have said the same Thing of Christianity in general, or the Existence of God, since both are confirmed by Acts of Parliament. But, the best is behind: For, in the next Line, having named the Church half a Dozen Times before, he now says, he meaneth only *the Polity and Discipline of it*: As if, having spoke in Praise of the Art of Physick, a Man should explain himself, that he meant only the Institution of a College of Physicians into a President and Fellows. And it will appear, that this Author, however versed in the Practice, hath grosly transgressed the Rules of Nonsense, (whose Property it is neither to affirm or deny) since every visible Assertion gathered from those few Lines is absolutely false: For where was the Necessity of excepting the Doctrines expressed in the Articles, since, these are equally Creatures of the Civil Power, having been established by Acts of Parliament as well as the others. But the Church of *England* is no Creature of the Civil Power, either as to its Polity or Doctrines. The Fundamentals of both were deduced from Christ and his Apostles, and the Instructions of the purest and earliest Ages, and were received as such by those Princes or States who embraced Christianity, whatever prudential Additions have been made to the former by human Laws, which alone can be justly altered or annulled by them.

WHAT I have already said, would, I think be a sufficient Answer to his whole Preface, and indeed to the greatest Part of his Book, which is wholely turned upon battering down a Sort of independent Power in the Clergy; which few or none of them ever claimed or defended. But there being certain Peculiarities in this Preface, that very much set off the Wit, the Learning, the Raillery, Reasoning and Sincerity of the Author; I shall take Notice of some of them as I pass. ———

BUT here I hope, it will not be expected, that I should bestow Remarks upon every Passage in this Book, that is liable to Exception for Ignorance, Falshood, Dulness, or Malice. Where he is so insipid, that nothing can be struck out for the Reader's Entertainment, I shall observe *Horace*'s Rule:

> *Quæ desperes tractata nitescere posse, relinques.*

Upon which Account I shall say nothing of that great Instance of his Candour and Judgment in Relation to Dr. *Stillingfleet*, who (happening to lie under his Displeasure upon the fatal Test of *Imperium in Imperio*) is High-Church and Jacobite, took the Oaths of Allegiance to save him from the Gallows * and subscribed the Articles only to keep his Preferment: Whereas the Character of that Prelate is universally known to have been directly the Reverse, of what this Writer gives him.

BUT before he can attempt to ruin this damnable Opinion of

---

* Page 5. *He quotes Bishop* STILLINGFLEET's *Vindication of the Doctrine of the Trinity, where the Bishop says, that a Man might be very right in the Belief of an Article, though mistaken in the Explication of it. Upon which* Tindal *observes*: These Men treat the Articles as they do the Oath of Allegiance, which, they say, obliges them not actually to assist the Government, but to do nothing against it; that is, nothing that would bring him to the Gallows.

two independent Powers, he telleth us; Page 6. *It will be necessary to shew what is contained in the Idea of Government*. Now, it is to be understood, that this refined Way of Speaking was introduced by Mr. *Locke*: After whom the Author limpeth as fast as he was able. All the former Philosophers in the World, from the Age of *Socrates* to ours, would have ignorantly put the Question, *Quid est Imperium?* But now it seemeth we must vary our Phrase; and since our modern Improvement of Human Understanding, instead of desiring a Philosopher to describe or define a Mousetrap, or tell me what it is; I must gravely ask, what is contained in the Idea of a Mouse-trap? But then to observe how deeply this new Way of putting Questions to a Man's Self, maketh him enter into the Nature of Things; his present Business is to shew us, what is contained in the Idea of Government. The Company knoweth nothing of the Matter, and would gladly be instructed; which he doth in the following Words, p. 6.

It would be in vain for one intelligent Being to pretend to set Rules to the Actions of another, if he had it not in his Power to reward the Compliance with, or punish the Deviations from his Rules by some Good, or Evil, which is not the natural Consequence of those Actions; since the forbidding Men to do or forbear an Action on the Account of that Convenience or Inconvenience which attendeth it, whether he who forbids it will or no, can be no more than Advice.

I SHALL not often draw such long Quotations as this, which I could not forbear to offer as a Specimen of the Propriety and Perspicuity of this Author's Style. And, indeed, what a Light breaketh out upon us all, as soon as we have read these Words! How thoroughly are we instructed in the whole Nature of Government? What mighty Truths are here discovered; and how clearly conveyed to our Understandings? And therefore let us melt this refined Jargon into the *Old Style*, for the Improvement of such, who are not enough conversant in the *New*.

IF the Author were one that used to talk like one of us, he would have spoke in this Manner: I think it necessary to give a full and perfect Definition of Government, such as will shew the Nature and all the Properties of it; and, my Definition is thus. One Man will never cure another of stealing Horses, merely by minding him of the Pains he hath taken, the Cold he hath got, and the Shoe-Leather he hath lost in stealing that Horse; nay, to warn him, that the Horse may kick or fling him, or cost him more than he is worth in Hay and Oats, can be no more than Advice. For the Gallows is not the natural Effect of robbing on the High-Way, as Heat is of Fire: And therefore, if you will govern a Man, you must find out some other Way of Punishment, than what he will inflict upon himself.

OR, if this will not do, let us try it in another Case (which I instanced before) and in his own Terms. Suppose he had thought it necessary (and I think it was as much so as the other) to shew us what is contained in the Idea of a Mouse-Trap, he must have proceeded in these Terms. It would be in vain for an intelligent Being, to set Rules for hindering a Mouse from eating his Cheese, unless he can inflict upon that Mouse some Punishment, which is not the natural Consequence of eating the Cheese. For, to tell her, it may lie heavy on her Stomach; that she will grow too big to get back into her Hole, and the like, can be no more than Advice: Therefore, we must find out some Way of punishing her, which hath more Inconveniencies than she will ever suffer by the mere eating of Cheese. After this, who is so slow of Understanding, not to have in his Mind a full and compleat Idea of a Mouse-trap? Well.—The Free-thinkers may talk what they please of Pedantry, and Cant, and Jargon of Schoolmen, and insignificant Terms in the Writings of the Clergy, if ever the most perplexed and perplexing Follower of *Aristotle* from *Scotus* to *Suarez* could be a Match for this Author.

BUT the Strength of his Arguments is equal to the Clearness of his Definitions. For, having most ignorantly divided Government into three Parts, whereof the first contains the other two; he attempteth to prove that the Clergy possess none of these by a Divine Right. And, he argueth thus, p. 7. *As to a legislative Power, if that belongs to the Clergy by Divine Right, it must be when they are assembled in Convocation: But the* 25 Hen. 8. c. 19. *is a Bar to any such Divine Right, because that Act makes it no less than a Præmunire for them, so much as to meet without the King's Writ,* &c. So that the Force of his Argument lieth here; if the Clergy had a Divine Right, it is taken away by the 25th of *Henry* the 8th. And as ridiculous as this Argument is, the Preface and Book are founded upon it.

ANOTHER Argument against the legislative Power in the

II g

Clergy of *England*, is, p. 8, that *Tacitus* telleth us; that in great Affairs, the *Germans* consulted the whole Body of the People. *De minoribus rebus Principes consultant, de majoribus omnes: Ita tamen, ut ea quoque, quorum penes plebem arbitrium est apud Principes pertractandum.* Tacitus *de moribus & populis Germaniæ.* Upon which, *Tindall* observeth thus. *De majoribus omnes,* was a Fundamental amongst our Ancestors long before they arrived in *Great-Britain,* and Matters of Religion were ever reckoned among their *Majora.* (See Pref. p. 8. and 9.) Now it is plain, that our Ancestors, the *Saxons,* came from *Germany*: It is likewise plain, that Religion was always reckoned by the Heathens among their *Majora*: And it is plain, the whole Body of the People could not be the Clergy, and therefore, the Clergy of *England* have no legislative Power.

Thirdly, p. 9. They have no legislative Power, because Mr. *Washington*, in his *Observations on the Ecclesiastical Jurisdiction of the Kings of* England, sheweth from *undeniable Authorities, that in the Time of* William *the Conqueror, and several of his Successors, there were no Laws enacted concerning Religion, but by the great Council of the Kingdom.* I hope likewise Mr. *Washington* observeth, that this great Council of the Kingdom, as appeareth by undeniable Authorities, was sometimes entirely composed of Bishops and Clergy, and called the Parliament, and often consulted upon Affairs of State, as well as Church, as it is agreed by twenty Writers of three Ages; and if Mr. *Washington* says otherwise, he is an Author just fit to be quoted by *Beaux*.

Fourthly,—But it is endless to pursue this Matter any further, in that, it is plain, the Clergy have no Divine Right to make Laws; because *Hen.* VIII. *Edward* VI. and Queen *Elizabeth,* with their Parliaments will not allow it them. Now, without examining what Divine Right the Clergy have, or how far it extendeth, is it any Sort of Proof that I have no Right, because a stronger Power will not let me exercise it? Or, doth all, that this Author says through his Preface, or Book itself, offer any other Sort of Argument but this, or what he deduces the same Way?

BUT his Arguments and Definitions are yet more supportable than the Grossness of historical Remarks, which are scattered so plentifully in his Book, that it would be tedious to enumerate or to shew the Fraud and Ignorance of them. I beg the Reader's Leave to take Notice of one here just in my Way; and, the rather, because I design for the future to let Hundreds of them pass without further Notice. *When*, says he, p. 10. *by the abolishing of the Pope's Power, Things were brought back to their antient Channel, the Parliament's Right in making ecclesiastical Laws revived of Course.* What can possibly be meant by this *antient Channel?* Why, the Channel that Things ran in before the Pope had any Power in *England*: That is to say, before *Austin* the Monk converted *England*, before which Time, it seems the Parliament had a Right to make Ecclesiastical Laws. And what Parliament could this be? Why, the Lords Spiritual and Temporal, and the Commons met at *Westminster*.

I CANNOT here forbear reproving the Folly and Pedantry of some Lawyers, whose Opinions this poor Creature blindly followeth, and rendereth yet more absurd by his Comments. The Knowledge of our Constitution can be only attained by consulting the earliest *English* Histories, of which those Gentlemen seem utterly ignorant, further than a Quotation or an Index. They would fain derive our Government as now constituted, from Antiquity: And, because they have seen *Tacitus* quoted for his *Majoribus omnes*; and have read of the *Goths* military Institution in their Progresses and Conquests, they presently dream of a Parliament. Had their Reading reached so far, they might have deduced it much more fairly from *Aristotle* and *Polybius*, who both distinctly name the Composition of *Rex, Seniores, et Populus*; and the latter, as I remember particularly, with the highest Approbation. The Princes in the *Saxon* Heptarchy, did indeed call their Nobles sometimes together upon weighty Affairs, as most other Princes of the World have done in all Ages. But they made War and Peace, and raised Money by their own Authority: They gave or mended Laws by their Charters, and they raised Armies by their Tenures. Besides, some of those Kingdoms fell in by Conquest, before *England* was reduced under one Head, and therefore could pretend no Rights, but by the Concessions of the Conqueror.

FURTHER, which is more material, upon the Admission of Christianity, great Quantities of Land were acquired by the

Clergy, so that the great Council of the Nation was often entirely of Churchmen, and ever a considerable Part. But, our present Constitution is an artificial Thing, not fairly to be traced, in my Opinion, beyond *Henry* I. Since which Time it hath in every Age admitted several Alterations; and differeth now as much, even from what it was then, as almost any two Species of Government described by *Aristotle*. And, it would be much more reasonable to affirm, that the Government of *Rome* continued the same under *Justinian*, as it was in the Time of *Scipio*, because the Senate and Consuls still remained, although the Power of both had been several hundred Years transferred to the Emperors.

REFERENCES to TINDALL'S Book, and Remarks upon it, which the Author left thus undigested, being Hints for himself to use in answering the said Book.

The PREFACE.

Page 4, 5. MAY not a Man subscribe the whole Articles, because he differs from another in the Explication of one? How many Oaths are prescribed, that Men may differ in the Explication of some Part of them? Instance, &c.

Page 6. *Idea of Government.* A canting, pedantic Way, learned from *Locke*; and how prettily he sheweth it. Instance---

Page 7. Absurd to argue against the Clergy's Divine Right, because of the Statute of *Henry* VIII. How doth that destroy Divine Right? The sottish Way of Arguing; from what the Parliament can do; from their Power, &c.

Page 8. *Damned all the Canons.* What doth he mean? A grave Divine could not answer all his Play-house and *Alsatia* Cant, &c. He hath read *Hudibras*, and many Plays.

Ibid. *If the Parliament can annul Ecclesiastical Laws, they must be able to make them.* Distinguish and shew the Sillyness, &c.

Ibid. All that he sayeth against the Discipline, he might say the same against the Doctrine, nay, against the Belief of a God, *viz.* That the Legislature might forbid it. The Church formeth and contriveth Canons; and the Civil Power, which is compulsive, confirms them.

Page 9. *The great Council of the Kingdom.* And that was very often, chiefly, only Bishops.

Ibid. *Laws settled by Parliament to punish the Clergy.* What Laws were those?

Page 10. *The People are bound to no Laws but of their own chusing.* It is fraudulent; for they may consent to what others chuse, and so People often do.

Page 14, Paragraph 6.—Answer it. No such Consequence at all. They have a Power exclusive from all others. Ordained to act as Clergy, but not govern in Civil Affairs; nor act without Leave of the Civil Power.

Page 25. *They suspected the Love of Power natural to Churchmen.* Truly, so is the Love of Pudding, and most other Things desirable in this Life; and in that they are like the Laity, as in all other Things that are not good. And, therefore, they are held not in Esteem for what they are like in, but for their Virtues. The true Way to abuse them with Effect, is to tell us some Faults of their's, that other Men have not, or not so much of as they, *&c.* Might not any Man speak full as bad of Senates, Dyets, and Parliaments, as he can do about Councils; and as bad of Princes, as he doth of Bishops?

Page 31. *They might as well have made Cardinals* Campegi *and* de Chinuchii, *Bishops of* Salisbury *and* Worcester, *as have enacted that their several Sees and Bishopricks were utterly void.* No. The Legislature might determine he should not be a Bishop there, but not make a Bishop.

Ibid. *Were not a great Number deprived by Parliament?* Does he mean Presbyters? What signifies that?

Ibid. *Have they not trusted this Power with our Princes?* Why, ay. But that argueth not Right, but Power. Have they not cut off a King's Head, *&c.* The Church must do the best they can, if not what they would.

Page 36. *If Tythes and First-Fruits are paid to spiritual Persons as such, the King or Queen is the most spiritual Person,* &c. As if the First-Fruits, *&c.* were paid to the King, as Tythes to a spiritual Person.

Page 43. *King* Charles II. *thought fit that the Bishops in* Scotland *should hold their Bishopricks during Will and Pleasure; I do not find that High Church complained of this as an Encroachment,* &c. No; but as a pernicious Council of Lord *Loch.*

Page 44. *The common Law Judges have a Power to determine, whether a Man has a legal Right to the Sacrament.* They pretend it, but that we complain of as a most abominable Hardship, *&c.*

Page 45. *Giving Men thus blindly to the Devil, is an extraordinary Piece of Complaisance to a Lay-Chancellor.* He is something in the right; and therefore it is a Pity there are any; and I hope the Church will provide against it. But, if the Sentence be just, it is not the Person, but the Contempt. And, if the Author attacketh a Man on the Highway, and taketh but Two-pence, he shall be sent to the Gallows, more terrible to him than the Devil, for his Contempt of the Law, *&c.* Therefore he need not complain of being sent to Hell.

Page 64. Mr. *Lesly* may carry Things too far, as it is natural, because the other Extreme is so great. But what he says of the King's Losses, since the Church Lands were given away, is too great a Truth, *&c.*

Page 76. *To which I have nothing to plead, except the Zeal I have for the Church of* England. You will see some Pages further, what he meaneth by the Church; but it is not fair not to begin with telling us what is contained in the Idea of a Church, *&c.*

Page 83. Ibid. *They will not be angry with me for thinking better of the Church than they do*, &c. No, but they will differ from you; because the worse the Queen is pleased, you think her better. I believe the Church will not concern themselves much about your Opinion of them, *&c.*

Page 84. *But the Popish, Eastern, Presbyterian and Jacobite Clergy*, &c. This is like a general Pardon, with such Exceptions as make it useless, if we compute it, *&c.*

Page 87. *Misapplying of the Word Church*, &c. This is cavilling. No doubt his Project is for exempting of the People: But that is not what in common Speech we usually mean by the Church. Besides, who doth not know that Distinction?

Ibid. *Constantly apply the same Ideas to them*. This is, in old *English*, meaning the same Thing.

Page 89. *Demonstrates I could have no Design but the promoting of Truth*, &c. Yes, several Designs, as Money, Spleen, Atheism, *&c.* What? Will any Man think Truth was his Design, and not Money and Malice? Doth he expect the House will go into a Committee for a Bill to bring Things to his Scheme, to confound every Thing, *&c*?

Some deny *Tindall* to be the Author, and produce Stories of his Dullness and Stupidity. But what is there in all this Book, that the dullest Man in *England* might not write, if he were angry and bold enough, and had no Regard to Truth?

REMARKS on the BOOK, beginning with the INTRODUCTION.

Page 4. WHETHER Louis XIV. *has such a Power over Philip V?* He speaketh here of the unlimited, uncontroulable Authority of Fathers. A very foolish Question; and his Discourse hitherto, of Government, weak and trivial, and liable to Objections.

Ibid. *Whom he is to consider not as his own, but the Almighty's Workmanship.* A very likely Consideration for the Ideas of the State of Nature. A very wrong Deduction of paternal Government; but that is nothing to the Dispute, *&c.*

Page 12. *And as such might justly be punished by every one in the State of Nature.* False; he doth not seem to understand the State of Nature, although he hath borrowed it from *Hobbes, &c.*

Page 14. *Merely speculative Points, and other indifferent Things,* &c. And why are speculative Opinions so insignificant? Do not Men proceed in their Practice according to their Speculations? So, if the Author were a Chancellor, and one of his Speculations were, that the poorer the Clergy the better; would not that be of great Use, if a Cause came before him of Tythes or Church-Lands?

Ibid. *Which can only be known by examining whether Men had any Power in the State of Nature over their own, or others Actions in these Matters.* No, that is a wrong Method, unless where Religion hath not been revealed; in natural Religion.

Ibid. *Nothing at first Sight can be more obvious, than that in all Religious Matters, none could make over the Right of judging for himself, since that would cause his Religion to be absolutely at the Disposal of another.* At his Rate of arguing (I think I do not misrepresent him, and I believe he will not deny the Consequence) a Man may profess Heathenism, Mahometanism, *&c.* and gain as many Proselytes as he can; and they may have their Assemblies, and the Magistrate ought to protect them, provided they do not disturb the State: And they may enjoy all Secular Preferments, be Lords Chancellors, Judges, *&c.* But there are some Opinions in several Religions, which, although they do not directly make Men rebel, yet lead to it. Instance some. Nay we might have

Temples for Idols, &c. A thousand such Absurdities follow from his general Notions, and ill-digested Schemes. And we see in the Old Testament, that Kings were reckoned good or ill, as they suffered or hindered Image-Worship and Idolatry, &c. which was limiting Conscience.

Page 15. *Men may form what Clubs, Companies, or Meetings they think fit*, &c. *which the Magistrate, as long as the Public sustains no Damage, cannot hinder*, &c. This is false; although the Public sustain no Damage, they will forbid Clubs, where they think Danger may happen.

Page 16. *The Magistrate is as much obliged to protect them in the Way they chuse of worshiping him, as in any other indifferent Matter.*—Page 17. *The Magistrate to treat all his Subjects alike, how much so ever they differ from him or one another in these Matters*. This shews, that although they be *Turks, Jews*, or *Heathens*, it is so. But we are sure Christianity is the only true Religion, &c. and therefore it should be the Magistrate's chief Care to propagate it; and that God should be worshipped in that Form, that those who are the Teachers think most proper, &c.

Page 18. *So that Persecution is the most comprehensive of all Crimes*, &c. But he hath not told us what is concluded in the Idea of Persecution. State it right.

Ibid. *But here it may be demanded, If a Man's Conscience make him do such Acts*, &c. This doth not answer the above Objection: For, if the Public be not disturbed with atheistical Principles preached, nor Immoralities, all is well. So that still, Men may be *Jews, Turks*, &c.

Page 22. *The same Reason which obliges them to make Statutes of Mortmain, and other Laws, against the People's giving Estates to the Clergy, will equally hold for their taking them away when given*. A great Security for Property! Will this hold to any other Society in a State, as Merchants, &c. or only to Ecclesiasticks? A pretty Project: Forming general Schemes requireth a deeper Head than this Man's.

Ibid. *But the Good of the Society being the only Reason of the Magistrates having any Power over Men's Properties, I cannot see why he should deprive his Subjects of any Part thereof, for the Maintenance of such Opinions as have no Tendency that Way*. Here is a Paragraph (*Vide* also *infra*) which hath a great deal in it. The Meaning is, that no Man ought to pay Tythes, who doth not believe what the Minister preacheth, But how came they by this Property? When they purchased the Land, they paid only for so much; and the Tythes were exempted. It is an older Title than any Man's Estate is, and if it were taken away To-morrow, it could not without a new Law belong to the Owners of the other nine Parts, any more than Impropriations do.

Ibid. *For the Maintenance of such Opinions, as no Ways contribute to the publick Good.* By such Opinions as the Publick receive no Advantage by, he must mean Christianity.

Page 23. *Who by Reason of such Articles are divided into different Sects.* A pretty Cause of Sects! &c.

Page 24. *So the same Reason as often as it occurs, will oblige him to leave that Church.* This is an Excuse for his turning Papist.

Ibid. *Unless you suppose Churches like Traps, easy to admit one; but when once he is in, there he must always stick, either for the Pleasure or Profit of the Trap-Setters.* Remark his Wit.

Page 29. *Nothing can be more absurd than maintaining there must be two independent Powers in the same Society,* &c. This abominably absurd; shew it.

Page 33. *The whole Hierarchy as built on it, must necessarily fall to to the Ground, and great will be the Fall of this spiritual* Babylon. I will do him Justice, and take Notice, when he is witty, &c.

Page 36. *For if there may be two such in every Society on Earth, why may there not be more than one in Heaven?* A delicate Consequence.

Page 37. *Without having the less, he could not have the greater, in which that is contained.* Sophistical; Instance wherein.

Page 42. *Some since, more subtle than the Jews, have managed their Commutations more to their own Advantage, by enriching themselves, and beggaring, if Fame be not a Liar, many an honest Dissenter.* It is fair to produce Witnesses, is she a Lyar or not? The Report is almost impossible. Commutations were contrived for roguish Registers and Proctors, and Lay-Chancellors, but not for the Clergy.

Page 43. *Kings and People, who (as the Indians do the Devil) adored the Pope out of Fear.* I am in Doubt whether I shall allow that for Wit or no, &c. Look you in these Cases, preface it thus; if one may use an old Saying.

Page 44. *One Reason why the Clergy make what they call Schism, to be so heinous a Sin.* There it is now; because he hath changed Churches, he ridiculeth Schism; as *Milton* wrote for Divorces, because he had an ill Wife. For ten Pages on, we must give the true Answer that makes all these Arguments of no Use.

Page 60. *It possibly will be said, I have all this while been doing these Gentlemen a great deal of Wrong.* To do him Justice, he sets forth the Objections of his Adversaries with great Strength, and much to their Advantage. No Doubt those are the very Objections we would offer.

Page 68. *Their Executioner.* He is fond of this Word in many Places, yet there is nothing in it, further than it is the Name for the Hangman, &c.

Page 69. *Since they exclude both from having any Thing in the order-ing of Church Matters.* Another Part of his Scheme: For by this the People ought to execute Ecclesiastical Offices without Distinction, for he brings the other Opinion as an absurd one.

Page 72. *They claim a judicial Power, and by Virtue of it, the Government of the Church, and thereby (pardon the Expression) become Traytors both to God and Man.* Who doth he desire to pardon him? or is this meant of the *English* Clergy? So it seemeth. Doth he desire them to pardon him? They do it as Christians. Doth he desire the Government to do it? But then how can they make Examples? He says, the Clergy do so, &c. so he means all.

Page 74. *I would gladly know what they mean by giving the Holy Ghost.* Explain what is really meant by giving the Holy Ghost, like a King impowering an Ambassador.

Page 76. *The Popish Clergy make very bold with the Three Persons of the Trinity.* Why then, do not mix them, but we see whom this glanceth on most. As to the *Conge d' Elire* and *nolo Episcopari*, not so absurd; and, if omitted, why changed?

Page 78. *But not to digress* —— Pray, doth he call Scurrility upon the Clergy, a Digression? The Apology needless, &c.

Ibid. *A Clergyman, it is said, is God's Ambassador.* But you know an Ambassador may leave a Secretary, &c.

Ibid. *Call their Pulpit Speeches, the Word of God.* That is a Mistake.

Page 79. *Such Persons to represent him.* Are not they that own his Power, fitter to represent him than others? Would the Author be a fitter Person?

Ibid. *Puft up with intolerable Pride and Insolence.* Not at all; For, where is the Pride to be employed by a Prince, whom so few own, and whose Being is disputed by such as this Author?

Ibid. *Perhaps from a Poor Servitor,* &c. *to be a Prime Minister in God's Kingdom.* That is right. God taketh Notice of the Difference between poor Servitors, *&c.* extremely foolish—shew it. The Argument lieth stronger against the Apostles, poor Fishermen, and St. Paul, a Tent-maker. So gross and idle!

Page 80. *The Formality of laying Hand over Head on a Man.* A Pun; but an old one. I remember when *Swan* made that Pun first, he was severely checked for it.

Ibid. *What is more required to give one a Right,* &c. Here shew, what Power is in the Church, and what in the State, to make Priests.

Page 85. *To bring Men into, and not turn them out of the ordinary Way of Salvation.* Yes; but as one rotten Sheep doth Mischief— And do you think it reasonable, that such a one as this Author, should converse with Christians, and weak ones?

Page 86. See his fine Account of Spiritual Punishment.

Page 87. *The Clergy affirm, that if they had not the Power to exclude Men from the Church, its Unity could not be preserved.* So, to expel an ill Member from a College, would be the Way to divide the College; as in *All-Souls,* &c. Apply it to him.

Page 88. *I cannot see but it is contrary to the Rules of Charity to exclude Men from the Church,* &c. All this turns upon the falsest Reasoning in the World. So if a Man be imprisoned for stealing a Horse, he is hindered from other Duties: And, you might argue, that a Man who doth ill, ought to be more diligent in minding other Duties, and not be debarred from them. It is for Contumacy and Rebellion against that Power in the Church, which the Law hath confirmed. So a Man is outlawed for a Trifle, upon Contumacy.

Page 92. *Obliging all by penal Laws to receive the Sacrament.* This is false.

Page 93. *The Want of which Means can only harden a Man in his Impenitence.* It is for his being hardened that he is excluded. Suppose a Son robbeth his Father in the High-Way, and his Father will not see him 'till he restoreth the Money and owneth his Fault. It is hard to deny him paying his Duty in other Things, *&c.* How absurd this!

Page 95. *And that only they had a Right to give it.* Another Part of his Scheme, that the People have a Right to give the Sacrament. See more of it, p. 135 and 137.

Page 96. *Made familiar to such Practices by the Heathen Priests.* Well; And this shews the Necessity of it for Peace Sake. A silly Objection of this and other Enemies to Religion, to think to disgrace it by applying Heathenism, which only concerns the political Part wherein they were as wise as others, and might give Rules. Instance in some, *&c.*

Page 98. *How differently from this do the great Pretenders to primitive Practice act*, &c. This a remarkable Passage. Doth he condemn or allow this mysterious Way? It seems the first———— and therefore these Words are a little turned, but infallibly stood in the first Draught as a great Argument for *Popery.*

Page 100. *They dress them up in a* Sanbenito. So, now we are to answer for the Inquisition. One Thing is; that he makes the Fathers guilty of asserting most of the Corruptions about the Power of Priests.

Page 104. *Some Priests assume to themselves an arbitrary Power of excluding Men from the Lord's Supper.* His Scheme; that any Body may administer the Sacraments, Women or Children, *&c.*

Page 108. *One no more than another can be reckoned a Priest.* See his Scheme. Here he disgraceth what the Law enacts, about the Manner of consecrating, *&c.*

Page 118. *Churches serve to worse Purposes than Bear-Gardens.* This from *Hudibras.*

Page 119. *In the Time of that wise Heathen* Ammianus Marcellinus. Here he runs down all Christianity in general.

Page 120. *I shall in the following Part of my Discourse, &c.* This independent Power in the Church, is like the Worms; being the Cause of all Diseases.

Page 124. *How easily could the* Roman *Emperors have destroyed the Church.* Just as if he had said; how easily could *Herod* kill *Christ* when a Child, *&c.*

Page 125. *The People were set against Bishops by Reason of their Tyranny.* Wrong. For the Bishops were no Tyrants: Their Power was swallowed up by the Popes, and the People desired they should have more. It were the Regulars that tyrannized and formed Priestcraft. He is ignorant.

Page 139. *He is not bound by the Laws of Christ to leave his Friends in order to be baptized,* &c. This directly against the Gospel.—One would think him an Emissary, by his preaching Schism.

Page 142. *Occasional Conformists only,* &c. So that all are wrong but they. The Scripture is full against Schism. *Tindall* promoteth it, and placeth in it all the present and future Happiness of Man.

Page 144. All he has hitherto said on this Matter, with a very little Turn, were Arguments for Popery: For, it is certain, that Religion had Share in very few Wars for many hundred Years before the Reformation, because they were all of a Mind. It is the Ambition of Rebels, preaching upon the Discontents of Sectaries, that they are not supream, which hath caused Wars for Religion. He is mistaken altogether. His little narrow Understanding and Want of Learning.

Page 145. *Tho' some say the High-flyers Lives might serve for a very good Rule, if Men would act quite contrary to them.* Is he one of that Some? Besides the new Turn of Wit, *&c.* all the Clergy in *England* come under his Notion of High-Flyers, as he states it.

Page 147. *None of them* (*Churchmen*) *could be brought to acknowledge it lawful, upon any Account whatever, to exclude the Duke of* York. This Account false in Fact.

Ibid. *And the Body Politick, whether Ecclesiastical, or Civil, must be dealt with after the same Manner as the Body natural.* What, because it is called a Body, and is a Simile, must it hold in all Circumstances.

Page 148. *We find all wise Legislators,* &c. This Paragraph false.———It was directly contrary in several, as *Lycurgus,* &c.

Page 152. *All the Skill of the Prelatists is not able to discover the least Distinction between Bishop and Presbyter.* Yet God knows this hath been done many a Time.

Page 158. *The Epistle to the* Philippians *is directed to the Bishops and Deacons, I mean in due Order after the People,* viz. *To the Saints with their Bishops and Deacons.* I hope, he would argue from another Place, that the People precede the King, because of these Words: *Ye shall be destroyed, both you and your King.*

Page 167. *The Pope, and other great Church Dons.* I suppose he meaneth Bishops: But I wish, he would explain himself, and not be so very witty in the midst of an Argument; it is like two Mediums; not fair in disputing.

Page 168. *Assuming a Power,* &c. His great Error all along is, that he doth not distinguish between a Power, and a Liberty of exercising that Power, *&c.* I would appeal to any Man, whether the Clergy have not too little Power, since a Book like his, that unsettleth Foundations, and would destroy all, goes unpunished, *&c.*

Page 171. *The whole Tenor of the Gospel directly contrary to it.* Then it is not an allowable Means: This carries it so far as to spoil his own System; it is a Sin to have Bishops as we have them.

Page 172. *No great Compliment to the Clergy of those Days.* Why so? It is the natural Effect of a worse Independency, that he keepeth such a Clatter about. An Independency of Churches on each other, which must naturally create Schism.

Page 183. *Their having a Right to the tenth Part.* Yes, that would have passed easy enough; for they could not imagine Teachers could live on Air; and their Heathen Priests were much more unreasonable.

Page 184. *Mens suffering for such Opinions is not sufficient to support the Weight of them.* This is a Glance against Christianity. State the Case of converting Infidels; the Converters are supposed few; the Bulk of the Priests must be of the converted Country. It is their own People therefore they maintain. What Project or End can a few Converters propose? they can leave no Power to their Families, *&c.* State this, I say, at Length, and give it a true Turn. Princes give Corporations Power to purchase Lands.

Page 187. *That it became an easy Prey to the barbarous Nations.* Ignorance in *Tindall.* The Empire long declined before Christianity was introduced. This a wrong Cause, if ever there was one.

Page 190. *It is the Clergy's Interest to have Religion corrupted.* Quite the contrary, prove it. How is it the Interest of the *English* Clergy to corrupt Religion? The more Justice and Piety the

People have, the better it is for them; for that would prevent the Penury of Farmers, and the Oppression of exacting covetous Landlords, &c. That which hath corrupted Religion, is the Liberty unlimited of professing all Opinions. Do not Lawyers render Law intricate by their Speculations, &c. And Physicians, &c.

Page 209. *The Spirit and Temper of the Clergy*, &c. What does this Man think the Clergy are made of? Answer generally to what he says against Councils in the ten Pages before. Suppose I should bring Quotations in their Praise.

Page 211. *As the Clergy were the Inventors of Corruptions*. His Scheme is, that the fewer and poorer the better, and the contrary among the Clergy. A noble Principle; and delicate Consequences from it.

Page 207. *Men are not always condemned for the Sake of Opinions, but Opinions sometimes for the Sake of Men*. And so he hopes, that if his Opinions are condemned, People will think, it is a Spite against him, as having been always scandalous.

Page 210. *The meanest Layman as good a Judge as the greatest Priest*. As if one should say, the meanest sick Man hath as much Interest in Health as a Physician, therefore is as good a Judge of Physick as a Physician, &c.

Ibid. *Had Synods been composed of Laymen, none of those Corruptions which tend to advance the Interest of the Clergy*, &c. True. But the Part the Laity had in reforming, was little more than plundering. He should understand, that the Nature of Things is this, that the Clergy are made of Men, and without some Encouragement, they will not have the best, but the worst.

Page 219. *They who gave Estates to, rather than they who took them from the Clergy, were guilty of Sacrilege*. Then the People are the Church, and the Clergy not; another Part of his Scheme.

Page 215. *The Clergy, as they subsisted by the Alms of the People*, &c. This he would have still. Shew the Folly of it. Not possible to shew any civilized Nation ever did it. Who would be Clergymen then? The Absurdity appears by putting the Case, that none were to be Statesmen, Lawyers or Physicians, but who were to subsist by Alms.

Page 222. *These subtle Clergymen work their Designs, who lately cut out such a tacking Job for them,* &c. He is mistaken——Every Body was for the Bill almost; though not for the Tack. The Bishop of *Sarum* was for it, as appears by his Speech against it. But it seems, the tacking is owing to metaphysical Speculations. I wonder whether is most perplexed, this Author in his Style, or the Writings of our Divines. In the Judgment of all People, our Divines have carried practical Preaching and Writing to the greatest Perfection it ever arrived to; which shews, that we may affirm in general our Clergy is excellent, although this or that Man be faulty. As if an Army be constantly victorious, regular, *&c.* we may say, it is an excellent, victorious Army: But *Tindall,* to disparage it, would say, such a Serjeant ran away, such an Ensign hid himself in a Ditch; nay, one Colonel turned his Back, therefore it is a corrupt, cowardly Army, *&c.*

Page 224. *The Work of a late Philosopher, which they are afraid will let too much Light into the World.* Yet just such another, only a Commentator on *Aristotle.* People who are likely to improve their Understanding much with *Locke*: It is not his *Human Understanding,* but other Works that People dislike, although in that there are some dangerous Tenets, as that of *innate Ideas.*

Page 226. *Could they, like the Popish Priests, add to this a Restraint on the Press, their Business would be done.* So it ought: For Example, to hinder his Book, because it is written to justify the Vices and Infidelity of the Age. There can be no other Design in it. For, is this a Way or Manner to do good? Railing doth but provoke. The Opinion of the whole Parliament is, the Clergy are too poor.

Ibid. *When some Nations could be no longer kept from prying into Learning, this miserable Gibberish of the Schools was contrived.* We have exploded Schoolmen as much as he, and in some People's Opinion too much, since the Liberty of embracing any Opinion is allowed. They following *Aristotle,* who is doubtless the greatest Master of Arguing in the World: But it hath been a Fashion of late Years to explode *Aristotle,* and therefore this Man hath fallen into it like others, for that Reason, without understanding him. *Aristotle's* Poetry, Rhetorick, and Politicks are admirable, and therefore it is likely, so are his Logicks.

Page 230. *In these freer Countries, as the Clergy have less Power,*

11 h

&c. Not generally. *Holland* not very famous. *Spain* hath been, and *France* famous. But it requireth more Knowledge, than his, to form general Rules, which People strain (when ignorant) to false Deductions to make them out.

Page 232. The Title of this Chapter, a Truism.

Page 234. *If God has not placed Mankind in Respect to civil Matters*, &c. Bad Parallels; bad Politicks; Want of due Distinction between Teaching and Government. The People may know when they are governed well, but not be wiser than their Instructers. Shew the Difference.

Ibid. *If God has allowed the Civil Society these Privileges, can we suppose he has less Kindness for his Church*, &c. Here they are distinguished; then here it makes for him. It is a Sort of Turn of Expression, which is scarce with him, and he contradicts himself to follow it.

Page 235. The seventh Paragraph furious and false. Were there no Tyrants before the Clergy, *&c?*

Page 236. *Therefore, in order to serve them, though I expect little Thanks*, &c. And, why so? Will they not, you say, follow their Interest? I thought you said so. He has three or four sprightly Turns of this Kind, that look, as if he thought, he had done Wonders, and had put all the Clergy in a Ferment. Whereas, I do assure him, there are but two Things wonderful in his Book: First, How any Man in a Christian Country could have the Boldness and Wickedness to write it. And, how any Government would neglect punishing the Author of it, if not as an Enemy of Religion, yet a profligate Trumpeter of Sedition. These are hard Words, got by reading his Book.

Ibid. *The Light of Nature, as well as the Gospel, obliges People to judge of themselves, &c. to avoid false Prophets, Seducers*, &c. The Legislature can turn out a Priest, and appoint another ready made, but not make one; as you discharge a Physician, and may take a Farrier; but he is no Physician, unless made as he ought to be.

Ibid. *Since no more Power is required for the one than the other.* That is, I dislike my Physician, and can turn him off, therefore I can make any Man a Physician, *&c. cujus est destruere*, &c. Jest on it: Therefore, because he lays Schemes for destroying the Church, we must employ him to raise it again. See, what Danger lies in applying Maxims at Random. So, because it is the Soldier's

Business to knock Men on the Head, it is their's likewise to raise them to Life, &c.

Page 237. *It can belong only to the People to appoint their own ecclesiastical Officers.* This Word *People* is so delicious in him, that I cannot tell what is included in the Idea of the *People.* Doth he mean the Rabble or the Legislature, &c.? In this Sense it may be true, that the Legislature giveth Leave to the Bishops to appoint, and they appoint themselves; I mean, the executive Power appoints, &c. He sheweth his Ignorance in Government. As to *High-Church* he carrieth it a prodigious Way, and includeth in the Idea of it more than others will allow.

Page 239. *Though it be customary to admit none to the Ministry who are not approved by the Bishops or Priests,* &c. One of his Principles to expose.

Ibid. *Every one has not an inherent Right to chuse his own Guide.* That would make delicate Work in a Nation: What would become of all our Churches? They must dwindle into Conventicles. Shew what would be the Consequence of his Scheme in several Points. This great Reformer, if his Projects were reduced to Practice, how many thousand Sects, and consequently Tumults, &c. Men must be governed in Speculations, at least not suffered to vent them, because Opinions tend to Actions, which are most governed by Opinions, &c. If those who write for the Church writ no better, they would succeed but scurvily. But to see whether he be a good Writer, let us see (after he hath published his second Part.)

Page 253. *An excellent Author in his Preface to the Account of* Denmark. This Man judgeth and writeth much of a Level. *Molesworth*'s Preface full of stale profligate Topicks.

That Author wrote his Book in Spite to a Nation as this doth to Religion, and both perhaps on poor personal Piques.

Ibid. *By which Means, and not by any Difference in speculative Matters, they are more rich and populous.* As if ever any Body thought that a Difference in Speculative Opinions made Men richer or poorer; for Example, &c.

Page 258. *Play the Devil for God's Sake.* If this meant for Wit; I would be glad to observe it, but in such Cases I first look whether there be common Sense, &c.

Page 261. *Christendom has been the Scene of perpetual Wars, Mas-*

sacres, &c. He doth not consider that most religious Wars have been caused by Schisms, when the dissenting Parties were ready to join with any ambitious discontented Men. The national Religion always desireth Peace, even in her Notions, for its Interests.

Page 270. *Some have taken the Liberty to compare a High Church Priest in Politicks to a Monkey in a Glass-Shop, where, as he can do no Good, so he never fails of doing Mischief enough.* That is his Modesty, it is his own Simile, and it rather fits a Man that does so and so, (meaning himself). Besides the Comparison is foolish. So it is with Men as with Stags.

Page 276. *Their Interest obliges them directly to promote Tyranny.* The Matter is, that Christianity is the Fault, which spoils the Priests, for they were like other Men before they were Priests. Among the *Romans*, Priests did not do so; for they had the greatest Power during the Republick. I wonder he did not prove, they spoiled *Nero*.

Page 277. *No Princes have been more insupportable and done greater Violence to the Commonwealth than those the Clergy have honoured for Saints and Martyrs.* For Example in our Country, the Princes most celebrated by our Clergy are, *&c. &c. &c.* And the Quarrels since the Conquest were nothing at all of the Clergy, but purely of Families, *&c.* wherein the Clergy only joined like other Men.

Page 279. *Whether the Conduct of the Clergy was any Ways altered for the better*, &c. Monstrous Misrepresentation. Does this Man's Spirit of declaiming let him forget all Truth of Fact, as here, *&c.* shew it. Or doth he flatter himself, a Time will come in future Ages, that Men will believe it on his Word. In short, between Declaiming, Misrepresenting, and Falseness, and charging Popish Things and Independency huddled together, his whole Book is employed.

Set forth at large the Necessity of Union in Religion, and the Disadvantage of the contrary, and answer the contrary in *Holland*, where they have no Religion, and are the worst constituted Government in the World to last. It is Ignorance of Causes and Appearances make shallow People judge so much to their Advantage. They are governed by the Administration and almost Legislature of *Holland* through Advantage of Property; nor are they fit to be set in Balance with a noble Kingdom, *&c.* like a Man that gets a hundred Pounds a Year by hard Labour, and one that hath it in Land.

Page 280. *It may be worth enquiring, whether the Difference between the several Sects in England,* &c. A noble Notion started, that Union in the Church must enslave the Kingdom; reflect on it. This Man hath somewhere heard, that it is a Point of Wit to advance Paradoxes, and the bolder the better. But the Wit lies in maintaining them, which he neglecteth, and formeth imaginary Conclusions from them, as if they were true and uncontested.

He adds, *That in the best constituted Church, the greatest Good which can be expected of the Ecclesiasticks is from their Divisions.* This is a Maxim deduced from a Gradation of false Suppositions. If a Man should turn the Tables, and argue that all the Debauchery, Atheism, Licentiousness, *&c.* of the Times, were owing to the Poverty of the Clergy, *&c.* what would he say? There have been more Wars of Religion since the Ruin of the Clergy, than before in *England.* All the Civil Wars before were from other Causes.

Page 283. *Prayers are made in the Loyal University of Oxford, to continue the Throne free from the Contagion of Schism.* See *Mather's* Sermon on the 29th of *May,* 1705. Thus he ridicules the University while he is eating their Bread. The whole University comes with the most loyal Addresses, yet that goes for nothing. If one indiscreet Man drops an indiscreet Word, all must answer for it.

Page 286. *By allowing all who hold no Opinions prejudicial to the State, and contribute equally with their Fellow-Subjects to its Support, equal Privileges in it.* But who denies that of the Dissenters? The Calvinist Scheme one would not think proper for Monarchy. Therefore, they fall in with the *Scotch, Geneva,* and *Holland*; and when they had Strength here, they pulled down the Monarchy. But I will tell an Opinion they hold prejudicial to the State in his Opinion; and that is, that they are against Toleration, of which, if I do not shew him ten Times more Instances from their greatest Writers, than he can do of passive Obedience among the Clergy, I have done.

Does not Justice demand, that they who alike contribute to the Burden, should alike receive the Advantage? Here is another of his Maxims loosely put without considering what Exceptions may be made. The Papists have contributed doubly (being so taxed) therefore by this Rule they ought to have double Advantage. Protection in Property, Leave to Trade and Purchase, &c. are enough for a Government to give. Employments in a State are a Reward for those who intirely agree with it, &c. For Example, a Man who upon all Occasions declared his Opinion, of a Commonwealth before a Monarchy, would not be a fit Man to have Employments; let him enjoy his Opinion, but not be in a Capacity of reducing it to Practice, &c.

Page 287. *There can be no Alteration in the established Mode of Church Discipline, which is not made in a legal Way.* Oh, but there are several Methods to compass this legal Way, by Cunning, Faction, Industry. The common People, he knows, may be wrought upon by Priests; these may influence the Faction, and so compass a very pernicious Law, and in a legal Way ruin the State; as King *Charles* I. began to be ruined in a legal Way, by passing Bills, &c.

Page 288. *As every Thing is Persecution, which puts a Man in a worse Condition than his Neighbours.* It is hard to think sometimes whether this Man is hired to write for or against Dissenters and the Sects. This is their Opinion, although they will not own it so roundly. Let this be brought to Practice. Make a Quaker Lord Chancellor, who thinketh paying Tythes unlawful, and bring other Instances to shew that several Employments affect the Church.

Ibid. *Great Advantage, which both Church and State have got by the Kindness already shewn to Dissenters.* Let them then be thankful for that. We humour Children for their Good sometimes, but too much may hurt. Observe that this 64th Paragraph just contradicts the former. For, if we advantage by Kindness shewn to Dissenters, then there is no Necessity of Banishment, or Death.

Page 290. *Christ never designed the Holy Sacrament should be prostituted to serve a Party. And then People should be bribed by a Place to receive unworthily.* Why, the Business is, to be sure, that those who are employed are of the national Church; and the Way to know it is by receiving the Sacrament, which all Men ought to do in their own Church; and if not, are hardly fit for an

Office, and if they have those moral Qualifications, he mention-eth, joined to Religion, no Fear of receiving unworthily. And for this there might be a Remedy. To take an Oath, that they are of the same Principles, *&c.* For that is the End of receiving. And that it might be no Bribe, the Bill against Occasional Confor-mity would prevent entirely.

Ibid. *Preferring Men not for their Capacity, but their Zeal to the Church.* The Misfortune is, that if we prefer Dissenters to great Posts, they will have an Inclination to make themselves the National Church, and so there will be perpetual Struggling; which Case may be dangerous to the State. For Men are naturally wishing to get over others to their own Opinion: Witness this Writer, who hath published as singular and absurd Notions as possible, yet hath a mighty Zeal to bring us over to them, *&c.*

Page 292. Here are two Pages of scurrilous Faction, with a deal of Reflections on great Persons. Under the Notion of High-Churchmen, he runs down all Uniformity and Church Govern-ment. Here is the whole lower House of Convocation, which represents the Body of the Clergy and both Universities, treated with Rudeness by an obscure, corrupt Member, while he is eat-ing their Bread.

Page 294. *The Reason why the middle Sort of People retain so much of their antient Virtue,* &c. *is because no such pernicious Notions are the Ingredients of their Education; which 'tis a Sign are infinitely absurd, when so many of the Gentry and Nobility, can notwithstanding their Prepossession, get clear of them.* Now the very same Argument lies against Religion, Morality, Honour, and Honesty, which are, it seems, but Prejudices of Education, and too many get clear of them. The middle Sort of People have other Things to mind than the Factions of the Age. He always assigneth many Causes, and sometimes with Reason, since he maketh imaginary Effects. He quarrels at Power being lodged in the Clergy: When there is no reasonable Protestant Clergy, or Lay, who will not readily own the Inconveniencies by too great Power and Wealth, in any one Body of Men, Ecclesiasticks, or Seculars; but on that Account to weed up the Wheat with the Tears; to banish all Religion, because it is capable of being corrupted; to give un-bounded Licence to all Sects, *&c.* And if Heresies had not been used with some Violence in the primitive Age, we should have had, instead of true Religion, the most corrupt one in the World.

Page 316. *The* Dutch, *and the rest of our Presbyterian Allies*, &c. The *Dutch* will hardly thank him for this Appellation. The *French* Huguenots, and *Geneva* Protestants themselves and others, have lamented the Want of Episcopacy, and approved ours, *&c.* In this and the next Paragraph, the Author introduceth the Arguments he formerly used, when he turned Papist in King *James*'s Time; and, loth to lose them, he gives them a new Turn; and they are the strongest in his Book, at least have most Artifice.

Page 333. *'Tis plain, all the Power the Bishops have, is derived from the People*, &c. In general the Distinction lies here. The permissive Power of exercising Jurisdiction, lies in the People, or Legislature, or Administrator of a Kingdom, but not of making him a Bishop; as a Physician that commenceth Abroad, may be suffered to practice in *London*, or be hindered; but they have not the Power of creating him a Doctor, which is peculiar to a University. This is some Allusion; but the Thing is plain, as it seemeth to me, and wanteth no Subterfuge, *&c.*

Page 338. *A Journeyman Bishop to ordain for him.* Doth any Man think, that writing at this Rate, does the Author's Cause any Service? Is it his Wit or his Spleen that he cannot govern?

Page 364. *Can any have a Right to an Office without having a Right to do those Things in which the Office consists?* I answer, the Ordination is valid. But a Man may prudentially forbid to do some Things. As a Clergyman may marry without Licence or Bans; the Marriage is good; yet he is punishable for it.

Page 368. *A Choice made by Persons who have no Right to chuse, is an Error of the first Concoction.* That battered Simile again; this is hard. I wish the Physicians had kept that a Secret, it lieth so ready for him to be witty with.

Page 370. *If Prescription can make mere Nullities to become good and valid*, &c. There is a Difference; for here the same Way is kept, although there might be Breaches; but it is quite otherwise if you alter the whole Method from what it was at first. We see Bishops. There always were Bishops. It is the old Way still. So a Family is still held the same, although we are not sure of the Purity of every one of the Race.

Page 380. It is said, *That every Nation is not a compleat Body Politick within itself as to Ecclesiastical. But the whole Church, say they, compose such a Body, and Christ is the Head of it. But Christ's Headship makes Christians no more one Body Politick with Respect to Ecclesiasticals than to Civils.* Here we must shew the Reason and Necessity of the Church being a Corporation all over the World: To avoid Heresies and preserve Fundamentals, and hinder corrupting of Scripture, *&c.* But there are no such Necessities in Government, to be the same every where, *&c.* It is something like the College in a University, they all are independent, yet joined, are one Body. So a general Council consisteth of many Persons independent of one another, *&c.*

HOWEVER there is such a Thing as *Jus Gentium,* &c. And he that is Doctor of Physick, or Laws, is so in any University in *Europe,* like the *Respublica Literaria.* Nor to me does there seem any Thing contradicting, or improper in this Notion of the Catholick Church, and for Want of such a Communion, Religion is so much corrupted, and would be more, if there were[not]more Communion in this than in Civils. It is of no Import to Mankind how Nations are governed; but the preserving the Purity of Religion is best held up by endeavouring to make it one Body over the World. Something like as there is in Trade. So to be able to communicate with all Christians we come among, is at least to be wished and aimed at as much as we can.

Page 384. *In a Word, if the Bishops are not supreme,* &c. Here he reassumeth his Arguments for Popery, that there cannot be a Body Politick of the Church through the whole World, without a visible Head to have Recourse to. These were formerly writ to advance Popery, and now to put an Absurdity upon the Hypothesis of a Catholick Church. As they say in *Ireland,* in King *James's* Time, they built Mass-houses which we make very good Barns of.

Page 388. *Bishops are under a Premunire obliged to confirm and consecrate the Person named in the* Conge d'Elire. This perhaps is complained of. He is permitted to do it. We allow the Legislature may hinder if they please; as they may turn out Christianity if they think fit.

Page 389. *It is the Magistrate who impowers them to do more for other Bishops than they can for themselves, since they cannot appoint their own Successors.* Yes they could, if the Magistrate would let them. Here is an endless Splutter, and a Parcel of perplexed Distinctions upon no Occasion. All that the Clergy pretend to, is a Right of qualifying Men for the Ministry, something like what a University doth with Degrees. This Power they claim from GOD, and that the Civil Power cannot do it as pleasing to God without them; but they may chuse whether they will suffer it or no. A Religion cannot be crammed down a Nation's Throat against their Will; but when they receive a Religion, it is supposed they receive it as their Converters give it; and, upon that Foot, they cannot justly mingle their own Methods, that contradict that Religion, *&c.*

Page 390. *With us the Bishops act only ministerially, and by Virtue of the regal Commission, by which the Prince firmly enjoins and commands them to proceed in chusing, confirming, and consecrating,* &c. Suppose we held it unlawful to do so: How can we help it? But does that make it rightful, if it be not so? Suppose the Author lived in a Heathen Country, where a Law would be made to call Christianity idolatrous; would that be a Topick for him to prove it so by, *&c.* And why do the Clergy incur a Premunire?——To frighten them——Because the Law understandeth, that, if they refuse, the Chosen cannot be a Bishop: But if the Clergy had an Order to do it otherwise than they have prescribed, they ought and would incur an Hundred rather.

Page 402. *I believe the Catholick Church,* &c. Here he ridicules the Apostles Creed.——Another Part of his Scheme.——By what he says in these Pages, it is certain, his Design is either to run down Christianity, or set up Popery; and the latter is more charitable to think, and, from his past Life, highly probable.

Page 405. *That which gave the Papists so great Advantage was, Clergymens talking so very inconsistent with themselves,* &c. State the Difference here between our Separation from *Rome,* and the Dissenters from us, and shew the Falseness of what he sayeth. I wish he would tell us what he leaveth for a Clergyman to do, if he may not instruct the People in Religion, and if they should not receive his Instructions.

Page 411. *The Restraint of the Press a Badge of Popery.* Why is that a Badge of Popery? Why not restrain the Press to those who would confound Religion, as in Civil Matters. But this toucheth himself. He would starve perhaps, &c. Let him get some honester Livelihood then. It is plain, all his Arguments against Constraint, &c. favour the Papists as much as Dissenters; for both have Opinions that may affect the Peace of the State.

Page 413. *Since this Discourse*, &c. And must we have another Volume on this one Subject of Independency? Or, is it to fright us? I am not of Dr. *Hicks*'s Mind, *Qu'il venge*. I pity the Readers, and the Clergy that must answer it, be it ever so insipid. Reflect on this sarcastic Conclusion, &c.

A
LETTER

FROM A
MEMBER of the
House of COMMONS
IN
IRELAND

TO A
MEMBER of the
House of COMMONS
IN
ENGLAND,

Concerning the
SACRAMENTAL TEST.

LONDON:

Printed for *John Morphew*, near *Stationers-Hall*, 1709.

THE
Publisher's Advertisement
TO THE
READER.

IN the second Volume of Doctor *Swift's* and Mr. *Pope's* Miscellanies, I found the following Treatise, which had been printed in *London,* with some other of the *Dean's* Works many Years before, but at first came out by it self in the Year 1708, as the Date shews: And it was at a Juncture, when the *Dissenters* were endeavouring to repeal the *Sacramental Test,* as by common Fame, and some Pamphlets published to the same Purpose, they seem to be now again attempting, with great Hope of Success. I have, therefore, taken the Liberty to make an Extract out of that Discourse, omitting only some Passages, which relate to certain Persons, and are of no Consequence to the Argument. But the Author's Way of Reasoning seems at present to have more Weight, than it had in those Times, when the Discourse first appeared.

The Author, in this Letter, personates a Member of Parliament here, to a Member of Parliament in *England.*

· The Speaker mentioned in this Letter was *Allen Broderick,* afterwards Chancellor and Lord *Middleton*; and the Prelate was Dr. *Lindsay,* afterwards Lord Primate.

A

LETTER

FROM A

MEMBER

OF THE

House of Commons

OF

IRELAND, &c.

SIR,

I RECEIVED your Letter, wherein you tell me of the strange Representations made of us on your Side of the Water. The Instance you are pleased to mention, is that of the Presbyterian *Missionary,* who, according to your Phrase, hath been lately *persecuted* in *Drogheda* for his Religion; but it is easy to observe, how mighty industrious some People have been for three or four Years past, to hand about Stories of the Hardships, the Merits, the Number, and the Power of the *Presbyterians* in *Ireland,* to raise formidable Ideas of the Dangers of *Popery* there, and to transmit all for *England,* improved by great Additions, and with special Care to have them inserted, with Comments, in those infamous weekly Papers that infest your Coffee-Houses. So, when the Clause enacting a *Sacramental Test* was put in Execution, it was given out in *England,* that half the Justices of Peace through this Kingdom had laid down their Commissions; whereas, upon Examination, the whole Number was found to amount only to a Dozen or Thirteen, and those generally of the lowest Rate in Fortune and Understanding, and some of them superannuated. So, when the Earl of *Pembroke* was in *Ireland,*

and the Parliament sitting, a formal Story was very gravely carried to his Excellency by some zealous Members, of a Priest newly arrived, from Abroad, to the *North-West* Parts of *Ireland*, who had publickly preached to his People, to fall a murthering the Protestants; which Abuse, although invented to serve an End they were then upon, and are still driving at, was presently handed over, and printed with shrewd Remarks by your worthy Scriblers. In like Manner, the Account of that Person, who was lately expelled our University for reflecting on the Memory of King *William*, what a Dust it raised, and how foully it was related, is fresh enough in Memory. Neither would People be convinced, till the University was at the Pains of publishing a *Latin* Paper to justify themselves. And, to mention no more, this Story of the *Persecution* at *Drogheda*, how it hath been spread and aggravated, what Consequences drawn from it, and what Reproaches fixed on those who have least deserved them, we are already informed. Now, if the End of all this Proceeding were a Secret and Mystery, I should not pretend to give it an Interpretation. But sufficient Care hath been taken to explain it. First, by Addresses artificially (if not illegally) procured, to shew the miserable State of the Dissenters in *Ireland*, by reason of the *Sacramental Test*, and to desire the Queen's Intercession that it might be repealed. Then it is manifest, that our * Speaker, when he was last Year in *England*, sollicited, in Person, several Members of both Houses, to have it repealed by an Act there, although it be a Matter purely national, that cannot possibly interfere with the Trade and Interest of *England*, and although he himself appeared formerly the most zealous of all Men against the Injustice of binding a Nation by Laws, to which they do not consent. And lastly, those weekly Libellers, whenever they get a Tale by the End relating to *Ireland*, without once troubling their Thoughts about the Truth, always end it with an Application against the *Sacramental Test*, and the absolute Necessity there is of repealing it in both Kingdoms. I know it may be reckoned a Weakness to say any thing of such Trifles as are below a serious Man's Notice: Much less would I disparage the

---

* Mr. *Broderick*, afterwards Chancellor.

Understanding of any Party, to think they would choose the Vilest and most Ignorant among Mankind, to employ them for Asserters of a Cause. I shall only say, that the scandalous Liberty those Wretches take, would hardly be allowed, if it were not mingled with Opinions that *some Men* would be glad to advance. Besides, how insipid soever those Papers are, they seem to be levelled to the Understandings of a great Number. They are grown a necessary Part in Coffee-house Furniture, and some Time or other happen to be read by Customers of all Ranks, for Curiosity or Amusement; because they lie always in the Way. One of these Authors (the Fellow that was † *pilloryed*, I have forgot his Name) is indeed so grave, sententious, dogmatical a Rogue, that there is no enduring him; the *Observator* is much the brisker of the two; and, I think, farther gone of late in Lies and Impudence than his *Presbyterian* Brother.

I NOW come to answer the other Part of your Letter, and shall give you my Opinion freely about repealing the *Sacramental Test*; only, whereas you desire my Thoughts as a Friend, and not as I am a Member of Parliament, I must assure you they are exactly the same in both Capacities.

I MUST begin by telling you, we are generally surprised at your wonderful Kindness to us on this Occasion, in being so very industrious to teach us to see our Interests, in a Point where we are so unable to see it our selves. This hath given us some Suspicion; and although, in my own Particular, I am hugely bent to believe, that whenever you concern your selves in our Affairs, it is certainly *for our Good*; yet I have the Misfortune to be something singular in this Belief, and therefore I never attempted to justify it, but content my self to possess my own Opinion in private, for fear of encountring Men of more Wit, or Words than I have to spare.

WE at this Distance, who see nothing of the Spring of Actions, are forced, by mere Conjecture, to assign two Reasons for your desiring us to repeal the *Sacramental Test*. One is, because you are said to imagine it will be a Step towards the like *good Work* in *England*: The other more immediate, that it will open a

---

† *Daniel Defoe.*

Way for rewarding *several Persons*, who have well deserved upon a *great Occasion*, but who are now unqualified through that Impediment.

I DO not frequently quote Poets, especially *English*, but I remember there is in some of Mr. *Cowley*'s Love Verses, a Strain that I thought extraordinary at Fifteen, and have often since imagined it to be spoken by *Ireland*.

> *Forbid it Heaven my Life should be*
> *Weigh'd with her least Conveniency.*

IN short, whatever Advantage you propose to your selves by repealing the *Sacramental Test*, speak it out plainly, it is the best Argument you can use, for we value your Interest much more than our own. If your little Finger be sore, and you think a Poultice made of our *Vitals* will give it any Ease, speak the Word, and it shall be done; the Interest of our whole Kingdom is, at any Time, ready to strike to that of your poorest *Fishing Town*; it is hard you will not accept our Services, unless we believe, at the same Time, that you are only consulting our Profit, and giving us Marks of your Love. If there be a Fire at some Distance, and I immediately blow up my House before there be Occasion, because you are a Man of Quality, and apprehend some Danger to a *Corner of your Stable*; yet why should you require me to attend next Morning at your Levee, with my humble Thanks for the Favour you have done me?

IF we might be allowed to judge for our selves, we had Abundance of Benefit by the *Sacramental Test*, and foresee a Number of Mischiefs would be the Consequence of repealing it; and we conceive the Objections made against it by the *Dissenters*, are of no Manner of Force: They tell us of their Merits in the late War in *Ireland*, and how chearfully they engaged for the Safety of the Nation; that if they had thought they were fighting only other Peoples Quarrels, perhaps it might have cooled their Zeal; and that, for the Future, they shall sit down quietly, and let us do our Work our selves; nay, that it is necessary they should do so, since they cannot take up Arms under the Penalty of High-Treason.

NOW, supposing them to have done their Duty, as I believe

they did, and not to trouble them about the *Fly on the Wheel*; I thought *Liberty, Property*, and *Religion* had been the three Subjects of the Quarrel: And have not all those been amply secured to them? Had they, at that Time, a *mental Reservation* for *Power* and *Employments*? And must these two Articles be added henceforward in our National Quarrels? It is grown a mighty Conceit, among some Men, to melt down the Phrase of a *Church established by Law*, into that of *the Religion of the Magistrate*; of which Appellation it is easier to find the Reason than the Sense: If, by the *Magistrate*, they mean the *Prince*, the Expression includes a Falshood; for when King *James* was *Prince*, the Established Church was the same it is now: If, by the same Word they mean the Legislature, we desire no more. Be that as it will, we of this Kingdom believe the Church of *Ireland* to be the National Church, and the only one established by Law; and are willing, by the same Law, to give a *Toleration* to Dissenters. But if once we repeal our *Sacramental Test*, and grant a *Toleration*, or suspend the Execution of the Penal Laws, I do not see how we can be said to have any Established Church remaining; or rather why there will not be as many Established Churches as there are Sects of Dissenters. No, say they, yours will still be the National Church, because your Bishops and Clergy are maintained by the Publick; but, *That*, I suppose, will be of no long Duration, and it would be very unjust it should; because, to speak in *Tindal's* Phrase, it is not reasonable that Revenues should be annexed to one Opinion more than another, when all are equally lawful; and it is the same Author's Maxim, That no free-born Subject ought to pay for maintaining Speculations he does not believe. *But why should any Man, upon Account of Opinions he cannot help, be deprived the Opportunity of serving his Queen and Country?* Their Zeal is commendable, and when Employments go a begging for want of Hands, they shall be sure to have the Refusal; only, upon Condition, that they will not pretend to them upon Maxims which equally include *Atheists, Turks, Jews, Infidels* and *Hereticks*; or which is still more dangerous, even *Papists* themselves; the former you allow, the other you deny, because these last own a foreign Power, and therefore must be shut out. But there is no great Weight in this; for their Religion can suit with free States, with limited or absolute Monarchies, as well as a better; and the *Pope's* Power in *France* is but a Shadow; so that, upon this Foot, there need be no great Danger to the Constitution, by admitting *Papists* to Employments. I will help you to enough of them, who shall be ready to allow the *Pope* as little Power here as you please; and the bare Opinion of his being Vicar of Christ, is but a *speculative Point*, for which no Man, it seems, ought to be deprived the Capacity of serving his Country.

BUT, if you please, I will tell you the great Objection we have against repealing this same *Sacramental Test*. It is, that we are verily perswaded the Consequence will be an entire Alteration of Religion among us, in a no great Compass of Years. And, pray observe, how we reason here in *Ireland* upon this Matter.

WE observe the *Scots*, in our *Northern* Parts, to be an industrious People, extreamly devoted to their Religion, and full of an *undisturbed* Affection towards each other. Numbers of that *noble Nation*, invited by the Fertilities of the Soil, are glad to exchange their barren Hills of *Loughabar*, by a Voyage of three Hours, for our fruitful Vales of *Down* and *Antrim*, so productive of that *Grain*, which, at little Trouble and less Expence, finds Diet and Lodging for themselves and their Cattle. These People by their extream Parsimony, wonderful *Dexterity in Dealing*, and firm Adherence to one another, soon grow into Wealth from the *smallest Beginnings*, never are rooted out where they once fix, and increase daily by new Supplies. Besides, when they are the superior Number in any Tract of Ground, they are not *over patient of Mixture*; but such, whom they cannot *assimilate*, soon find it their Interest to remove. I have done all in my Power, on some Land of my own, to preserve two or three *English* Fellows in their Neighbourhood, but found it impossible, although one of them thought he had sufficiently made his Court by turning *Presbyterian*. Add to all this, that they bring along with them from *Scotland*, a most formidable Notion of our Church, which they look upon, at least, three Degrees worse than *Popery*; and it is natural it should be so, since they come over full fraught with that Spirit which taught them to abolish Episcopacy at home.

THEN we proceed farther, and observe, that the Gentlemen

of Employments here, make a very considerable Number in the House of Commons, and have no *other Merit* but that of doing their Duty in their several Stations; therefore, when the *Test* is repealed, it will be highly reasonable they should give Place to those who have much *greater Services* to plead. The Commissions of the Revenue are soon disposed of, and the Collectors, and other Officers throughout the Kingdom, are generally appointed by the Commissioners, which gives them a mighty Influence in every County. As much may be said of the great Offices in the Law; and when this Door is open to let *Dissenters* into the Commissions of the Peace, to make them High-Sheriffs, Mayors of Corporations, and Officers of the Army and Militia; I do not see how it can be otherwise, considering their Industry and our Supineness, but that they may, in a very few Years, grow to a Majority in the House of Commons, and consequently make themselves the National Religion, and have a fair Pretence to demand the Revenues of the Church for their Teachers. I know it will be objected, that if all this should happen as I describe, yet the *Presbyterian* Religion could never be made the National by Act of Parliament, because our Bishops are so great a Number in the House of Lords; and without a Majority there, the Church could not be abolished. But I have *two very good Expedients* for that, which I shall leave you to guess, and, I dare swear, our Speaker here has often thought on, especially having endeavoured at *one of them* so lately. That this Design is not so foreign from *some Peoples* Thoughts, I must let you know that an honest * *Bell-weather* of our House (you have him now in *England*, I wish you could keep him there) had the Impudence, some Years ago, in Parliament Time, to shake my Lord Bishop of *Killaloo* by his Lawn Sleeve, and tell him in a threatening Manner, *That he hoped to live to see the Day, when there should not be one of his Order in the Kingdom.*

THESE last Lines, perhaps, you think a Digression; therefore to return, I have told you the Consequences we fully reckon upon, from repealing the *Sacramental Test*, which although the greatest Number of such as are for doing it, are actually in no

---

* Supposed to be Mr. *Broderick.*

Manner of Pain about, and many of them care not three Pence
whether there be any *Church* or no; yet, because they pretend to
argue from Conscience as well as Policy and Interest, I thought
it proper to understand and answer them accordingly.

Now, Sir, in Answer to your Question, Whether if any
Attempt should be made here for repealing the *Sacramental Test*,
it would be likely to succeed? The Number of profest *Dissenters*
in this Parliament was, as I remember, something under a
Dozen, and I cannot call to mind above Thirty others who were
expected to fall in with them. This is certain, that the *Presbyterian*
Party having with great Industry mustered up their Forces, did
endeavour one Day, upon Occasion of a Hint in my Lord
Pembroke's Speech, to introduce a Debate about repealing the
Test Clause, when there appeared, at least, four to one Odds
against them; and the ablest of those, who were reckoned the
most stanch and thorough-paced *Whigs* upon all other Occasions, fell off with an Abhorrence at the first Mention of this.

I must desire you to take Notice, that the Terms of *Whig* and
Tory, do not properly express the different Interests in our
Parliament.

Whoever bears a true Veneration for the Glorious Memory
of King *William*, as our great Deliverer from *Popery* and *Slavery*;
whoever is firmly loyal to our present Queen, with an utter
Abhorrence and Detestation of the *Pretender*; whoever approves
the Succession to the Crown in the House of *Hanover*, and is for
preserving the Doctrine and Discipline of the Church of *England*, with an *Indulgence* for scrupulous Consciences; such a Man,
we think, acts upon right Principles, and may be justly allowed
a *Whig*; and, I believe, there are not six Members in our House of
Commons, who may not fairly come under this Description.
So that the Parties among us are made up, on one side, of
moderate Whigs, and, on the other, of *Presbyterians* and their
Abettors; by which last I mean, such who can equally go to a
Church, or a *Conventicle*; or such who are indifferent to all Religion in general; or, lastly, such who affect to bear a personal
Rancor towards the Clergy. These last, are a Set of Men not of
our own Growth; their Principles, at least, have been *imported*
of late Years; yet this whole Party, put together, will not, I am

confident, amount to above fifty Men in Parliament, which can hardly be worked up into a Majority of three Hundred.

As to the House of Lords, the Difficulty there is conceived, at least, as great as in ours. So many of our Temporal Peers live in *England*, that the Bishops are generally pretty near a *Par* of the House, and we reckon † they will be all to a Man against repealing the *Test*; and yet their Lordships are generally thought as good *Whigs* upon our Principles as any in the Kingdom. There are, indeed, a few Lay Lords who appear to have no great Devotion for *Episcopacy*; and perhaps one or two more, with whom *certain powerful Motives* might be used for removing any Difficulty whatsoever; but these are in no sort of a Number to carry any Point against a Conjunction of the rest, with the whole Bench of Bishops.

Besides, the intire Body of our Clergy is utterly against repealing the *Test*, although they are entirely devoted to her Majesty, and hardly One in a Hundred who are not very good *Whigs*, in our Acceptation of the Word. And I must let you know, that we of *Ireland*, are not yet come up to *other Folks Refinement*: For we generally love and esteem our Clergy, and think they deserve it; nay, we are apt to lay some Weight upon their Opinions, and would not willingly disoblige them, at least, unless it were upon some greater Point of Interest than this. And their Judgment, in the present Affair, is the more to be regarded, because they are the last Persons who will be affected by it: This makes us think them impartial, and that their Concern is only for Religion and the Interest of the Kingdom. Because, the Act which repeals the *Test*, will only qualify a *Layman* for an Employment, but not a *Presbyterian* or *Anabaptist* Preacher for a Church Living. Now I must take Leave to inform you, that several Members of our House, and my self among the rest, knowing, some Time ago, what was upon the Anvil, went to all the Clergy we knew of any Distinction, and desired their Judgment in the Matter, wherein we found a most wonderful Agreement; there being but *one Divine*, that we could hear of,

---

† *N.B.* Things are quite altered in that Bench, since this Discourse was written.

in the whole Kingdom, who appeared of a contrary Sentiment; wherein he afterwards stood alone in the *Convocation*, very little to his *Credit*, although, as he hoped, very much to his *Interest*.

I WILL now consider, a little, the Arguments offered to shew the Advantages, or rather Necessity of repealing the *Test* in *Ireland*. We are told, the *Popish* Interest is here so formidable; that all Hands should be joined to keep it under; that the only Names of Distinctions among us, ought to be those of *Protestant* and *Papist*; and that this Expedient is the only Means to *unite* all Protestants upon one common Bottom. All which is nothing but Misrepresentation and Mistake.

I F we were under any real Fear of the *Papists* in this Kingdom, it would be hard to think us so stupid, as not to be equally apprehensive with *others*, since we are likely to be the greatest, and more immediate Sufferers; but, on the contrary, we look upon them to be altogether as inconsiderable as the Women and Children. Their Lands are almost entirely taken from them, and they are rendered uncapable of purchasing any more; and for the little that remains, Provision is made by the late Act against Popery, that it will daily crumble away: To prevent which, some of the most considerable among them are already turned Protestants, and so, in all Probability, will many more. Then, the Popish Priests are all registered, and without Permission (which, I hope, will not be granted) they can have no Successors; so that the Protestant Clergy will find it, perhaps, no difficult Matter to bring great Numbers over to the Church; and, in the mean Time, the common People without Leaders, without Discipline, or natural Courage, being little better than *Hewers of Wood, and Drawers of Water*, are out of all Capacity of doing any Mischief, if they were ever so well inclined. Neither are they, at all, likely to join in any considerable Numbers with an *Invader*, having found so ill Success when they were much more numerous and powerful; when they had a Prince of their own Religion to head them, had been trained for some Years under a *Popish Deputy*, and received such mighty Aids from the *French* King.

A s to that Argument used for repealing the *Test*; that it will unite all Protestants against the *common Enemy*; I wonder by what Figure those Gentlemen speak, who are pleased to advance it: Suppose, in order to encrease the Friendship between you and me, a Law should pass that I must have Half your Estate; do you think that would much advance the Union between us? Or, suppose I share my Fortune equally between my own *Children*, and a *Stranger*, whom I take into my Protection; will that be a Method to unite them? It is an odd way of uniting Parties, to deprive a *Majority* of Part of their antient Right, by conferring it on a *Faction* who had never any Right at all, and therefore cannot be said to suffer any Loss or Injury, if it be refused them. Neither is it very clear, how far some People may stretch the Term of *common Enemy*: How many are there of those that call themselves Protestants, who look upon our Worship to be idolatrous as well as that of the *Papists*, and with great Charity put *Prelacy* and *Popery* together, as Terms convertible?

AND, therefore, there is one small Doubt I would be willingly satisfied in, before I agree to the repealing of the *Test*; that is, whether these same Protestants, when they have, by their Dexterity, made themselves the National Religion, and disposed the Church Revenues among their *Pastors* or *Themselves*, will be so kind to allow *us Dissenters*, I do not say a Share in Employments, but a bare *Toleration* by Law. The Reason of my Doubt is, because I have been so very idle as to read above fifty Pamphlets, written by as many *Presbyterian* Divines, loudly disclaiming this Idol *Toleration*; some of them calling it (I know not how properly) a *Rag of Popery*, and all agreeing, it was to *establish Iniquity by a Law*. Now, I would be glad to know when and where *their Successors* have renounced this Doctrine, and before what Witnesses. Because, methinks, I should be loath to see my poor titular Bishop *in partibus*, seized on by Mistake in the Dark for a Jesuit, or be forced my self to keep a Chaplain disguised like my Butler, and steal to Prayers in a back Room, as my Grandfather used in those Times when the Church of *England* was *malignant*.

BUT this is ripping up old Quarrels long forgot; *Popery* is now the *common Enemy*, against which we must all unite: I have been tired in History with the perpetual Folly of those States, who called in Foreigners to assist them against a *common Enemy*: But the Mischief was, these *Allies* would never be brought to allow that the *common Enemy* was quite subdued: And they had

Reason; for it proved at last, that one Part of the *common Enemy* was those who called them in; and so the *Allies* became at length the *Masters*.

IT is agreed, among Naturalists, that a *Lyon* is a larger, a stronger, and more dangerous Enemy than a *Cat*; yet if a Man were to have his Choice, either a *Lyon* at his Foot, bound fast with three or four Chains, his Teeth drawn out, and his Claws pared to the Quick, or an angry *Cat* in full Liberty at his Throat; he would take no long Time to determine.

I HAVE been sometimes admiring the wonderful Significancy of that Word *Persecution*, and what various Interpretations it hath acquired even within my Memory. When I was a Boy, I often heard the *Presbyterians* complain, that they were not permitted to serve God in their own Way; they said, they did not repine at our Employments, but thought that all Men, who live peaceably, ought to have Liberty of Conscience, and Leave to assemble. That Impediment being removed at the Revolution, they soon learned to swallow the *Sacramental Test*, and began to take very large Steps, wherein all who offered to oppose them, were called Men of a *persecuting Spirit*. During the Time the Bill against Occasional Conformity was on Foot, *Persecution* was every Day rung in our Ears, and now at last the *Sacramental Test* it self has the same Name. Where then is this Matter likely to end, when the obtaining of one Request is only used as a Step to demand another? A Lover is ever complaining of *Cruelty*, while any thing is denied him; and when the Lady ceases to be *cruel*, she is from the next Moment at his Mercy: So *Persecution*, it seems, is every Thing that will not leave it in Men's Power to *persecute others*.

THERE is one Argument offered against a *Sacramental Test*, by a Sort of Men who are content to be stiled of the Church of *England*, who, perhaps, attend its Service in the Morning, and go with their Wives to a *Conventicle* in the Afternoon, confessing they hear very good Doctrine in both. These Men are much offended, that so holy an Institution as that of the Lord's Supper, should be made subservient to such mercenary Purposes, as the getting of an Employment. Now, it seems, the Law concluding all Men to be Members of that Church where they receive the

Sacrament; and supposing all Men to live like Christians (especially those who are to have Employments) did imagine they received the Sacrament, in Course, about four Times a Year, and therefore only desired it might appear by Certificate to the Publick, that such who took an Office, were Members of the Church established, by doing their ordinary Duty. However, *lest we should offend them*, we have often desired they would deal candidly with us; for if the Matter stuck only there, we would propose it in Parliament, that every Man who takes an Employment, should, instead of receiving the Sacrament, be obliged to swear, that he is a Member of the Church of *Ireland* by Law established, with *Episcopacy, and so forth*; and as they do now in *Scotland, to be true to the Kirk*. But when we drive them thus far, they always retire to the main Body of the Argument, urge the Hardship that Men should be deprived the Liberty of serving their Queen and Country, on Account of their Conscience: And, in short, have Recourse to the common Stile of their half Brethren. Now, whether this be a sincere Way of arguing, I will appeal to any other Judgment but theirs.

THERE is another Topick of Clamour somewhat parallel to the foregoing; it seems, by the Test Clause, the *Military* Officers are obliged to receive the Sacrament as well as the *Civil*. And it is a Matter of some Patience, to hear the *Dissenters* declaiming upon this Occasion: They cry they are *disarmed*, they are used like *Papists*; when an Enemy appears at Home, or from Abroad, they must sit still, and see their Throats cut, or be hanged for High Treason if they offer to defend themselves. Miserable Condition! Woeful Dilemma! It is happy for us all, that the Pretender was not apprised of this *passive Presbyterian* Principle, else he would have infallibly landed in our *Northern* Parts, and found them all sat down in their Formalities, as the *Gauls* did the *Roman* Senators, ready to die with Honour in their Callings. Sometimes, to appease their Indignation, we venture to give them Hopes, that, in such a Case, the Government will perhaps connive, and hardly be so severe to hang them for defending it against the Letter of the Law; to which they readily answer, that they will not lie at our Mercy, but let us fight our Battles our selves. Sometimes we offer to get an Act, by which,

upon all *Popish* Insurrections at Home, or *Popish* Invasions from
Abroad, the Government shall be impowered to grant Com-
missions to all Protestants whatsoever, without that *persecuting*
Circumstance of obliging them to *say their Prayers* when they
receive the Sacrament; but they abhor all Thoughts of *occasional*
Commissions, they will not do our Drudgery, and we reap the
Benefit; it is not worth their while to fight *pro Aris & focis*;
and they had rather lose their Estates, Liberties, Religion and
Lives, than the Pleasure of *governing*.

But to bring this Discourse towards a Conclusion. If the
Dissenters will be satisfied with such a *Toleration* by Law, as
hath been granted them in *England*, I believe the Majority of
both Houses will fall readily in with it; farther it will be hard to
perswade this House of Commons, and, perhaps, much harder
the next. For, to say the Truth, we make a mighty Difference
here between suffering *Thistles* to grow among us, and wearing
them for *Posies*. We are fully convinced in our Consciences, that
We shall always *tolerate them*, but not quite so fully, that *They*
will always *tolerate us*, when it comes to their Turn; and *We* are
the Majority, and *We* are in Possession.

He who argues in Defence of a Law in Force, not antiquated
or obsolete, but lately enacted, is certainly on the safer Side, and
may be allowed to point out the Dangers he conceives to foresee
in the Abrogation of it.

For if the Consequences of repealing this Clause, should, at
some time or other, enable the *Presbyterians* to work themselves
up into the National Church; instead of *uniting* Protestants, it
would sow eternal Divisions among them. First, their own
Sects which now lie dormant, would be soon at Cuffs *again* with
each other, about Power and Preferment; and the *Dissenting
Episcopals*, perhaps, discontented to such a Degree, as, upon
some *fair unhappy* Occasion, would be able to shake the firmest
Loyalty, which none can deny theirs to be.

Neither is it very difficult to conjecture, from some late
Proceedings, at what a Rate this *Faction* is like to drive wherever
it gets the *Whip* and the *Seat*. They have already set up Courts of
Spiritual Judicature, in open Contempt of the Law: They send
Missionaries every where, without being invited, in order to

convert the Church of *England* Folks to *Christianity*. They are as vigilant as *I know who*, to attend Persons on their Death-Beds, and for Purposes much alike. And what Practices such Principles as these (with many others that might be invidious to mention) may spawn, when they are *laid out to the Sun*, you may determine at Leisure.

LASTLY, whether we are so entirely sure of their Loyalty upon the present Foot of Government as you may imagine, their Detractors make a Question, which, however, does, I think, by no Means affect the Body of *Dissenters*; but the Instance produced, is of some among their leading Teachers in the *North*, who refused the *Abjuration Oath*, yet continue their Preaching, and have Abundance of Followers. The Particulars are out of my Head, but the Fact is notorious enough, and, I believe, hath been published; I think it a Pity it has not been *remedied*.

THUS I have fairly given you, Sir, my own Opinion, as well as that of a great Majority in both Houses here, relating to this weighty Affair, upon which, I am confident, you may securely reckon. I will leave you to make what Use of it you please.

A Letter *to a*
Member of Parliament
1708

A

LETTER

TO

A MEMBER OF PARLIAMENT

In IRELAND.

Upon the chusing a new SPEAKER there.

Written in the Year 1708.

SIR,

YOU may easily believe I am not at all surprised at what you tell me, since it is but a Confirmation of my own Conjecture that I sent you last week, and made you my Reproaches upon it at a Venture. It looks exceeding strange, yet I believe it to be a great Truth, that, in order to carry a Point in your House, the two following Circumstances are of great Advantage: first, to have an ill Cause; and, secondly, to be a Minority. For both these Circumstances are extreamly apt to unite men, to make them assiduous in their Attendance, watchfull of Opportunityes, zealous for gaining over Proselytes, and often successfull; which is not to be wondred at, when Favour and Interest are on the side of their Opinion. Wheras, on the contrary, A Majority with a good Cause are negligent and supine. They think it sufficient to declare themselves upon Occasion in Favor of their Party; but, sailing against the Tide of Favor and Preferment, they are easily scattred and driven back. In short, they want a common Principle to cement, and Motive to spirit them. For the bare acting upon a Principle from the Dictates of a good Conscience, or prospect of Serving the Publick, will not go very far under the present Dispositions of Mankind. This was amply verifyed last Sessions of Parliament, upon Occasion of the Money-bill, the Merits of which I shall not pretend to examine. It is enough that, upon the first News of its Transmission hither, in the Form it afterwards appeared, the Members, upon discourse with their Friends, seemed unanimous against it; I mean those of both Partyes, except a few, who were lookt upon as Persons ready to go any Lengths prescribed them by the Court. Yet with onely a weeks canvassing among a very few Hands, the Bill past after a full Debate, by a very great Majority. Yet, I believe, you will hardly attempt persuading me, or any body else, that one man in ten, of those who changed their Language, were moved by Reasons any way affecting the Merits of the Cause, but meerly through Hope, Fear, Indolence, or good Manners. Nay, I have been assured from good Hands, that there was still a number sufficient to make a majority against the Bill, if they had not apprehended the other Side to be secure, and therefore thought it imprudence, by declaring themselves, to disoblige the Government to no purpose.

Reflecting upon this, and fourty other Passages, in the severall Houses of Commons since the Revolution, makes me apt to think, there is nothing a chief Governor can be commanded to attempt here wherein he may not succeed, with a very competent share of Address, and with such Assistance as he will allways find ready at his Devotion. And therefore I repeat what I said at first, that I am not at all surprized at what you tell me. For, if there had been the least Spark of publick Spirit left, those who wisht well to their Country and its Constitution in Church and State, should, upon the first News of the late Speaker's Promotion, (and you and I know it might have been done a great deal sooner) have immediatly gone together, and consulted about the fittest Person to succeed him. But, by all I can comprehend, you have been so far from proceeding thus, that it hardly ever came into any of your Heads. And the Reason you give is the worst in the World: That none offered themselves, and you knew not whom to pitch upon. It seems, however, the other Party was more resolved, or at least not so modest: For you say your Vote is engaged against your Opinion, and severall Gentlemen in my Neighborhood, tell me the same Story of themselves. This, I confess, is of an unusuall Strain, and a good many Steps below any Condescensions a Court will, I hope, ever require from you. I shall not trouble my self to inquire who is the Person for whom you and others are engaged, or whether there be more Candidates from that Side than One. You tell me nothing of either, and I never thought it worth the Question to any body else. But, in so weighty an Affair, and against your Judgment, I cannot look upon you as irrevocably determined. Therefore I desire you will give me leave to reason with you a little upon the Subject, lest your Complyance, or Inadvertency, should put you upon what you may have Cause to Repent as long as you live.

You know very well, the great Business of the High-flying Whigs, at this Juncture, is to endeavor a Repeal of the Test Clause. You know likewise that the Moderate Men, both of High and Low Church, profess to be wholly averse from this Design, as thinking it beneath the Policy of common Gardners to cutt down the onely Hedge that shelters from the North. Now, I will put the Case: If the Person to whom you have promised your Vote, be one of whom you have the least Apprehension that he will promote or assent to the Repealing of that Clause, whether it be decent or proper he should be the Mouth of an Assembly, whereof a very great Majority pretend to abhor his opinion. Can a Body, whose Mouth and Heart must go so contrary ways, ever act with Sincerity, or hardly with Consistence? Such a man is no proper vehicle to retain or convey the Sense of the House, which, in so many Points of the greatest moment, will be directly contrary to His. It is full as absurd, as to prefer a man to a Bishoprick, who denyes revealed Religion. But it may possibly be a great deal worse. What if the Person You design to vote into that Important Post, should not only be a declared Enemy of the Sacramental Test, but should prove to be a Sollicitor, an Encourager, or even a Penner of Addresses to complain of it? Do you think it so indifferent a Thing, that a Promise of Course, the Effect of Compliance, Importunity, Shame of Refusing, or any the like motive, shall oblidge you past the Power of Retracting?

Perhaps you will tell me, as some have already had the Weakness to do, that it is of little Importance to either Party to have a Speaker of their side, his business being onely to take the Sense of the House and report it; that you often, at Committees, put an able Speaker into the Chair, on Purpose to prevent him from stopping a Bill. Why, if it were no more than this; I believe I should hardly chuse, even among my Footmen, such a one to deliver a Message, whose Interest and Opinion led him to wish it might miscarry. But I remember to have heard old Colonel Birch of Herefordshire say, that he was a very sorry Speaker, whose single vote was not better than fifty common ones. I am sure it is reckoned in England the first great Test of the Pre- valency of either Party in the House. Sir Thomas Littleton thought, that a House of Commons, with a stinking Breath (supposing the Speaker to be the Mouth) would go near to infect every thing within the Walls, and a great deal without. It is the smallest Part of an able Speaker's Business, what he per- forms in the House, at least if he be in with the Court, when it is hard to say how many Converts may be made in a Circle of Dinners, or private Cabals. And you and I can easily call to mind a Gentleman in that Station in England, who, by his own Arts and personall Credit, was able to draw over a Majority, and change the whole Power of a prevailing Side in a nice Juncture of Affairs, and made a Parliament expire in one Party who had lived in another.

I am far from an Inclination to multiply Party Causes, but surely the best of us can with very ill Grace make that an Objec- tion, who have not been so nice in Matters of much less Import- ance. Yet I have heard some Persons of both sides gravely de- liver themselves in this manner; Why should we make the Chusing a Speaker a Party Cause? Let us fix upon one who is well versed in the Practices and Methods of Parliament. And I believe there are too many who would talk at the same Rate if the Ques- tion were, not onely about abolishing the Sacramental Test, but the Sacrament itself.

But suppose the Principles of the most artfull Speaker could have no Influence either to obtain or obstruct any Point in Parliament, who can answer what Effects such a Choice may produce without doors? It is obvious how small a Matter serves to raise the Spirits and Hopes of the Dissenters and their high- flying Advocates, what Lengths they run, what Conclusions they form, and what Hopes they entertain. Do they hear of a new Friend in Office? That is encouragement enough to practice the City, against the Opinion of a Majority, into an Address to the Queen for repealing the Sacramentall Test; or issue out their Orders to the next fanatick Parson to furbish up his old Sermons, and preach and print new ones directly against Episcopacy. I would lay a good Wager, that, if the Choice of a new Speaker succeeds exactly to their liking, we shall see it soon followd by many new Attempts, either in the form of Pamphlet, Sermon, or Address to the same or perhaps more dangerous Purposes.

Supposing the Speaker's office to be only an Employment of Profit and Honour, and a Step to a Better; since it is in your own Gift, will you not chuse to bestow it upon some Person whose Principles the Majority of you pretends to approve, if it were only to be sure of a worthy man hereafter in a high Station, on the Bench or at the Bar?

I confess, if it were a Thing possible to be compassed, it would seem most reasonable to fill the Chair with some Person who would be entirely devoted to neither Party: But, since there are so few of that Character, and those either unqualifyed or unfriended, I cannot see how a Majority will answer it to their Reputation, to be so ill provided of able Persons, that they must have recourse for a Leader to their Adversaryes, a Proceeding of which I never mett with above one Example, and even that succeeded but ill, though it was recommended by an Oracle, which advised some City in Greece to beg a Generall from their Enemyes, who, in scorn, sent them either a Fidler or a Poet, I have forgot which; but so much I remember, that his Conduct was such, as they soon grew weary of him.

You pretend to be heartily resolved against repealing the Sacramentall Test, yet, at the same Time, give the onely great Employment You have to dispose of to a Person who will take that Test against his Stomach, (by which word I understand many a man's Conscience) who earnestly wisheth it repealed, and will endeavor it to the utmost of his Power; so that the First Action after you meet, will be a sort of contravention to that Test: And will any body go further than your Practice to judge of your Principles?

And now I am upon this Subject, I cannot conclude without saying something to a very popular Argument against that

Sacramental Test, which may be apt to shake many of those who would otherwise wish well enough to it. They say it was a new Hardship putt upon the Dissenters, without any Provocation; and, it is plain, could be no way necessary, because we had peaceably lived together so long without it. They add some other Circumstances of the Arts by which it was obtained, and the Person by whom it was inserted. Surely such People do not consider, that the Penall Laws against Dissenters were made wholly ineffectual by the Connivance and Mercy of the Government, so that all Employments of the State lay as open to them, as they did to the best and most legall Subjects. And what Progress they would have made by the Advantages of a late Conjuncture, is obvious to imagine; which I take to be a full Answer to that Objection.

I remember, upon the Transmission of that bill with the Test Clause inserted, the Dissenters and their Partizans, among other Topicks, spoke much of the good Effects produced by the Lenity of the Government: That the Presbyterians were grown very inconsiderable in their Number and Quality, and would daily come in to the Church, if we did not fright them from it by new Severityes. When the Act was passt, they presently changed their Style, and raisd a Clamor through both kingdoms of the great numbers of considerable Gentry who were layd aside, and could no longer serve their Queen and Country: which hyperbolicall way of reckoning, when it came to be melted down into Truth, amounted to about fifteen Country Justices, most of them of the lowest Size for Estate, Quality, or Understanding. However, this putt me in mind of a Passage told me by a great man, although I know not whether it be any where recorded. That a Complaint was made to the King and Council in Sweden of a prodigious Swarm of Scots, who, under the Condition of Pedlars, infested that Kingdom to such a degree, as, if not suddenly prevented, might in time prove dangerous to the State, by joyning with any discontented Party. Meanwhile the Scots, by their Agents, placed a good Sum of money to engage the offices of the Prime Minister in their behalf; who, in order to their defence, told the Councill, he was assured they were but a few inconsiderable People, that lived honestly and poorly, and were not of any Consequence. Their enemyes offered to prove the contrary: Whereupon an Order was made to take their Numbers, which was found to amount, as I remember, to about thirty thousand. The Affair was again brought before the Council, and great Reproaches made the first Minister, for his ill Computation; who presently took the other handle, said he had reason to believe the number yet greater than what was returned; and then gravely offered to the King's Consideration, whether it were safe to render desperate so great a Body of able Men, who had little to lose, and whom any hard Treatment would onely serve to unite into a Power capable of disturbing, if not destroying the Peace of the Kingdom. And so they were suffered to continue.

IOHN PARTRIDGE.
Fatis agimur: Cedite Fatis.

Originally engraved for Frontispiece to Merlinus Liberatus 1708.

The Partridge *Papers*

PREDICTIONS

FOR THE

YEAR 1708.

Wherein the Month and Day of the
Month are set down, the Persons
named, and the great Actions and
Events of next Year particularly
related, as they will come to pass.

Written to prevent the People of England *from
being further impos'd on by vulgar Almanack-
makers.*

By ISAAC BICKERSTAFF *Esq;*

Sold by *John Morphew* near *Stationers-Hall.*
MDCCVIII.

PREDICTIONS *for the* Year 1708.

Wherein the Month, and Day of the Month, are set down, the Persons named, and the great Actions and Events of next Year particularly related as they will come to pass.

Written to prevent the People of England *from being farther imposed on by vulgar Almanack-Makers.*

By Isaac Bickerstaff,* Esq;

HAVING long considered the gross Abuse of Astrology in this Kingdom; upon debating the Matter with my self, I could not possibly lay the Fault upon the Art, but upon those gross Impostors, who set up to be the Artists. I know, several learned Men have contended, that the whole is a Cheat; that it is absurd and ridiculous to imagine, the Stars can have any Influence at all upon human Actions, Thoughts, or Inclinations: And whoever hath not bent his Studies that Way, may be excused for thinking so, when he sees in how wretched a Manner this noble Art is treated, by a few mean illiterate Traders between us and the Stars; who import a yearly Stock of Nonsense, Lies, Folly, and Impertinence, which they offer to the World as genuine from the Planets; although they descend from no greater a Height than their own Brains.

I INTEND, in a short Time, to publish a large and rational

It is said, that the Author, when he had writ the following Paper, and being at a Loss what Name to prefix to it; passing through Long-Acre, *observed a Sign over a House where a Locksmith dwelt, and found the Name* Bickerstaff *written under it: Which being a Name somewhat uncommon, he chose to call himself* Isaac Bickerstaff. *This Name was sometime afterward made Use of by Sir* Richard Steele, *and Mr.* Addison, *in the* TATLERS; *in which Papers, as well as many of the* SPECTATORS, *it is well known, that the Author had a considerable Part.*

Defence of this Art; and, therefore, shall say no more in its Justification at present, than that it hath been in all Ages defended by many learned Men; and among the rest, by *Socrates* himself; whom I look upon as undoubtedly the wisest of uninspired Mortals: To which if we add, that those who have condemned this Art, although otherwise learned, having been such as either did not apply their Studies this Way; or at least did not succeed in their Applications; their Testimony will not be of much Weight to its Disadvantage, since they are liable to the common Objection of condemning what they did not understand.

Nor am I at all offended, or think it an Injury to the Art, when I see the common Dealers in it, the *Students in Astrology*, the *Philomaths*, and the rest of that Tribe, treated by wise Men with the utmost Scorn and Contempt: But I rather wonder, when I observe Gentlemen in the Country, rich enough to serve the Nation in Parliament, poring in *Partrige's* Almanack, to find out the Events of the Year at Home and Abroad; not daring to propose a Hunting-Match, until *Gadbury*, or he, hath fixed the Weather.

I will allow either of the Two I have mentioned, or any other of the Fraternity, to be not only Astrologers, but Conjurers too; if I do not produce an Hundred Instances in all their Almanacks, to convince any reasonable Man, that they do not so much as understand Grammar and Syntax; that they are not able to spell any Word out of the usual Road; nor even in their Prefaces to write common Sense, or intelligible *English*. Then, for their Observations and Predictions, they are such as will equally suit any Age, or Country in the World. *This Month a certain great Person will be threatned with Death, or Sickness.* This the News-Paper will tell them; for there we find at the End of the Year, that no Month passes without the Death of some Person of Note; and it would be hard, if it should be otherwise, when there are at least two Thousand Persons of Note in this Kingdom, many of them old; and the Almanack-maker has the Liberty of chusing the sickliest Season of the Year, where he may fix his Prediction. Again, *This Month an eminent Clergyman will be preferred*; of which there may be some Hundreds, Half of them with one Foot in the Grave. Then, *Such a Planet in such a House shews great Machinations, Plots and Conspiracies, that may in Time be brought to Light*: After which, if we hear of any Discovery, the Astrologer gets the Honour; if not, his Prediction still stands good. And at last, *God preserve King* William *from all his open and secret Enemies, Amen.* When if the King should happen to have died, the Astrologer plainly foretold it; otherwise, it passeth but for the pious Ejaculation of a loyal Subject: Although it unluckily happened in some of their Almanacks, that poor King *William* was prayed for many Months after he was dead; because, it fell out that he died about the Beginning of the Year.

To mention no more of their impertinent Predictions: What have we to do with their Advertisements about *Pills, and Drinks for the Venereal Disease,* or their mutual Quarrels in Verse and Prose of *Whig* and *Tory?* wherewith the Stars have little to do.

HAVING long observed and lamented these, and a hundred other Abuses of this Art, too tedious to repeat; I resolved to proceed in a new Way; which I doubt not will be to the general Satisfaction of the Kingdom. I can this Year produce but a Specimen of what I design for the future; having employed most Part of my Time in adjusting and correcting the Calculations I made for some Years past; because I would offer nothing to the World of which I am not as fully satisfied, as that I am now alive. For these two last Years I have not failed in above one or two Particulars, and those of no very great Moment. I exactly foretold the Miscarriage at *Toulon,* with all its Particulars; and the Loss of Admiral *Shovel*; although I was mistaken as to the Day, placing that Accident about thirty six Hours sooner than it happened; but upon reviewing my Schemes, I quickly found the Cause of that Error. I likewise foretold the Battle at *Almanza* to the very Day and Hour, with the Loss on both Sides, and the Consequences thereof. All which I shewed to some Friends many Months before they happened; that is, I gave them Papers sealed up, to open at such a Time, after which they were at liberty to read them; and there they found my Predictions true in every Article, except one or two, very minute.

As for the few following Predictions I now offer the World,

I forbore to publish them, till I had perused the several Almanacks for the Year we are now entered upon: I found them all in the usual Strain, and I beg the Reader will compare their Manner with mine: And here I make bold to tell the World, that I lay the whole Credit of my Art upon the Truth of these Predictions; and I will be content that *Partrige*, and the rest of his Clan, may hoot me for a Cheat and Impostor, if I fail in any single Particular of Moment. I believe any Man, who reads this Paper, will look upon me to be at least a Person of as much Honesty and Understanding, as a common Maker of Almanacks. I do not lurk in the Dark; I am not wholly unknown in the World: I have set my Name at length, to be a Mark of Infamy to Mankind, if they shall find I deceive them.

IN one Point I must desire to be forgiven; that I talk more sparingly of Home-Affairs. As it would be Imprudence to discover Secrets of State, so it might be dangerous to my Person: But in smaller Matters, and such as are not of publick Consequence, I shall be very free: And the Truth of my Conjectures will as much appear from these as the other. As for the most signal Events abroad in *France*, *Flanders*, *Italy* and *Spain*, I shall make no Scruple to predict them in plain Terms: Some of them are of Importance, and I hope, I shall seldom mistake the Day they will happen: Therefore, I think good to inform the Reader, that I all along make use of the *Old Stile* observed in *England*; which I desire he will compare with that of the News-Papers, at the Time they relate the Actions I mention.

I MUST add one Word more: I know it hath been the Opinion of several learned Persons, who think well enough of the true Art of Astrology, That the Stars do only *incline*, and not force the Actions or Wills of Men: And therefore, however I may proceed by right Rules, yet I cannot in Prudence so confidently assure that the Events will follow exactly as I predict them.

I HOPE, I have maturely considered this Objection, which in some Cases is of no little Weight. For Example: A Man may, by the Influence of an over-ruling Planet, be disposed or inclined to Lust, Rage, or Avarice; and yet by the Force of Reason overcome that evil Influence. And this was the Case of *Socrates*: But the the great Events of the World usually depending upon Numbers of Men, it cannot be expected they should all unite to cross their Inclinations, from pursuing a general Design, wherein they unanimously agree. Besides, the Influence of the Stars reacheth to many Actions and Events, which are not any way in the Power of Reason; as Sickness, Death, and what we commonly call Accidents; with many more needless to repeat.

But now it is Time to proceed to my Predictions; which I have begun to calculate from the Time that the *Sun* enters into *Aries*. And this I take to be properly the Beginning of the natural Year. I pursue them to the Time that he enters *Libra*, or somewhat more, which is the busy Period of the Year. The Remainder I have not yet adjusted upon Account of several Impediments needless here to mention. Besides, I must remind the Reader again, that this is but a Specimen of what I design in succeeding Years to treat more at large, if I may have Liberty and Encouragement.

My first Prediction is but a Trifle; yet I will mention it, to shew how ignorant those sottish Pretenders to Astrology are in their own Concerns: It relates to *Partrige* the Almanack-Maker; I have consulted the Star of his Nativity by my own Rules; and find he will infallibly die upon the 29th of *March* next, about eleven at Night, of a raging Fever: Therefore I advise him to consider of it, and settle his Affairs in Time.

The Month of *APRIL* will be observable for the Death of many great Persons. On the 4th will die the Cardinal *de Noailles*, Archbishop of *Paris*: On the 11th the young Prince of *Asturias*, Son to the Duke of *Anjou*: On the 14th a great Peer of this Realm will die at his Country-House: On the 19th an old *Layman* of great Fame for Learning: And on the 23rd an eminent Goldsmith in *Lombard Street*. I could mention others, both at home and abroad, if I did not consider such Events of very little Use or Instruction to the Reader, or to the World.

As to publick Affairs: On the 7th of this Month, there will be an Insurrection in *Dauphine*, occasioned by the Oppressions of the People; which will not be quieted in some Months.

On the 15th will be a violent Storm on the South-East Coast of *France*; which will destroy many of their Ships, and some in the very Harbour.

THE 19th will be famous for the Revolt of a whole Province or Kingdom, excepting one City; by which the Affairs of a certain Prince in the Alliance will take a better Face.

MAY, Against common Conjectures, will be no very busy Month in *Europe*; but very signal for the Death of the *Dauphine*, which will happen on the 7th, after a short Fit of Sickness, and grievous Torments with the Strangury. He dies less lamented by the Court than the Kingdom.

ON the 9th a *Mareschal* of *France* will break his Leg by a Fall from his Horse. I have not been able to discover whether he will then die or not.

ON the 11th will begin a most important Siege, which the Eyes of all *Europe* will be upon: I cannot be more particular; for in relating Affairs that so nearly concern the *Confederates*, and consequently this Kingdom; I am forced to confine my self, for several Reasons very obvious to the Reader.

ON the 15th News will arrive of a very *surprizing Event*, than which nothing could be more unexpected.

ON the 19th, three Noble Ladies of this Kingdom, will against all Expectation, prove with Child, to the great Joy of their Husbands.

ON the 23d, a famous Buffoon of the Play-House will die a ridiculous Death, suitable to his Vocation.

JUNE. This Month will be distinguished at home, by the utter dispersing of those ridiculous deluded Enthusiasts, commonly called the *Prophets*; occasioned chiefly by seeing the Time come, when many of their Prophecies were to be fulfilled; and then finding themselves deceived by contrary Events. It is indeed to be admired how any Deceiver can be so weak to foretel Things near at hand; when a very few Months must of Necessity discover the Imposture to all the World: In this Point less prudent than common Almanack-Makers, who are so wise to wander in Generals, talk dubiously, and leave to the Reader the Business of interpreting.

ON the 1st of this Month a *French* General will be killed by random Shot of a Cannon-Ball.

ON the 6th a Fire will break out in the Suburbs of *Paris*, which will destroy above a thousand Houses; and seems to be the

Foreboding of what will happen, to the Surprize of all *Europe*, about the End of the following Month.

ON the 10th a great Battle will be fought, which will begin at four of the Clock in the Afternoon, and last till nine at Night with great Obstinacy, but no very decisive Event. I shall not name the Place, for the Reasons aforesaid; but the Commanders on each left Wing will be killed. —— I see Bonfires and hear the Noise of Guns for a Victory.

ON the 14th there will be a false Report of the *French* King's Death.

ON the 20th Cardinal *Portocarero* will die of a Dissentery, with great Suspicion of Poison; but the Report of his Intention to revolt to King *Charles* will prove false.

JULY. The 6th of this Month a *certain General* will, by a glorious Action, recover the Reputation he lost by former Misfortunes.

ON the 12th a *great Commander* will die a Prisoner in the Hands of his Enemies.

ON the 14th a shameful Discovery will be made of a *French* Jesuit giving Poison to a great Foreign General; and when he is put to the Torture, will make wonderful Discoveries.

IN short, this will prove a Month of great Action, if I might have Liberty to relate the Particulars.

AT home, the Death of an old famous Senator will happen on the 15th at his Country-House, worn with Age and Diseases.

BUT that which will make this Month memorable to all Posterity, is the Death of the *French* King *Lewis* the Fourteenth, after a Week's Sickness at *Marli*; which will happen on the 29th, about six a-Clock in the Evening. It seems to be an Effect of the Gout in his Stomach, followed by a Flux. And in three Days after Monsieur *Chamillard* will follow his Master, dying suddenly of an Apoplexy.

IN this Month likewise an *Ambassador* will die in *London*; but I cannot assign the Day.

AUGUST. The affairs of *France* will seem to suffer no Change for a while under the Duke of *Burgundy*'s Administration. But the Genius that animated the whole Machine being gone, will be the Cause of mighty Turns and Revolutions in the following Year. The new King makes yet little Change either in the Army or the Ministry; but the Libels against his Grandfather, that fly about his very Court, give him Uneasiness.

I SEE an Express in mighty Haste, with Joy and Wonder in his Looks, arriving by the Break of Day, on the 26th of this Month, having travelled in three Days a prodigious Journey by Land and Sea. In the Evening I hear Bells and Guns, and see the Blazing of a Thousand Bonfires.

A YOUNG Admiral, of noble Birth, does likewise this Month gain immortal Honour, by a great Atchievement.

THE Affairs of *Poland* are this Month entirely settled: *Augustus* resigns his Pretensions, which he had again taken up for some Time: *Stanislaus* is peaceably possessed of the Throne; and the King of *Sweden* declares for the Emperor.

I CANNOT omit one particular Accident here at home; that near the End of this Month, much Mischief will be done at *Bartholomew* Fair, by the Fall of a Booth.

SEPTEMBER. This Month begins with a very surprizing Fit of frosty Weather, which will last near twelve Days.

THE Pope having long languished last Month; the Swellings in his Legs breaking, and the Flesh mortifying, will die on the 11th Instant: And in three Weeks Time, after a mighty Contest, be succeeded by a Cardinal of the *Imperial* Faction, but Native of *Tuscany*, who is now about Sixty-One Years old.

THE *French* Army acts now wholly on the Defensive, strongly fortified in their Trenches; and the young *French* King sends Overtures for a Treaty of Peace, by the Duke of *Mantua*; which, because it is a Matter of State that concerns us here at home, I shall speak no farther of it.

I SHALL add but one Prediction more, and that in mystical Terms, which shall be included in a Verse out of *Virgil.*

> *Alter erit jam Tethys, & altera quæ vehat Argo,*
> *Dilectos Heroas.*

UPON the 25th Day of this Month, the fulfilling of this Prediction will be manifest to every Body.

THIS is the farthest I have proceeded in my Calculations for the present Year. I do not pretend, that these are all the grea

Events which will happen in this Period; but that those I have set down will infallibly come to pass. It may, perhaps, still be objected, why I have not spoke more particularly of Affairs at home; or of the Success of our Armies abroad, which I might, and could very largely have done. But those in Power have wisely discouraged Men from meddling in publick Concerns; and I was resolved, by no Means, to give the least Offence. This I will venture to say; that it will be a glorious Campaign for the Allies; wherein the *English* Forces, both by Sea and Land, will have their full Share of Honour: That Her Majesty Queen ANNE will continue in Health and Prosperity: And that no ill Accident will arrive to any in the chief Ministry.

As to the particular Events I have mentioned, the Readers may judge by the fulfilling of them, whether I am of the Level with common Astrologers; who, with an old paultry Cant, and a few Pot-hooks for Planets to amuse the Vulgar, have, in my Opinion, too long been suffered to abuse the World. But an honest Physician ought not to be despised, because there are such Things as Mountebanks. I hope, I have some Share of Reputation, which I would not willingly forfeit for a Frolick, or Humour: And I believe no Gentleman, who reads this Paper, will look upon it to be of the same Cast, or Mold, with the common Scribbles that are every Day hawked about. My Fortune hath placed me above the little Regard of writing for a few Pence, which I neither value nor want: Therefore, let not wise Men too hastily condemn this Essay, intended for a good Design, to cultivate and improve an antient Art, long in Disgrace by having fallen into mean unskilful Hands. A little Time will determine whether I have deceived others, or my self; and I think it is no very unreasonable Request, that Men would please to suspend their Judgments till then. I was once of the Opinion with those who despise all Predictions from the Stars, till in the Year 1686, a Man of Quality shewed me, written in his *Album*, that the most learned Astronomer Captain *Hally*, assured him, he would never believe any thing of the Stars Influence, if there were not a great Revolution in *England* in the Year 1688. Since that Time I began to have other Thoughts; and after Eighteen Years diligent Study and Application, I think I have no Reason to repent of my Pains. I shall detain the Reader no longer than to let him know, that the Account I design to give of next Year's Events, shall take in the principal Affairs that happen in *Europe*: And if I be denied the Liberty of offering it to my own Country, I shall appeal to the learned World, by publishing it in *Latin*, and giving Order to have it printed in *Holland*.

THE
ACCOMPLISHMENT
Of the First of
Mr. *Bickerstaff*'s Predictions.
Being an
ACCOUNT
Of the Death of
Mr. *PARTRIGE*, the Almanack-maker,

Upon the 29th Instant.

In a Letter to a Person of Honour.

My LORD,

IN Obedience to your Lordship's Commands, as well as to satisfie may own Curiosity, I have for some Days past enquired constantly after *Partrige*, the Almanack-maker, of whom it was foretold in Mr. *Bickerstaff*'s Predictions,
                                                    publish'd

THE
ACCOMPLISHMENT
Of the First of
Mr. *Bickerstaff*'s PREDICTIONS.
BEING AN
ACCOUNT
OF THE

Death of Mr. *Partrige*, the Almanack-maker, upon the 29th Inst.

In a Letter to a Person of Honour.

Written in the Year 1708.

My LORD,

IN Obedience to your Lordship's Commands, as well as to satisfy my own Curiosity, I have for some Days past enquired constantly after *Partrige* the Almanack-maker; of whom it was foretold in Mr. *Bickerstaff*'s Predictions, published about a Month ago, that he should die the 29th Instant, about Eleven at Night, of a raging Fever. I had some Sort of Knowledge of him when I was employed in the Revenue; because he used every Year to present me with his Almanack, as he did other Gentlemen upon the score of some little Gratuity we gave him. I saw him accidentally once or twice about ten Days before he died; and observed he began very much to droop and languish, although I hear his Friends did not seem to apprehend him in any Danger. About two or three Days ago he grew ill; was confined first to his Chamber, and in a few Hours after to his Bed; where Dr. *Case* and Mrs. *Kirleus** were sent for to visit, and to prescribe

* *Two famous Quacks at that Time in* London.

to him. Upon this Intelligence I sent thrice every Day one Servant or other to enquire after his Health; and Yesterday about four in the Afternoon, Word was brought me that he was past Hopes: Upon which I prevailed with my self to go and see him; partly out of Commiseration, and, I confess, partly out of Curiosity. He knew me very well, seemed surprized at my Condescension, and made me Compliments upon it as well as he could in the Condition he was. The People about him said, he had been for some Hours delirious; but when I saw him, he had his Understanding as well as ever I knew, and spoke strong and hearty, without any seeming Uneasiness or Constraint. After I had told him I was sorry to see him in those melancholly Circumstances, and said some other Civilities, suitable to the Occasion; I desired him to tell me freely and ingenuously whether the Predictions Mr. *Bickerstaff* had published relating to his Death, had not too much affected and worked on his Imagination. He confessed he had often had it in his Head, but never with much Apprehension till about a Fortnight before; since which Time it had the perpetual Possession of his Mind and Thoughts; and he did verily believe was the true natural Cause of his present Distemper: For, said he, I am thoroughly persuaded, and I think I have very good Reasons, that Mr. *Bickerstaff* spoke altogether by guess, and knew no more what will happen this Year than I did my self. I told him his Discourse surprized me; and I would be glad he were in a State of Health to be able to tell me what Reason he had to be convinced of Mr. *Bickerstaff*'s Ignorance. He replied, I am a poor ignorant Fellow, bred to a mean Trade; yet I have Sense enough to know, that all Pretences of foretelling by Astrology are Deceits; for this manifest Reason, because the Wise and Learned, who can only judge whether there be any Truth in this Science, do all unanimously agree to laugh at and despise it; and none but the poor ignorant Vulgar give it any Credit, and that only upon the Word of such silly Wretches as I and my Fellows, who can hardly write or read. I then asked him, why he had not calculated his own Nativity, to see whether it agreed with *Bickerstaff*'s Predictions? At which he shook his Head, and said, O! Sir, this is no Time for jesting, but for repenting those Fooleries, as I do now from the very Bottom of my Heart. By what I can gather from you, said I, the Observations and Predictions you printed with your Almanacks were meer Impositions upon the People. He replied, if it were otherwise, I should have the less to answer for. We have a common Form for all those Things: As to foretelling the Weather, we never meddle with that, but leave it to the Printer, who takes it out of any old Almanack as he thinks fit: The rest was my own Invention to make my Almanack sell; having a Wife to maintain, and no other Way to get my Bread; for mending old Shoes is a poor Livelihood: And (added he, sighing) I wish I may not have done more Mischief by my Physick than my Astrology; although I had some good Receipts from my Grandmother, and my own Compositions were such, as I thought could at least do no Hurt.

I HAD some other Discourse with him, which now I cannot call to Mind; and I fear I have already tired your Lordship. I shall only add one Circumstance, That on his Death-Bed he declared himself a Nonconformist, and had a fanatick Preacher to be his spiritual Guide. After half an Hour's Conversation, I took my Leave, being almost stifled by the Closeness of the Room. I imagined he could not hold out long; and therefore withdrew to a little Coffee-House hard by, leaving a Servant at the House with Orders to come immediately, and tell me, as near as he could, the Minute when *Partrige* should expire, which was not above two Hours after; when looking upon my Watch, I found it to be above five Minutes after Seven: By which it is clear, that Mr. *Bickerstaff* was mistaken almost four Hours in his Calculation. In the other Circumstances he was exact enough. But whether he hath not been the Cause of this poor Man's Death, as well as the Predictor, may be very reasonably disputed. However, it must be confessed, the Matter is odd enough, whether we should endeavour to account for it by Chance or the Effect of Imagination: For my own Part, although I believe no Man hath less Faith in these Matters; yet I shall wait with some Impatience, and not without Expectation, the fulfilling of Mr. *Bickerstaff*'s second Prediction; that the Cardinal *de Noailles* is to die upon the 4th of *April*; and if that should be verified as exactly as this of poor *Partrige*; I must own, I should be wholly surprized, and at a Loss; and should infallibly expect the Accomplishment of all the rest.

A
VINDICATION

O F

Iſaac Bickerſtaff Eſq;

A G A I N S T

What is Objected to Him by
Mr. *Partridge,* in his Almanack
for the preſent Year 1709.

By the ſaid ISAAC BICKERSTAFF *Eſq;*

LONDON:
Printed in the Year MDCCIX.

A

VINDICATION

OF

Isaac Bickerstaff, Esq;

AGAINST

What is objected to him by Mr. *Partrige*, in his Almanack for the present Year 1709.

By the said ISAAC BICKERSTAFF, *Esq*;

Written in the YEAR 1709.

MR. *Partrige* hath been lately pleased to treat me after a very rough Manner, in *that which is called*, His Almanack for the present Year: Such Usage is very undecent from *one Gentleman to another*, and doth not at all contribute to the Discovery of Truth; which ought to be the great End in all Disputes of the *Learned*. To call a Man *Fool* and *Villain*, and *impudent Fellow*, only for differing from him in a Point meerly speculative, is, in my humble Opinion, a very improper Stile for a Person of *his Education*. I appeal to the *learned World*, whether in my last Year's Predictions, I gave him the least Provocation for such unworthy Treatment. Philosophers have differed in all Ages, but the discreetest among them have always differed as became Philosophers. Scurrility and Passion, in a Controversy among *Scholars*, is just so much of nothing to the Purpose; and, at best, a tacit Confession of a weak Cause: My Concern is not so much for my own Reputation, as that of the *Republick of Letters*, which Mr. *Partrige* hath endeavoured to wound through my Sides. If Men of publick Spirit must be superciliously treated for their ingenuous Attempts; how will true useful Knowledge be ever advanced? I wish Mr. *Partrige* knew the Thoughts which *foreign Universities* have conceived of his ungenerous Proceedings with me; but I am too tender of his Reputation to publish them to the World. That Spirit of Envy and Pride, which blasts so many rising Genius's in our Nation, is yet unknown among *Professors* abroad: The Necessity of justifying my self, will excuse my Vanity, when I tell the Reader, that I have near an Hundred *honorary* Letters from several Parts of *Europe*, (some as far as *Muscovy*) in Praise of my Performance. Besides several others, which, as I have been credibly informed, were opened in the Post-Office, and never sent me. * It is true, the *Inquisition* in *Portugal* was pleased to burn my Predictions, and condemn the Author and Readers of them; but, I hope, at the same Time, it will be considered in how deplorable a State *Learning* lies at present in that Kingdom: And with the profoundest Veneration for *crowned Heads*, I will presume to add; that it a little concerned *his Majesty of Portugal*, to interpose his Authority in Behalf of a *Scholar* and a *Gentleman*, the Subject of a Nation with which he is now in so strict an Alliance. But, the other Kingdoms and States of *Europe* have treated me with more Candour and Generosity. If I had leave to print the *Latin* Letters transmitted to me from foreign Parts, they would fill a Volume, and be a full Defence against all that Mr. *Partrige*, or his Accomplices of the *Portugal Inquisition*, will be ever able to object; who, by the way, are the only Enemies my Predictions have ever met with at home or abroad. But, I hope, I know better what is due to the Honour of a *learned Correspondence*, in so tender a Point. Yet, some of those illustrious Persons will, perhaps, excuse me for transcribing a Passage or two in my own Vindication. The † most learned Monsieur *Leibnitz* thus addresseth to me his third Letter: *Illustrissimo Bickerstaffio Astrologiæ Instauratori*, &c. Monsieur *le Clerc* quoting my Predictions in a Treatise he published last Year, is pleased to say, *Ità nuperime Bickerstaffius*

* *This is Fact, as the Author was assured by Sir* Paul Methuen, *then Ambassador to that Crown.*

† *The Quotations here inserted, are in Imitation of Dr.* Bentley, *in some Part of the famous Controversy between him and* Charles Boyle, *Esq; afterwards Earl of* Orrery.

magnum illud Angliæ sidus. Another great Professor writing of me, has these Words: *Bickerstaffius, nobilis Anglus, Astrologorum hujusce Seculi facilè Princeps.* Signior *Magliabecchi*, the *Great Duke's* famous Library-keeper, spends almost his whole Letter in Compliments and Praises. It is true, the renowned *Professor* of Astronomy at *Utrecht*, seems to differ from me in one Article; but it is after the modest Manner that becomes a Philosopher; as, *Pace tanti viri dixerim*: And, *Page* 55, he seems to lay the Error upon the Printer, (as indeed it ought) and says, *vel forsan error Typographi, cum alioquin Bickerstaffius vir doctissimus,* &c.

IF Mr. *Partrige* had followed these Examples in the Controversy between us, he might have spared me the Trouble of justifying my self in so publick a Manner. I believe few Men are readier to own their Errors than I, or more thankful to those who will please to inform him of them. But it seems this Gentleman, instead of encouraging the Progress of his own Art, is pleased to look upon all Attempts of that Kind, as an Invasion of his Province. He hath been indeed so wise, to make no Objection against the Truth of my Predictions, except in one single Point, relating to himself: And to demonstrate how much Men are blinded by their own Partiality; I do solemnly assure the Reader, that he is the *only* Person from whom I ever heard that Objection offered; which Consideration alone, I think, will take off all its Weight.

WITH my utmost Endeavours, I have not been able to trace above two Objections ever made against the Truth of my last Year's Prophecies: The first is of a *French* Man, who was pleased to publish to the World, that *the Cardinal* de Noailles *was still alive, notwithstanding the pretended Prophecy of Monsieur* Biquerstaffe: But how far a *French* Man, a *Papist*, and an *Enemy* is to be believed, in his own Cause, against an *English Protestant*, who is *true to the Government*, I shall leave to the candid and impartial Reader.

THE other Objection, is the unhappy Occasion of this Discourse; and relates to an Article in my Predictions, which foretold the Death of Mr. *Partrige* to happen on *March* 29, 1708. This he is pleased to contradict absolutely in the Almanack he hath published for the present Year; and in that ungentlemanly

II m

Manner, (pardon the Expression) as I have above related. In
that Work, he very roundly asserts, That he *is not only now alive,
but was likewise alive upon that very 29th of* March, *when I had
foretold* he *should die.* This is the Subject of the present Controversy between us; which I design to handle with all Brevity, Perspicuity, and Calmness: In this Dispute, I am sensible, the Eyes
not only of *England*, but of all *Europe*, will be upon us: And the
Learned in every Country will, I doubt not, take Part on that
Side where they find most Appearance of Reason and Truth.

WITHOUT entering into Criticisms of *Chronology* about the
Hour of his Death; I shall only prove, that Mr. *Partrige* is not
alive. And my first Argument is thus: Above a Thousand Gentlemen having bought his Almanacks for this Year, meerly to
find what he said against me; at every Line they read, they would
lift up their Eyes, and cry out, betwixt Rage and Laughter,
They were sure no Man alive *ever writ such damned Stuff as this.*
Neither did I ever hear that Opinion disputed: So that Mr.
Partrige lies under a *Dilemma*, either of disowning his Almanack,
or allowing himself to be *no Man alive.* But now, if an *uninformed*
Carcass walks still about, and is pleased to call it self *Partrige*;
Mr. *Bickerstaff* does not think himself any way answerable for
that. Neither had the said Carcass any Right to beat the poor Boy,
who happened to pass by it in the Street, crying, *A full and true
Account of Dr.* Partrige'*s Death*, &c.

SECONDLY, Mr. *Partridge* pretends to tell Fortunes, and
recover stolen Goods; which all the Parish says he must do by
conversing with the Devil, and other evil Spirits: And no wise
Man will ever allow he could converse personally with either,
till after he was dead.

THIRDLY, I will plainly prove him to be dead, out of his
own Almanack for this Year, and from the very Passage which
he produceth to make us think him alive. He there says, *He is not
only* now *alive, but was also alive upon that very 29th of* March, *which
I foretold* he *should die on*: By this, he declares his Opinion, that a
Man may be alive *now*, who was not alive a Twelve-month ago.
And, indeed, there lies the Sophistry of his Argument. He dares
not assert, he was alive ever since the 29th of *March*, but that he
is now alive, and was so on that Day: I grant the latter, for he did

not die till Night, as appears by the printed Account of his Death, in a *Letter to a Lord*; and whether he be since revived, I leave the World to judge. This, indeed, is perfect cavilling, and I am ashamed to dwell any longer upon it.

FOURTHLY, I will appeal to Mr. *Partrige* himself, whether it be probable I could have been so indiscreet, to begin my Predictions with the *only* Falshood that ever was pretended to be in them; and this is an Affair at Home, where I had so many Opportunities to be exact; and must have given such Advantages against me to a Person of Mr. *Partrige*'s Wit and Learning, who, if he could possibly have raised one single Objection more against the Truth of my Prophecies, would hardly have spared me.

AND here I must take Occasion to reprove the abovementioned Writer of the Relation of Mr. *Partrige*'s Death, in a *Letter to a Lord*; who was pleased to tax me with a Mistake of *four whole Hours* in my Calculation of that Event. I must confess, this Censure, pronounced with an Air of Certainty, in a Matter that so nearly concerned me, and by a *grave judicious Author*, moved me not a little. But although I was at that Time out of Town, yet several of my Friends, whose Curiosity had led them to be exactly informed, (for as to my own Part, having no doubt at all in the Matter, I never once thought of it,) assured me I computed to something under half an Hour; which (I speak my private Opinion) is an Error of no very great Magnitude, that Men should raise Clamour about it. I shall only say, it would not be amiss, if that Author would henceforth be more tender of other Mens Reputation as well as his own. It is well there were no more Mistakes of that Kind; if there had, I presume he would have told me of them with as little Ceremony.

THERE is one Objection against Mr. *Partrige*'s Death, which I have sometimes met with, although indeed very slightly offered; That he still continues to write Almanacks. But this is no more than what is common to all of that Profession; *Gadbury*, *Poor Robin*, *Dove*, *Wing*, and several others, do yearly publish their Almanacks, although several of them have been dead since before the *Revolution*. Now the natural Reason of this I take to be, that whereas it is the Privilege of other Authors, *to live after their Deaths*; Almanack-makers are alone excluded; because their Dissertations treating only upon the Minutes as they pass, become useless as those go off. In consideration of which, *Time*, whose *Registers* they are, gives them a Lease in Reversion, to continue their Works after their Death.

I SHOULD not have given the Publick or my self the Trouble of this Vindication, if my Name had not been made use of by several Persons, to whom I never lent it; one of which, a few Days ago, was pleased to father on me a new Set of Predictions. But I think these are Things too serious to be trifled with. It grieved me to the Heart, when I saw my Labours, which had cost me so much Thought and Watching, bawled about by common Hawkers, which I only intended for the weighty Consideration of the gravest Persons. This prejudiced the World so much at first, that several of my Friends had the Assurance to ask me, Whether I were in jest? To which I only answered coldly, *That the Event will shew*. But it is the Talent of our Age and Nation, to turn Things of the greatest Importance into Ridicule. When the End of the Year had *verified all my Predictions*; out comes Mr. *Partrige*'s Almanack, disputing the Point of his Death; so that I am employed, like the General who was forced to kill his Enemies twice over, whom a *Necromancer* had raised to Life. If Mr. *Partrige* hath practised the same Experiment upon himself, and be again alive; long may he continue so; but that doth not in the least contradict my Veracity: For I think I have clearly proved, by *invincible Demonstration*, that he died at farthest within half an Hour of the Time I foretold; and not four Hours sooner, as the above-mentioned Author, in his Letter to a Lord, hath maliciously suggested, with Design to blast my Credit, by charging me with so gross a Mistake.

Merlinus Verax.

A Famous Prediction of *MERLIN*, the *British* Wizard, written above a Thousand Years ago, and relating to this present Year.

With Explanatory Notes. By *T. N.* Philomath.

LAST Year was publish'd a Paper of Predictions pretended to be written by one *Isaac Bickerstaff*, Esq; but the true Design of it was to Ridicule the Art of Astrology, and Expose its Professors as Ignorant, or Impostors. Against this Imputation, Dr. *Partridge* hath vindicated himself in his Almanack for the present Year.

For a further Vindication of this famous Art, I have thought fit to present the World with the following Prophecy. The Original is said to be of the famous *Merlin*, who lived about a Thousand Years ago: And the following Translation is Two Hundred Years old; for it seems to be written near the End of *Henry* the Seventh's Reign. I found it in an Old Edition of *Merlin's* Prophecies; imprinted at *London* by *Johan Haukyns*, in the Year 1530. *Page* 39. I set it down Word for Word in the Old Orthography, and shall take Leave to subjoin a few Explanatory Notes.

> Seben and Ten addyd to nyne,
> Of Fraunce hir woe thys is the sygne,
> Tamys riuere twys y-frozen,
> Walke sans wetynge shoes ne hosen.
> Then comyth foorthe, Ich understonde,
> From Towne of Stoffe to fattyn Londe
> An herdie Chiftan, woe the morne
> To Fraunce, that euere he was borne.
> Than shall the Fryshe bewryle his Boste;
> For shall grin Berris make up the Loste
> Yonge Symnele shall agayne miscarrye:
> And Norways Pryd agayne shall marrye.
> And from the Tree where Blosmes blie,
> Ripe frute shall come, and all tis wele.
> Reaums shall daunce honde in honde,
> And it shall be merye in olde Inglonde.
> Then olde Inglonde shall be noe more,
> And no Man shall be sorie therefore.
> Gerron shall haue three Hedes agayne,
> Till Hapsburge makyth them but twayne.

Expla-

A Famous

PREDICTION

OF

MERLIN,

THE

British WIZARD,

Written above a thousand Years ago, and
relating to the Year 1709.

With Explanatory Notes. By T. N. *Philomath.*

Written in the YEAR 1709.

LAST Year was published a Paper of Predictions, pretended to be written by one *Isaac Bickerstaff*, Esq; but the
true Design of it was to ridicule the Art of Astrology, and
expose its Professors as ignorant, or Impostors. Against this
Imputation, Dr. *Partrige* hath learnedly vindicated himself in his
Almanack for that Year.

FOR a farther Defence of this famous Art, I have thought fit
to present the World with the following Prophecy. The Original
is said to be of the famous *Merlin*, who lived about a thousand
Years ago: And the following Translation is two hundred
Years old; for it seems to be written near the End of *Henry* the
Seventh's Reign. I found it in an old Edition of *Merlin*'s Prophecies; imprinted at *London* by *Johan Haukyns*, in the Year 1530.
Page 39. I set it down Word for Word in the old Orthography,
and shall take leave to subjoin a few explanatory Notes.

SEUEN and TEN addyd to NINE,
  Of Fraunce hir Woe thys is the Sygne,
Tamys Ryvere twys y-frozen,
Walke sans wetyng Shoes ne Hosen.
Then cometh foorthe, Ich understonde,
From Toune of Stoffe to fattyn Londe,
An herdie Chiftan, woe the Morne
To Fraunce, that evere he was borne.
Then shall the Fyshe beweyle his Bosse;
Nor shall grin Berrys make up the Losse.
Yonge Symnele shall again miscarrye:
And Norways Pryd again shall marrey.
And from the Tree where Blosums fele,
Ripe Fruit shall come, and all is wele.
Reaums shall daunce Honde in Honde,
And it shall be merye in old Inglonde.
Then old Inglonde shall be no more,
And no Man shall be sorie therefore.
Geryon shall have three Hedes agayne,
Till Hapsburge makyth them but twayne.

Explanatory NOTES.

Seven and Ten. This Line describes the Year when these Events
shall happen. Seven and Ten make Seventeen, which I explain
seventeen Hundred, and this Number added to Nine makes the
Year we are now in; for it must be understood of the Natural
Year, which begins the First of *January.*

Tamys Ryvere twys, &c. The River *Thames* frozen twice in one
Year, so as Men to walk on it, is a very signal Accident; which
perhaps hath not fallen out for several Hundred Years before;
and is the Reason why some Astrologers have thought that this
Prophecy could never be fulfilled; because they imagined such a
Thing could never happen in our Climate.

From Toune of Stoffe, &c. This is a plain Designation of the Duke of *Marlborough*. One Kind of stuff used to fatten Land is called *Marle*, and every Body knows, that *Borough* is a Name for a Town; and this Way of Expression is after the usual dark Manner of old Astrological Predictions.

Then shall the Fyshe, &c. By the *Fish* is understood the *Dauphin* of *France*, as the Kings eldest Sons are called: It is here said, he shall lament the Loss of the Duke of *Burgundy*, called the *Bosse*, which is an old *English* Word for *Hump-shoulder*, or *Crook-back*, as that Duke is known to be: And the Prophecy seems to mean, that he should be overcome, or slain. By the *Grin Berrys*, in the next Line, is meant the young Duke of *Berry*, the *Dauphin's* third Son, who shall not have Valour or Fortune enough to supply the Loss of his eldest Brother.

Yonge Symnele, &c. By *Symnele* is meant the pretended Prince of *Wales*; who, if he offers to attempt any Thing against *England*, shall miscarry as he did before. *Lambert Symnel* is the Name of a young Man noted in our Histories for personating the Son (as I remember) of *Edward* the Fourth.

And Norways Pryd, &c. I cannot guess who is meant by *Norways Pride*, perhaps the Reader may, as well as the Sense of the two following Lines.

Reaums shall, &c. *Reaums*, or as the Word is now, *Realms*, is the old Name for *Kingdoms*: And this is a very plain Prediction of our happy *Union*, with the Felicities that shall attend it. It is added, that *Old England* shall be no more, and yet no Man shall be sorry for it. And, indeed, properly speaking, *England* is now no more; for the whole Island is one Kingdom, under the Name of *Britain*.

Geryon shall, &c. This Prediction, though somewhat obscure, is wonderfully adapt. *Geryon* is said to have been a King of *Spain*, whom *Hercules* slew. It was a Fiction of the Poets, that he had three Heads, which the Author says he shall have again. That is, *Spain* shall have three Kings; which is now wonderfully verified: For, besides the King of *Portugal*, which properly is

---

* *Queen* Anne. *The Prophecy means, that she should marry a second Time, and have Children that would live.*

Part of *Spain*, there are now two Rivals for *Spain*; *Charles* and *Philip*. But *Charles* being descended from the Count of *Hapsburgh*, Founder of the *Austrian* Family, shall soon make those Heads but two; by overturning *Philip*, and driving him out of *Spain*.

SOME of these Predictions are already fulfilled; and it is highly probable the rest may be in due Time: And, I think, I have not forced the Words, by my Explication, into any other Sense than what they will naturally bear. If this be granted, I am sure it must be also allowed, that the Author (whoever he were) was a Person of extraordinary Sagacity; and that Astrology brought to such Perfection as this, is, by no Means, an Art to be despised; whatever Mr. *Bickerstaff*, or other merry Gentlemen are pleased to think. As to the Tradition of these Lines, having been writ in the Original by *Merlin*; I confess, I lay not much Weight upon it: But it is enough to justify their Authority, that the Book from whence I have transcribed them, was printed 170 Years ago, as appears by the Title-Page. For the Satisfaction of any Gentleman, who may be either doubtful of the Truth, or curious to be informed; I shall give Order to have the very Book sent to the Printer of this Paper, with Directions to let any Body see it that pleases; because I believe it is pretty scarce.

ISAAC BICKERSTAFF Esqr.

B. Lens sen.r delineavit

*Frontispiece to the Collected Edition of The Tatler, 1710 in the
King's Library, British Museum*

Papers
Contributed by Swift
to The Tatler

THE PUBLISHER'S PREFACE

We have added out of the Preface to the fourth
Volume of TATLERS, what is there said of
the Author.

IN *the last* TATLER, *I promised some Explanations of Passages
and Persons mentioned in this Work, as well as some Account of
the Assistances I have had in the Performance. I shall do this in
very few Words; for when a Man has no Design but to speak plain
Truth, he may say a great Deal in a very narrow Compass. I have, in the
Dedication of the first Volume, made my Acknowledgments to Dr.*
SWIFT, *whose pleasant Writings, in the Name of* Bickerstaff, *created
an Inclination in the Town towards any Thing that could appear in the
same Disguise. I must acknowledge also, that at my first entering upon
this Work, a certain uncommon Way of Thinking, and a Turn in Conversation peculiar to that agreeable Gentleman, rendered his Company
very advantageous to one, whose Imagination was to be continually employed upon obvious and common Subjects, though at the same Time
obliged to treat of them in a new and unbeaten Method. His Verses on
the* Shower in Town, *and the* Description of the Morning, *are
Instances of the Happiness of that Genius, which could raise such pleasing Ideas upon Occasions so barren to an ordinary Invention.*

THE
TATLER.

NUMBER CCXXX.*

Thursday, September 28, 1710.

From my own Apartment, Sept. 27.

THE following Letter hath laid before me many great and manifest Evils, in the World of Letters which I had over-looked; but they open to me a very busy Scene, and it will require no small Care and Application to amend Errors which are become so universal. The Affectation of Politeness, is exposed in this Epistle with a great deal of Wit and Discernment; so that, whatever Discourses I may fall into hereafter upon the Subjects the Writer treats of, I shall at present lay the Matter before the World, without the least Alteration from the Words of my Correspondent.

To ISAAC BICKERSTAFF, *Esq;*

SIR,

THERE *are some Abuses among us of great Consequence, the Reformation of which is properly your Province; although, as far as I have been conversant in your Papers, you have not yet considered them. These are the deplorable Ignorance that for some Years hath reigned among our* English *Writers; the great Depravity of our*

---

*This TATLER, *relating to the same Subject contained in the Letter to the Lord High-Treasurer, was thought proper to be prefixed to the said Letter. It is well known, that the Author writ several* Tatlers, *and some* Spectators: *and furnished Hints for many more. Particularly,* The Tables of Fame, The Life and Adventures of a Shilling, The Account of England *by an* Indian King, *and some others. But, as we are informed, he would never tell his best Friends the particular Papers.*

Taste; and the continual Corruption of our Style. I say nothing here of those who handle particular Sciences, Divinity, Law, Physick, and the like; I mean the Traders in History and Politicks, and the Belles Lettres; *together with those by whom Books are not translated, but (as the common Expressions are)* Done out of French, Latin, or other Language, and *made English. I cannot but observe to you, that until of late Years, a* Grub-street Book *was always bound in Sheep-skin, with suitable Print and Paper; the Price never above a Shilling; and taken off wholly by common Tradesmen, or Country Pedlars. But now they appear in all Sizes and Shapes, and in all Places: They are handed about from Lapfulls in every Coffee-house to Persons of Quality; are shewn in* Westminster-Hall, *and the Court of Requests. You may see them gilt, and in Royal Paper of five or six Hundred Pages, and rated accordingly. I would engage to furnish you with a Catalogue of* English *Books published within the Compass of seven Years past, which at the first Hand would cost you an Hundred Pounds; wherein you shall not be able to find ten Lines together of common Grammar, or common Sense.*

THESE two Evils, Ignorance, and want of Taste, have produced a Third; I mean the continual Corruption of our English *Tongue; which, without some timely Remedy, will suffer more by the false Refinements of Twenty Years past, than it hath been improved in the foregoing Hundred. And this is what I design chiefly to enlarge upon; leaving the former Evils to your Animadversion.*

BUT, instead of giving you a List of the late Refinements crept into our Language; I here send you the Copy of a Letter I received some Time ago from a most accomplished Person in this Way of Writing; upon which I shall make some Remarks. It is in these Terms:

SIR,

'I Cou'dn't get the Things you sent for all *about Town.*—*I* thot 'to ha' come down my self, and then *I'd ha'* bro't 'um; but I 'ha'n't don't, *and I believe I* can't do't, *that's* pozz——*Tom* 'begins to gi'mself *Airs, because* he's *going with the* Plenipo's. '—— 'Tis said the *French* King will *bamboozel us agen,* which 'causes many Speculations. *The* Jacks, *and others of that* Kidney, *are* 'very uppish, *and* alert upon't, *as you may see by their* Phizz's.—— 'Will Hazard *has got the* Hipps, *having lost* to the Tune *of five* 'Hundr'd Pound, tho' *he understands Play very well,* no Body

'*better*. He has promis't me upon *Rep*, to leave off Play; but you
'know 'tis a Weakness *he*'s too apt to *give into, tho'* he has as much
'Wit as any Man, *no body more*. He has lain *incog* ever since.——
'The *Mob*'s very quiet with us now.——I believe you *tho't* I
'*banter'd* you in my last like a *Country Put*.——I *shan't* leave
'Town this Month, *&c.*

THIS Letter is in every Point an admirable Pattern of the
present polite Way of Writing; nor is it of less Authority for
being an Epistle: You may gather every Flower of it, with a
Thousand more of equal Sweetness, from the Books, Pamphlets,
and single Papers, offered us every Day in the Coffee-houses:
And these are the Beauties introduced to supply the Want of
Wit, Sense, Humour and Learning; which formerly were looked
upon as Qualifications for a Writer. If a Man of Wit, who died
Forty Years ago, were to rise from the Grave on Purpose; how
would he be able to read this Letter? And after he had got
through that Difficulty, how would he be able to understand it?
The first Thing that strikes your Eye, is the *Breaks* at the End of
almost every Sentence; of which I know not the Use, only that
it is a Refinement, and very frequently practised. Then you will
observe the Abbreviations and Elisions, by which Consonants
of most obdurate Sound are joined together, without one soften-
ing Vowel to intervene: And all this only to make one Syllable
of two, directly contrary to the Example of the *Greeks* and
Romans; altogether of the *Gothick* Strain, and a natural Tendency
towards relapsing into Barbarity, which delights in Monosyllables, and uniting of mute Consonants; as it is observable in
all the *Northern* Languages. And this is still more visible in the
next Refinement, which consisteth in pronouncing the first Syllable in a Word that hath many, and dismissing the rest; such as
Phizz, Hipps, Mobb, Pozz, Rep, and many more; when we are
already over-loaded with Monosyllables, which are the Disgrace
of our Language. Thus we cram one Syllable, and cut off the
rest; as the Owl fattened her Mice after she had bit off their
Legs, to prevent them from running away; and if ours be the
same Reason for maiming of Words, it will certainly answer the
End, for I am sure no other Nation will desire to borrow them.
Some Words are hitherto but fairly split; and therefore only in

their Way to Perfection; as *Incog.* and *Plenipo's*: But in a short Time, it is to be hoped, they will be further docked to *Inc* and *Plen.* This Reflection had made me, of late Years, very impatient for a Peace; which I believe would save the Lives of many brave Words, as well as Men. The War hath introduced abundance of Polysyllables, which will never be able to live many more Campaigns. *Speculations, Operations, Preliminaries, Ambassadors, Pallisadoes, Communication, Circumvallation, Battallions,* as numerous as they are, if they attack us too frequently in our Coffee-houses, we shall certainly put them to Flight, and cut off the Rear.

THE third Refinement observeable in the Letter I send you, consisteth in the Choice of certain Words invented by some *pretty Fellows,* such as *Banter, Bamboozle, Country Put,* and *Kidney,* as it is there applied; some of which are now struggling for the Vogue, and others are in Possession of it. I have done my utmost for some Years past, to stop the Progress of *Mob* and *Banter*; but have been plainly born down by Numbers, and betrayed by those who promised to assist me.

IN the last Place, you are to take Notice of certain choice Phrases scattered through the Letter; some of them tolerable enough, till they were worn to Rags by servile Imitators. You might easily find them, although they were not in a different Print; and therefore I need not disturb them.

THESE are the false Refinements in our Style, which you ought to correct: First, by Arguments and fair Means; but if those fail, I think you are to make Use of your Authority as Censor, and by an annual *Index Expurgatorius,* expunge all Words and Phrases that are offensive to good Sense, and condemn those barbarous Mutilations of Vowels and Syllables. In this last Point, the usual Pretence is, that they spell as they speak: A noble Standard for Language! To depend upon the Caprice of every Coxcomb; who, because Words are the Cloathing of our Thoughts, cuts them out, and shapes them as he pleases, and changes them oftner than his Dress. I believe, all reasonable People would be content, that such Refiners were more sparing of their Words, and liberal in their Syllables. On this Head, I should be glad you would bestow some Advice upon several young Readers in our Churches; who coming up from the University, full fraught with Admiration of our Town Politeness, will needs correct the Style of their Prayer-Books. In reading the Absolution, they are very careful to say *Pardons* and *Absolves*; and in the Prayer for the Royal Family, it must be *endue'm, enrich'um, prosper'um,* and *bring'um*. Then, in their Sermons they use all the modern Terms of Art; *Sham, Banter, Mob, Bubble, Bully, Cutting, Shuffling,* and *Palming*: All which, and many more of the like Stamp, as I have heard them often in the Pulpit from some young Sophisters; so I have read them in some of *those Sermons that have made a great Noise of late*. The Design, it seems, is to avoid the dreadful Imputation of Pedantry; to shew us, that they *know the Town, understand Men and Manners,* and have not been poring upon old unfashionable Books in the University.

I SHOULD be glad to see you the Instrument of introducing into our Style, that Simplicity which is the best and truest Ornament of most Things in human Life, which the politer Ages always aimed at in their Building and Dress, (*Simplex munditiis*) as well as their Productions of Wit. It is manifest, that all new affected Modes of Speech, whether borrowed from the Court, the Town, or the Theatre, are the first perishing Parts in any Language; and, as I could prove by many Hundred Instances, have been so in ours. The Writings of *Hooker*, who was a Country Clergyman, and of *Parsons* the Jesuit, both in the Reign of Queen *Elizabeth*; are in a Style that, with very few Allowances, would not offend any present Reader; much more clear and intelligible than those of Sir *H. Wooton*, Sir *Robert Naunton*, *Osborn*, *Daniel* the Historian, and several others who writ later; but being Men of the Court, and affecting the Phrases then in Fashion; they are often either not to be understood, or appear perfectly ridiculous.

WHAT Remedies are to be applied to these Evils, I have not Room to consider; having, I fear, already taken up most of your Paper. Besides, I think it is our Office only to represent Abuses, and yours to redress them. I am, with great Respect,

SIR,

Yours, &c.

[Harrison's Continuation]

THE

TATLER

NUMBER 5*

—— *Laceratque, trahitque*
Molle pecus. ——   Vir.

From *Tuesday Jan.* 23, to *Saturday Jan.* 27, 1710.

AMONGST other Severities I have met with from some
Criticks, the cruellest for an old Man is, that they will not
let me be at quiet in my Bed, but pursue me to my very
Dreams. I must not dream but when they please, nor upon long
continued Subjects, however visionary in their own Nature,
because there is a manifest Moral quite through them, which to
produce as a Dream is improbable and unnatural. The Pain
might have had from this Objection, is prevented by considering
they have missed another, against which I should have been at
a Loss to defend my self. They might have asked me, whether
the Dreams I publish can properly be called *Lucubrations*, which
is the Name I have given to all my Papers, whether in Volume
or Half-sheets: So manifest a Contradiction *in Terminis*, that I
wonder no Sophister ever thought of it: But the other is a Cavil.
I remember when I was a Boy at School, I have often dreamed
out the whole Passages of a Day; that I rode a Journey, baited,
supped, went to Bed, and rose the next Morning: And I have
known young Ladies who could dream a whole Contexture of
Adventures in one Night, large enough to make a Novel. In
Youth the Imagination is strong, not mixed with Cares, nor

The Printer and Publisher hereof having been in London *after the first
Volume was printed off, met with the following* TATLERS, *which are
supposed to be wrote by the Author of the foregoing Works; and as they
were never printed in this Kingdom, we hope they will be acceptable to our
Readers.*

tinged with those Passions that most disturb and confound it; such as Avarice, Ambition, and many others. Now, as old Men are said to grow Children again, so in this Article of Dreaming, I am returned to my Childhood. My Imagination is at full Ease, without Care, Avarice or Ambition, to clog it; by which, among many others, I have this Advantage, of doubling the small Remainder of my Time, and living four and twenty Hours in the Day. However, the Dream I am now going to relate, is as wild as can well be imagined, and adapted to please these Refiners upon Sleep, without any Moral that I can discover.

'It happened that my Maid left on the Table in my Bed-'Chamber, one of her Story-Books (as she calls them) which I 'took up, and found full of strange Impertinence, fitted to her 'Taste and Condition; of poor Servants who came to be Ladies, 'and *Serving-Men of low Degree*, who married Kings Daughters. 'Among other things, I met this sage Observation; That a Lion 'would never hurt a true Virgin. With this Medly of Nonsense 'in my Fancy I went to Bed, and dreamed that a Friend waked me 'in the Morning, and proposed for Pastime to spend a few Hours 'in seeing the Parish Lions, which he had not done since he came 'to Town; and because they showed but once a Week, he would 'not miss the Opportunity. I said I would humour him; although, 'to speak the Truth, I was not fond of those cruel Spectacles; 'and if it were not so ancient a Custom, founded, as I had heard, 'upon the wisest Maxims, I should be apt to censure the In-'humanity of those who introduced it. All this will be a Riddle 'to the waking Reader, until I discover the Scene my Imagina-'tion had formed upon the Maxim, That a Lion would never 'hurt a true Virgin. I dreamed, that by a Law of immemorial 'Time, a He-Lion was kept in every Parish at the common 'Charge, and in a Place provided, adjoyning to the Church-yard: 'That, before any one of the Fair Sex was married, if she affirmed 'her self to be a Virgin, she must on her Wedding-Day, and in 'her Wedding-Clothes, perform the Ceremony of going alone 'into the Den, and stay an Hour with the Lion let loose, and kept 'fasting four and twenty Hours on purpose. At a proper Height, 'above the Den, were convenient Galleries for the Relations and 'Friends of the young Couple, and open to all Spectators. No

'Maiden was forced to offer her self to the Lion; but if she re-
'fused, it was a Disgrace to marry her, and every one might have
' Liberty of calling her a Whore. And methought it was as usual
'a Diversion to see the Parish-Lions, as with us to go to a Play or
'an Opera. And it was reckoned convenient to be near the
'Church, either for marrying the Virgin if she escaped the Trial,
'or for burying her Bones when the Lion had devoured the rest,
'as he constantly did.

   To go on therefore with the Dream: 'We called first (as I re-
'member) to see St. *Dunstan's* Lion, but we were told they did
'not shew To-day: From thence we went to that of *Covent-*
'*Garden*, which, to my great Surprize, we found as lean as a
'Skeleton, when I expected quite the contrary; but the Keeper
'said it was no Wonder at all, because the poor Beast had not got
'an Ounce of Woman's Flesh since he came into the Parish. This
'amazed me more than the other, and I was forming to my self a
'mighty Veneration for the Ladies in that Quarter of the Town;
'when the Keeper went on, and said, he wondered the Parish
'would be at the Charge of maintaining a Lion for nothing.
'Friend, (said I) do you call it nothing, to justify the Virtue of so
'many Ladies, or hath your Lion lost his distinguishing Faculty?
'Can there be any thing more for the Honour of your Parish,
'than that all the Ladies married in your Church were pure Vir-
'gins? That is true, (said he) and the Doctor knows it to his
'Sorrow; for there hath not been a Couple married in our Church
'since his Worship came amongst us. The Virgins hereabouts
'are too wise to venture the Claws of the Lion; and because no
'body will marry them, have all entered into Vows of Virginity.
'So that in Proportion we have much the largest Nunnery in the
'whole Town. This Manner of Ladies entering into a Vow of
'*Virginity*, because they were not *Virgins*, I easily conceived; and
'my Dream told me, that the whole Kingdom was full of Nun-
'neries, plentifully stocked from the same Reason.

   'WE went to see another Lion, where we found much Com-
'pany met in the Gallery: The Keeper told us, we should see
'*Sport* enough, as he called it; and in a little time, we saw a young
'beautiful Lady put into the Den, who walked up towards the
'Lion with all imaginable Security in her Countenance, and

'looked smiling upon her Lover and Friends in the Gallery;
'which I thought nothing extraordinary, because it was never
'known that any Lion had been mistaken. But however, we were
'all disappointed; for the Lion lifted up his right Paw, which was
'the fatal Sign, and advancing forward, seized her by the Arm,
'and began to tear it: The poor Lady gave a terrible Shriek, and
'cryed out, *The Lion is just, I am no true Virgin!* Oh! *Sappho*,
'*Sappho*. She could say no more; for the Lion gave her the *Coup*
'*de Grace*, by a Squeeze in the Throat, and she expired at his Feet.
'The Keeper dragged away her Body to feed the Animal after
'the Company should be gone; for the Parish-Lions never used
'to eat in publick. After a little Pause, another Lady came on
'towards the Lion in the same Manner as the former: We ob-
'served the Beast smell her with great Diligence; he scratched
'both her Hands with lifting them to his Nose, and laying one
'of his Claws on her Bosom, drew Blood: However he let her go,
'and at the same time turned from her with a Sort of Contempt,
'at which she was not a little mortified, and retired with some
'Confusion to her Friends in the Gallery. Methought the whole
'Company immediately understood the Meaning of this; that the
'Easiness of the Lady had suffered her to admit certain impru-
'dent and dangerous Familiarities, bordering too much upon
'what is criminal; neither was it sure whether the Lover then
'present had not some Sharers with him in those Freedoms, of
'which a Lady can never be too sparing.

'THIS happened to be an extraordinary Day; for a third Lady
'came into the Den, laughing loud, playing with her Fan, tossing
'her Head, and smiling round on the young Fellows in the Gal-
'lery. However, the Lion leaped on her with great Fury, and we
'gave her for gone; but on a sudden he let go his Hold, turned
'from her as if he were nauseated, then gave her a Lash with his
'Tail; after which she returned to the Gallery, not the least out
'of Countenance: And this, it seems, was the usual Treatment of
'Coquets.

'I THOUGHT we had now seen enough; but my Friend would
'needs have us go and visit one or two Lions in the City. We
'called at two or three Dens where they happened not to shew;
'but we generally found half a Score young Girls, between Eight

'and Eleven Years old, playing with each Lion, sitting on his
'Back, and putting their Hands into his Mouth; some of them
'would now and then get a Scratch, but we always discovered,
'upon examining, that they had been hoydening with the young
'Apprentices. One of them was calling to a pretty Girl about
'twelve Years old, who stood by us in the Gallery, to come down
'to the Lion, and upon her Refusal, said, *Ah, Miss* Betty, *we could
'never get you to come near the Lion, since you played at Hoop and Hide
'with my Brother in the Garret.*

   'WE followed a Couple, with the Wedding Folks, going to
'the Church of St. *Mary Ax.* The Lady although well stricken in
'Years, extremely crooked and deformed, was dressed out be-
'yond the Gaiety of Fifteen; having jumbled together, as I imag-
'ined, all the tawdry Remains of Aunts, Godmothers, and
'Grandmothers, for some Generations past: One of the Neigh-
'bours whispered me, that she was an old Maid, and had the
'clearest Reputation of any in the Parish. There is nothing
'strange in that, thought I, but was much surprized, when I ob-
'served afterwards that she went towards the Lion with Distrust
'and Concern. The Beast was lying down; but upon Sight of her,
'snuffed up his Nose two or three Times, and then giving the
'Sign of Death, proceeded instantly to Execution. In the Midst
'of her Agonies, she was heard to name the Words, *Italy* and
'*Artifices*, with the utmost Horror, and several repeated Execra-
'tions: And at last concluded, *Fool that I was, to put so much
'Confidence in the Toughness of my Skin.*

   'THE Keeper immediately set all in Order again for another
'Customer, which happened to be a famous Prude, whom her
'Parents after long Threatnings, and much Persuasion, had with
'the extremest Difficulty prevailed on to accept a young hand-
'some Goldsmith, who might have pretended to five times her
'Fortune. The Fathers and Mothers in the Neighbourhood used
'to quote her for an Example to their Daughters. Her Elbows
'were rivitted to her Sides; and her whole Person so ordered as
'to inform every Body that she was afraid they should touch her.
'She only dreaded to approach the Lion, because it was a He
'One, and abhorred to think a Male Animal should presume to
'breathe on her. The Sight of a Man at twenty Yards Distance

'made her draw back her Head. She always sat upon the farther
'Corner of the Chair, although there were six Chairs between
'her and her Lover, and with the Door wide open, and her little
'Sister in the Room. She was never saluted but at the Tip of her
'Ear; and her Father had much ado to make her dine without her
'Gloves, when there was a Man at Table. She entered the Den
'with some Fear, which we took to proceed from the Height of
'her Modesty, offended at the Sight of so many Men in the
'Gallery. The Lion beholding her at a Distance, immediately
'gave the deadly Sign; at which the poor Creature (methinks I
'see her still) miscarried in a Fright before us all. The Lion
'seemed to be surprized as much as we, and gave her time to
'make her Confession; *That she was five Months gone, by the Fore-*
'*man of her Father's Shop; that this was her third big Belly*; and when
'her Friends asked, why she would venture the Trial? She said,
'*her Nurse assured her, that a Lion would never hurt a Woman with*
'*Child.*' Upon this I immediately awaked, and could not help
'wishing, that the Deputy-Censors of my late Institution were
'indued with the same Instinct as these Parish-Lions.

[Harrison's Continuation]

THE

TATLER.

NUMBER 20

——— *Ingenuas didicisse fideliter Artes*
Emollit Mores. ———   Ovid.

From *Saturd. Mar.* 3, to *Tuesd. Mar.* 6, 1710.

From my own Apartment in Channel-Row, March 5.

THOSE inferior Duties of Life which the *French* call *les petites Morales,* or the smaller Morals, are with us distinguished by the Name of Good Manners, or Breeding. This I look upon, in the general Notion of it, to be a Sort of artificial good Sense, adapted to the meanest Capacities; and introduced to make Mankind easy in their Commerce with each other. Low and little Understandings, without some Rules of this Kind, would be perpetually wandering into a Thousand Indecencies and Irregularities in Behaviour; and in their ordinary Conversation fall into the same boisterous Familiarities that one observes amongst them, when a Debauch has quite taken away the Use of their Reason. In other Instances, it is odd to consider, that for want of common Discretion, the very End of Good Breeding is wholly perverted; and Civility, intended to make us easy, is employed in laying Chains and Fetters upon us, in debarring us of our Wishes, and in crossing our most reasonable Desires and Inclinations. This Abuse reigns chiefly in the Country, as I found to my Vexation, when I was last there, in a Visit I made to a Neighbour about two Miles from my Cousin. As soon as I entered the Parlour, they put me into the great Chair that stood close by a huge Fire, and kept me there by Force, untill I was almost stifled. Then, a Boy came in great Hurry to pull off my Boots, which I in vain opposed, urging, that I must return soon after Dinner. In the mean time, the good Lady whispered her eldest Daughter, and slipped a Key into her Hand. The Girl returned instantly with a Beer-Glass half full of *Aqua Mirabilis* and Syrup of Gillyflowers. I took as much as I had a mind for; but Madam vowed I should drink it off, (for she was sure it would do me good after coming out of the cold Air) and I was forced to obey; which absolutely took away my Stomach. When Dinner came in, I had a mind to sit at a Distance from the Fire; but they told me, it was as much as my Life was worth, and set me with my Back just against it. Although my Appetite were quite gone, I resolved to force down as much as I could; and desired the Leg of a Pullet. Indeed, Mr. *Bickerstaff*, says the Lady, you must eat a Wing to oblige me; and so put a Couple upon my Plate. I was persecuted at this Rate, during the whole Meal. As often as I called for Small Beer, the Master tipped the Wink, and the Servant brought me a Brimmer of *October*. Some time after Dinner, I ordered my Cousin's Man who came with me, to get ready the Horses; but it was resolved I should not stir that Night; and when I seemed pretty much bent upon going, they ordered the Stable Door to be locked; and the Children hid my Cloak and Boots. The next Question was, what I would have for Supper? I said I never eat any thing at Night, but was at last in my own Defence obliged to name the first thing that came into my Head. After three Hours spent chiefly in Apologies for my Entertainment, insinuating to me, 'That this was the worst time of the Year for Provisions; that 'they were at a great Distance from any Market; that they were 'afraid I should be starved; and that they knew they kept me to 'my Loss;' the Lady went, and left me to her Husband (for they took special Care I should never be alone.) As soon as her Back was turned, the little Misses ran backwards and forwards every Moment; and constantly as they came in or went out, made a Courtesy directly at me, which in good Manners I was forced to return with a Bow, and, *Your humble Servant pretty Miss*. Exactly at Eight the Mother came up, and discovered by the Redness of her Face, that Supper was not far off. It was twice as large as the Dinner; and my Persecution doubled in Proportion. I desired at my usual Hour to go to my Repose, and was conducted to my

Chamber by the Gentleman, his Lady, and the whole Train of Children. They importuned me to drink something before I went to Bed; and upon my refusing, at last left a Bottle of *Stingo*, as they called it, for fear I should wake and be thirsty in the Night. I was forced in the Morning to rise and dress myself in the Dark, because they would not suffer my Kinsman's Servant to disturb me at the Hour I desired to be called. I was now resolved to break through all Measures to get away; and after sitting down to a monstrous Breakfast of cold Beef, Mutton, Neats-Tongues, Venison-Pasty, and stale Beer, took Leave of the Family. But the Gentleman would needs see me Part of my Way; and carry me a short Cut through his own Grounds, which he told me would save half a Mile's Riding. This last Piece of Civility had like to have cost me dear, being once or twice in Danger of my Neck, by leaping over his Ditches, and at last forced to alight in the Dirt; when my Horse having slipped his Bridle, ran away, and took us up more than an Hour to recover him again.

It is evident, that none of the Absurdities I met with in this Visit proceeded from an ill Intention, but from a wrong Judgment of Complaisance, and a Misapplication in the Rules of it. I cannot so easily excuse the more refined Criticks upon Behaviour, who having professed no other Study, are yet infinitely defective in the most material Parts of it. *Ned Fashion* hath been bred all his Life about Court, and understands to a Tittle all the Punctilio's of a Drawing-Room. He visits most of the fine Women near *St. James*'s; and upon every Occasion says the civilest and softest Things to them of any Man breathing. To Mr. *Isaac he owes an easy Slide in his Bow, and a graceful Manner of coming into a Room. But in some other Cases he is very far from being a well-bred Person: He laughs at Men of far superior Understanding to his own, for not being as well dressed as himself; despiseth all his Acquaintance who are not of Quality; and in publick Places hath on that Account often avoided taking Notice of some among the best Speakers in the House of Commons. He raileth strenuously at both Universities before the

---

* *A famous Dancing-Master in those Days.*

Members of either; and is never heard to swear an Oath, or break in upon Religion and Morality, except in the Company of Divines. On the other Hand, a Man of right Sense hath all the Essentials of good Breeding, although he may be wanting in the Forms of it. *Horatio* hath spent most of his time at *Oxford*. He hath a great deal of Learning, an agreeable Wit, and as much Modesty as may serve to adorn without concealing his other good Qualities. In that retired way of living, he seemeth to have formed a Notion of human Nature, as he hath found it described in the Writings of the greatest Men; not as he is likely to meet with it in the common Course of Life. Hence it is, that he giveth no Offence; but converseth with great Deference, Candor, and Humanity. His Bow, I must confess, is somewhat aukward; but then he hath an extensive, universal, and unaffected Knowledge, which may perhaps a little excuse him. He would make no extraordinary Figure at a Ball; but I can assure the Ladies in his Behalf, and for their own Consolation, that he has writ better Verses on the Sex than any Man now living, and is preparing such a Poem for the Press as will transmit their Praises and his own to many Generations.

The PRESENTMENT *of the* GRAND JURY *for the County of* MIDDLESEX, *of the Author,* Printer *and* Publisher *of a* Book *intitled,* The Rights of the Christian Church Asserted, *&c.*

The PRESENTMENT of the GRAND JURY for the County of MIDDLESEX, of the Author, Printer and Publisher of a Book, intitled, *The Rights of the Christian Church asserted*, &c.

Which said Presentment is as followeth:

WHEREAS it is daily perceived that the free printing, publishing and dispersing of scandalous Books and Pamphlets, tendeth greatly to the propagating of Sedition and Profaneness, and particularly in a Book lately printed, and the Preface thereof, entitled, 'The Rights of the Christian 'Church, asserted against the *Romish*, and all other Priests who 'claim an independent Power over it; with a Preface concerning 'the Government of the Church of *England* as by Law estab-'lished.' In which Book, and the Preface thereof, are contained many Passages reflecting upon the Truth and Honour of our Christian Religion, and tending to disturb the Minds of her Majesty's good People, to the great Offence of well-disposed Christians, and giving great Advantage to Atheists, Papists, and the wildest Sectaries, and tending greatly to the disquieting the settled Peace and Unity of this Church and Nation, and particu-larly in several Parts and Passages hereunto referred, *viz*.—(Pre-face p. 30.) 'The Church, a private Society, and no more Power 'belonging to it than to other private Companies and Clubs, and, 'consequently, that all the Right any one has to be an Ecclesiasti-'cal Officer, and the Power he is intrusted with, depends on the 'Consent of the Parties concerned, and is no greater than they 'can bestow.—(The Book, P. 104.) 'The Scriptures no where 'make the receiving the Lord's Supper from the Hands of a 'Priest necessary.—(Page 105.) 'The Remembrance of Christ's 'Sufferings a mere Grace-Cup delivered to be handed about.—'(Page 108.) 'Among Christians, one no more than another can 'be reckoned a Priest from Scripture.—And the Clark hath as 'good a Title to the Priesthood as the Parson.—Every one as well 'as the Minister rightly consecrateth the Elements to himself.—'Any Thing further than this may rather be called Conjuration

'than Consecration.—(Page 313.) The Absurdities of Bishops
'being by Divine Appointment, Governors of the Christian
'Church, and Others, are capable of being of that Number, who
'derive not their Right by an uninterrupted Succession of
'Bishops in the Catholick Church.—(Page 255.) The Supream
'Powers had no Way to escape the heavier Oppressions, and
'more insupportable Usurpations of their own Clergy, than by
'submitting to the Pope's milder Yoke and gentler Authority.—
'(Page 151.) One grand Cause of Mistake is, not considering
'when God acts as Governor of the Universe, and when as
'Prince of a particular Nation. The *Jews* when they came out of
'the Land of Bondage, were under no settled Government, until
'God was pleased to offer himself to be their King, to which all
'the People expressly consented.—God's Laws bound no Na-
'tion, except those that agreed to the *Horeb* Contract.—(Page
'47.) Not only an Independent Power of Excommunication, but
'of Ordination in the Clergy, is inconsistent with the Magis-
'trate's Right to protect the Commonwealth.—(Page 118.)
'Priests no more than Spiritual, make Baits, Bareters, Boutefeuxs
'and Incendiaries, and who make Churches serve to worse Pur-
'poses than Bear-Gardens.—(Page 15.) It is a grand Mistake to
'suppose the Magistrate's Power extends to indifferent Things.
'—Men have Liberty as they please, and a Right—to form what
'Clubs, Companies or Meetings they think fit, either for Business
'or Pleasure, which the Magistrates—cannot hinder without
'manifest Injustice.—(Page 312.) God—interposed not amongst
'the *Jews*, untill they had chose him for their King.'

WE therefore present the Author, Printer, and Publisher of the
    said scandalous Book and Preface thereto, as dangerous
    and disaffected Persons to her Majesty and Government,
    and Promoters of Sedition and Profaneness.

Additional

BICKERSTAFF PAPERS

not written by

Swift

AN

ANSWER

TO

BICKERSTAFF

*Some Reflections upon Mr. Bickerstaff's Predictions
for the Year* MDCCVIII

BY A PERSON OF QUALITY.

I HAVE not observed, for some years past, any insignificant paper to have made more noise, or be more greedily bought, than that of these predictions. They are the wonder of the common people, an amusement for the better sort, and a jest only to the wise: yet, among these last, I have heard some very much in doubt, whether the author meant to deceive others, or is deceived himself. Whoever he was, he seems to have with great art adjusted his paper both to please the rabble and to entertain persons of condition. The writer is, without question, a gentleman of wit and learning, although the piece seems hastily written in a sudden frolic, with the scornful thought of the pleasure he will have, in putting this great town into a wonderment about nothing: Nor do I doubt but he and his friends in the secret, laugh often and plentifully in a corner, to reflect how many hundred thousand fools they have already made. And he has them fast for some time: For so they are like to continue until his prophecies begin to fail in the events. Nay, it is a great question, whether the miscarriage of the two or three first will so entirely undeceive people, as to hinder them from expecting the accomplishing of the rest. I doubt not but some thousands of these papers are carefully preserved by as many persons, to confront with the events, and try whether the astrologer exactly keeps the day and the hour. And these I take to be Mr. Bicker-

staff's choicest cullies, for whose sake chiefly he writ his amusement. Meanwhile he hath seven weeks good, during which time
the world is to be kept in suspense; for it is so long before the
almanack-maker is to die, which is the first prediction: And, if
that fellow happens to be a splenetic visionary fop, or hath any
faith in his own art, the prophesy may punctually come to pass
by very natural means. As a gentleman of my acquaintance, who
was ill-used by a mercer in town, writ him a letter in an unknown
hand, to give him notice that care had been taken to convey a
slow poison into his drink, which would infallibly kill him in a
month; after which the man began in earnest to languish and
decay, by the mere strength of imagination, and would certainly
have died, if care had not been taken to undeceive him before
the jest went too far. The like effect upon Partridge would wonderfully raise Mr. Bickerstaff's reputation for a fortnight longer,
until we could hear from France whether the Cardinal de
Noailles were dead or alive upon the fourth of April, which is
the second of his predictions.

FOR a piece so carelessly written, the observations upon
astrology are reasonable and pertinent, the remarks just; and, as
the paper is partly designed, in my opinion, for a satire upon the
credulity of the vulgar, and that idle itch of peeping into futur-
ities, so it is no more than what we all of us deserve. And, since
we must be teazed with perpetual hawkers of *strange and wonderful
things*, I am glad to see a man of sense find leisure and humour to
take up the trade for his own and our diversion. To speak in the
town-phrase, it is a *bite*; he has fully had his jest, and may be
satisfied.

I VERY much approve the serious air he gives himself in his
introduction and conclusion, which hath gone far to give some
people of no mean rank an opinion, that the author believes himself. He telleth us, 'He places the whole credit of his art on the
'truth of these predictions, and will be content to be hooted by
'Partridge and the rest for a cheat, if he fails in any one particu-
'lar;' with several other strains of the same kind, wherein I perfectly believe him; and that he is very indifferent whether *Isaac
Bickerstaff* be a *mark of infamy* or not. But, it seems, although he
hath joined an odd sirname to no very common Christian one.

that in this large town there is a man found to own both the names, although I believe, not the paper.

I BELIEVE it is no small mortification to this gentleman astrologer, as well as his bookseller, to find their piece, which they sent out in a tolerable print and paper, immediately seized on by three or four interloping printers of Grub-street, the title stuffed with an abstract of the whole matter, together with the standard epithets of *strange and wonderful,* the price brought down a full half, which was but a penny in its prime, and bawled about by hawkers of the inferior class, with the concluding cadence of *A halfpenny apiece.* But *sic cecidit Phaeton*; and, to comfort him a little, this production of mine will have the same fate: To-morrow will my ears be grated by the *little boys* and *wenches in straw-hats,* and I must an hundred times undergo the mortificaton to have my own work offered me to sale at an under-value. Then, which is a great deal worse, my acquaintance in the coffee-house will ask me, whether I have seen the Answer to 'Squire Bickerstaff's predictions, and whether I know the puppy that wrote it? And how to keep a man's countenance in such a junc-ture, is no easy point of conduct. When, in this case, you see a man shy either in praising or condemning, ready to turn off the discourse to another subject, standing as little in the light as he can to hide his blushing, pretending to sneeze or take snuff, or go off as if sudden business called him; then ply him close, ob-serve his looks narrowly, see whether his speech be constrained or affected, then charge him suddenly, or whisper and smile, and you will soon discover whether he be guilty. Although this seem not to the purpose I am discoursing on, yet I think it to be so; for I am much deceived if I do not know the true author of Bicker-staff's Predictions, and did not meet with him some days ago in a coffee-house at Covent-garden.

As to the matter of the Predictions themselves, I shall not enter upon the examination of them; but think it very incumbent upon the learned Mr. Partridge to take them into his considera-tion, and lay as many errors in astrology as possible to Mr. Bickerstaff's account. He may justly, I think, challenge the 'Squire to publish the calculation he hath made of Partridge's nativity, by the credit of which he so determinately pronounces the time and the manner of his death; and Mr. Bickerstaff can do no less, in honour, than give Mr. Partridge the same advantage of calculating *his*, by sending him an account of the time and place of his birth, with other particulars necessary for such a work. By which, no doubt, the learned world will be engaged in the dispute, and take part on each side according as they are inclined.

I SHOULD likewise advise Mr. Partridge to enquire, why Mr. Bickerstaff doth not so much as offer at one prediction to be fulfilled until two months after the time of publishing his paper? This looks a little suspicious, as if he were desirous to keep the world in play as long as he decently could, else it were hard he could not afford us one prediction between this and the 29th of March; which is not so fair dealing as we have, even from Mr. Partridge and his brethren, who give us their predictions (such as they are indeed) for every month in the year.

THERE is one passage in Mr. Bickerstaff's paper that seems to be as high a strain of assurance as I have any where met with. It is that prediction for the month of June which relates to the French Prophets here in town; where he telleth us, 'They will 'utterly disperse, by seeing the time come wherein their pro-'phecies should be fulfilled, and then finding themselves de-'ceived by contrary events.' Upon which he adds, with great reason, 'his wonder how any deceiver can be so weak, to fortel 'things near at hand, when a very few months must discover the 'imposture to all the world.' This is spoken with a great deal of affected unconcernedness, as if he would have us think himself to be not under the least apprehension, that the same in two months will be his own case. With respect to the gentleman, I do not remember to have heard of so refined and pleasant a piece of impudence, which I hope the author will not resent as an uncivil word, because I am sure I enter into his taste, and take it as he meant it. However, he half deserveth a reprimand for writing with so much scorn and contempt for the understandings of the majority.

FOR the month of July, he telleth us of 'a general, who, by a 'glorious action, will recover the reputation he lost by former 'misfortunes.' This is commonly understood to be Lord Galloway; who, if he be already dead, as some news-papers have it, Mr. Bickerstaff hath made a trip. But this I do not much insist on; for it is hard if *another general* cannot be found under the *same circumstances*, to whom this prediction may be as well applied.

THE French King's death is very punctually related; but it was unfortunate to make him die at Marli, where he never goes at that season of the year, as I observed myself during three years I passed in that kingdom: And, discoursing some months ago with Monsieur Tallard, about the French court, I find that King never goes to Marli for any time, but about the season of hunting there, which is not until August. So that here was an unlucky slip of Mr. Bickerstaff, for want of foreign education.

HE concludes with resuming his promise, of publishing entire predictions for the next year; of which the other astrologers need not be in very much pain. I suppose we shall have them much about the same time with *The General History of Ears*. I believe we have done with him for ever in this kind; and, although I am no astrologer, may venture to prophesy that Isaac Bickerstaff, Esq; is now dead, and died just at the time his Predictions were ready for the press: That he dropt out of the clouds about nine days ago, and, in about four hours after, mounted up thither again like a vapour; and will, one day or other, perhaps descend a second time, when he hath some new, agreeable, or amusing whimsy to pass upon the town; wherein, it is very probable, he will succeed as often as he is disposed to try the experiment, that is, as long as he can preserve a thorough contempt for his own time and other people's understandings, and is resolved not to laugh cheaper than at the expence of a million of people.

Mr. PARTRIDGE's

ANSWER

TO

Esquire *BICKERSTAFF's*

Strange and Wonderful

PREDICTIONS

FOR

The YEAR 1708.

When *Foxes* Preach, the *Geese* must have a care,
When *Knaves* find Fault, let Honest *Men* beware;
When Common *Fools* believe a Common *Liar*,
The worst of *Shams* will please a hasty Buyer.

Licenc'd according to Order.

LONDON:

Printed by *E. Beer*, near *Ludgate.* 1708.

Mr. Partridge's *Answer*, &c.

THIS Wonder-working Fortune Teller, comes Blustring into the World, under the Name of *Isaac Bickerstaffe*, Esq; though, I believe, there's no such Man in Being, so presumptuous as to own himself the Author of such a medley of Predictions; and therefore *John an Oakes*, Esq; has as true Claim to those Predictions as the disguised Worshipful *Isaac Bickerstaff*. However, the better to surprize and impose on the hasty, eager and unthinking Multitude, he falls foul, right or wrong, on the whole Tribe of Almanack-makers (and in the exact Language of a Common Strumpet, who calls all Women Whores, because she is a great one her self) Brands them with odious Names of Lyars, Fools, Cheats, and the like; and what is all this but to set up himself for the greatest of them all? He says at the very Beginning of his large Introduction, that many Learned Men have Condemn'd the whole Art of *Astrology* as a Cheat; but I dare be bold to assure his Worship, than any Man without Learning will prove him so, and a Lyar into the Bargain, if he lives but till the 30th of the next Month; for 'tis plain, he knows no more of the Art of *Astrology* (in Comparison) than he knows when his Wife will make him a Cuckold.

And yet, Mountebank-like, he boasts of what Wonders he has perform'd, foretold the Battle of *Almanza*, Miscarriage at *Thoulon*, Loss of Admiral *Shovel*; and all those Secrets of Nature (says he) were Seal'd up and given some Friends many Months before these Accidents happen'd. Oh rare Conjurer! But pray, Mr. Esquire, where are these Friends to be seen or heard of, that had the Possession of these Seal'd up Oracles: I believe it would puzzel you, and a much greater Conjurer than your World besides your self, to vouch the least Syllable of all this. 'Tis an easie matter for a pretended Conjurer to say he foretold this or that Victory or Disaster, when 'tis past and over, but it's quite another thing to discover such Surprising Accidents before they happen or come to pass. I will here relate his own Words, p. 3. 'I make bold to tell the World, that I lay the whole Credit of my 'Art upon the Truth of these Predictions; and I will be content,

'that *Partridge* and the rest of his Clan, may Hoot me for a Cheat
'and Imposture, if I fail in any single particular of Moment. I
'believe, any Man who reads this Paper will look upon me to be
'at least a Person of as much Honesty and Understanding, as a
'Common Maker of Almanacks. I do not lurk in the Dark; I am
'not wholly unknown in the World; I have set my Name at
'length, to be a Mark of Infamy to Mankind, if they shall find I
'deceive them.

As to the Honesty of common Almanack-makers I have nothing to say to, neither am I their Advocate, but I am certain
none of them has more Impudence, whatever they may have of
Understanding; and notwithstanding your Name at Length,
'twill I fear be a dark piece of Work to bring to Light, otherwise
Partridge is as likely a Man to Hoot at Squire *Conjurer* for a Cheat,
as any Person Living, and a thousand to one, but you will
deserve it. But now for your Predictions.

MARCH.

'Tis but a Trifle its only the Death of a Poor Cobling *Alman-
ack-maker*, the 29 *Day* at 11 *a Clock* at Night. Look about you
Partridge, here's a Philistian Goliah comes out against you with
Hercules's Club to beat your Brains out; you may Lawfully
Swear the Peace against him for you go in Danger of your Life.
However it looks something odd, that the Stars can find no body
else to kill all over Christendom, but a Poor *Almanack-maker*.

APRIL.

In this Month Squire *Conjurer* has made the Devil to do among
the *French* and *Spaniards*, Cardinals, Princes, Peers, Lay-men,
and a Goldsmith in *Lombard-street*, comes in for a Snack too;
Death is to be their Portion this very Month, unless they can get
a Reprieve from this Governour of the Stars, or else Remove
themselves in the mean time by a *Habeas Corpus* into some other
Country.

MAY.

This he says, will be no busy month, and yet the *Dauphine* of

France will Dye on the 7th, and a *Mareschal* of that Kingdom break his Leg, by a Fall from a Horse. *Also a* great Siege, which he does not know what to say of, because I conceive he thinks the Confederates will be Beaten, otherwise what harm will the particulars do the Government, which he seems affraid to offend. On the 15th a surprizing Event, but no particulars, which makes this look like bad News too. But on the 19th, Three Noble Ladies will prove with Child against all Expectation; and yet to the Joy of their Husbands, who were Fumblers to be sure, or else why contrary to Expectation? Therefore Cuckolds by Consequence, and being 3 of them, *Cuckolds a Row.* 23 *A Buffoon at the Play-house will dye of a Ridiculous Death suitable to his Vocation.* I am sure this is a Ridiculous Prediction, and as true as the Candle Eat the Cat.

JUNE.

The fury of the Stars this Month is Spent on the French Prophets in *Barbacan* whom he Blames for *fortelling particulars*, and *wonders how any Deceiver can be so weak to do so, when a few Months will Discover the Imposture to all the World*: and yet at the same time has made himself lyable to the same Scandal. On the 1st, of this Month (Says he) a French General will be Kill'd by a random Schot of a Cannon Ball; but this looks like (all his other Stuff) a Random Prediction.

On the 6 he Says *a Fire will break out in the Subburbs* of *Paris*, which will destroy a Thousand Houses; but I am sure there is no Reason in Art to lay a Foundation for such a Prediction; no more then there is for a Battel to be fought on the 10th from 5 till 9 at Night, which he says will be a Drawn Battel, but dares not name the Place, so that take him every way he much out-does his Brother Shuffler *J. P.* On the 20th (he says) *Portocarero* will dye, by great Suspicion of Poyson, which is as true as all the rest.

JULY.

On the 6th (he says,) a certain General will by a Glorious Action recover the Reputation he lost by former Misfortunes. I hope he does not mean the Elector of *Bavaria*, if he do he ought to tell us the Consequences of it which he wilfully omitted at the Battle of *Almanza* in *Spain*, Miscarriages at *Thoulon*; and the Death of Sir *Cloudsly Shovel*. On the 12th he says, a great Commander will dye in the Hands of his Enemies. Here's another Jacobite S[h]uffle, as if this would be one of the Confederates, or why would not such a positive and infallible Fortune-teller as this, [have] discovered who he belong'd to? On the 14th a shameful Discovery will be made of a *French* Jesuite giving Poison to a Foreign General, *&c.* But I think this Worshipful Conjurer a great Knave to conceal such a Villany, if he knows on whom it will fall; it not being likely that *French* Jesuites will do any hurt to their own side, therefore consequently one of the Allies; but I believe this Prediction is hatch'd in his own Noddle without any Advice from the Stars. On the 29th he Choaks the *French* King to death with the Gout in his Stomach and that he should not want Company Monsieur *Camillard* is prick'd down to go along with him; an Ambassador will also dye in *London*, but the day he's forgot.

AUGUST.

Having killed the *Dauphine*, and Old *Lewis* the preceeding Month, he makes the Duke of *Burgundy* a King in this: At which time he hears Bells and Guns, and sees the Blazing of a 1000 Bonefires. The Conjurer sure is in a mighty Rapture, at the News of the *French* King's Coronation, that he can hear nothing but Joy and Transport, here's Loyalty in Perfection.

But the worst Job of all is, the Downfal of a Booth in *Bartholomew-Fair*, which he ought to be more particular in, because the Actors are like to have but a bad time on't, for no body will be so hardy to venture in a Booth to be knock'd on the Head. And therefore *Finley* and *Pinkeman* may shut up their Shops, if the Conjurer be so ill-natured as not to discover the piece of Ground, where this unfortunate Fabrick is to be Erected.

SEPTEMBER.

And here Mr. Positive has betray'd himself with a Witness, for he asserts a great Frost at the beginning, which holds 12 Days together, which is quite contrary to the Order of Nature, such a thing never yet happened in the Memory of any Man living; I suppose by the same Rules he predicts the Death of the Pope, which if so, no doubt but his Holiness is safe enough. But the greatest Wonder of all, the *French* Fortifie themselves in their Trenches, and act Defensively; and pray Mr. *Bug-bear*, when do they do otherwise, unless on a manifest Advantage.

He Concludes his Predictions with Promise of a Glorious Campaign for the Allies, and yet in the whole course of his Monthly Guesses, though very Particular and Positive, on other insignificant absurdities, he gives not so much as a hint of any Success to the Confederates, but on the contrary, leaves us in the Dark, and seems all along as if our Enemies wou'd out-do us.

As for his next Years Predictions, let him Print it in *Holland* and Welcome, for by that time the *English* will know him too well to believe him.

> *His whole Design was nothing but Deceit,*
> *The End of* March *will plainly show the Cheat.*

FINIS.

A

CONTINUATION

OF THE

PRDICTIONS

For the Remaining Part of the

YEAR 1708.

From the Month of *September*, till the Month of *March*, which compleats the whole Year; wherein the Month, and day of the Month are set down, the Persons nam'd, and the great Actions and Events of the next year, particularly related as they will come to pass.

--- --- --- --- ---

Written to prevent the People of *England*, from being farther impos'd on by Vulgar *Almanack-Makers*.

--- --- --- --- ---

By ISAAC BICKERSTAFF, *Esq*;

--- --- --- --- ---

LONDON:

Printed and Sold by *H. Hills* in *Black Fryars*, near the Water-side. 1708.]

A CONTINUATION of the PREDICTIONS FOR the REMAINING PART of the YEAR, 1708, &c.

HAVING found, by the Reception, which my Predictions from *March*, to the end of *September*, have met with, that I am no ways distasteful to the Publick, and the Importunities of Friends are of much more weight than the most fix'd Resolutions; I have been forc'd to set my self to Work sooner than I design'd, and to look into the Events of the end of a Year, which has given us such Amazing Results of Astrological Knowledge, in its *Vernal* and *Summer* Quarters.

BUT before I enter into the Detail of more material Occurrences, I must ask the Reader not to hold me in the wrong, if I Answer some Objections that have been made to my last, which, though of little moment, if duly consider'd, may have a more than ordinary Influence upon such as will not give themselves time for well digested Reflections.

IN the first place I am charg'd with pointing out the *Day and Hour of Death*, which the *Scripture* says, *no Man knoweth*, and upon that Account tax'd with the highest Presumption. In Answer to which, I must beg leave to distinguish, upon the latter part of the Text, *No Man knoweth*, and produce what the Commentators have said on that Head: Which is, that God withholds that Knowledge from Mankind, *quatenus* Mankind, as inscrutable by such as are of Corrupt and Deprav'd Natures; but sometimes Condescends out of his especial Grace and Favour, to Communicate his Divine Influence to some particular Persons, and teaches them how to *call the Stars by their Names*, and deduce *Certaintys* from those Orbs which to Men of less Enlighten'd Capacitys are of *uncertain Stations*.

Secondly. As I was before censur'd for want of Christianity, and not giving my Assent to what has been penn'd down to us in sacred Writ, so I am Arraigned for want of Charity, and Condemn'd unheard, for dispiriting her Majesty's *Subjects*, by pointing out the time when they are to die, and putting them into a

Consternation concerning their latter end. To reply to this, requires no more than that I ought to have their thanks for so doing, for from hence they are awaken'd into a true sense of their mortal Condition, and [are] caution'd to prepare themselves for another World, though I hear my Friend *John Partridge*, takes other Measures, and is Tooth and Nail at Work in composing a Medicine call'd *Elixir Lethifugum*, or the *Death-driving Elixir*, to chase the Fate away which he is threatned with on the 29th of *March* next. I have consulted the Planets more distinctly since my last, and find by the Inclination of *Berenice's* Hair, towards the *North-Pole*, an Indication that has never yet fail'd me, that he gives up the Ghost at a Quarter after Eleven at Night, to less than a second of a Minute, and if I might advise him, he should rather fling by his intended Preparations, and fall a lamenting his sins of Rebellion, than attempt to alter what is unchangeable, since if he is minded not to die before the time appointed, the only Method he is to make use of for so doing, is not to take his own Medicines. I have another Reply to this Objection; which is, granting that this Fellow is her Majesty's subject, and one or two more put into the Dead Warrant in my last, I have made the Nation amends, in killing more of our Enemies, than treble the Number, and Persons of much greater Quality than we are likely to lose by these Predictions; if our Intestine Divisions don't make *Sagitarius* give *Orion* the slip in the Winter-Quarter, and by that means leave us defenceless in one Element that shall be successful in another.

Other Objections, I might say Cavils, have been rais'd against the Justice of my Design, but these are dismiss'd without Answer, till my Latin Book in Folio comes out, entituled, *De Naturà & certitudine Rerum Astrologicarum Libri duo*, which I design to dedicate to the Right Reverend and most Learned the L. B. of *W*. contenting my self in the mean while with giving the Occurrences from the Month of *October*, till *March*, which are all that are wanting for the year, 1708.

OCTOBER.

THE 13th of this Month will be remarkable for the K. of *Sweden's* making his publick Entrance into *Muscow*, after having

defeated the *Czar*, in a pitch'd Battel, Six Leagues from the Celebrated City on the 9th. The 15th will be signaliz'd in the taking
of *Ipres* from the *French*, after 22 days Open Trenches, in the
sight of their whole Army. The 23d, in the detection of Evil
Practices, against a certain Government, the Authors of which
will be Imprison'd, and suffer according to their Demerits. 24th
the City Poet will dye for Grief that the Lord-Mayors have left
off being harangued from gilded Pageants, in most Heroical
Metre, and the 31 will conclude the Month with the Death of
an Alderman that had exercis'd his Grinders too laboriously at a
City Feast on the 29th.

NOVEMBER.

OPENS it self with very hard Frosts, and the first day of it
gives us an account of P. *Ragotski*'s being taken Prisoner in his
endeavouring to relieve *Newhausel*, then distressed, and afterwards taken by the *Imperialists*. Heavens preserve a certain great
Potentate on the 2d, [from] his emissaries in his Court that threaten his life, if not timely prevented. *Dii talem avertite pestem.* The
8th will be rendred famous by burning the great Magazines of
Hay and Oats, at *Strasburgh*, and the Death of the Mareschal de
Villars, who shall dye of an Asthma to the great Joy of the *Imperialists*, whose Countrys have suffer'd by his Depradations,
and great disappointment of the young *French* King and his
whole Ministry. The 17th, the Elector of *Bavaria* shall make
Overtures to come into the Grand Alliance, but shall not be
trusted. *Equo ne Credite Teneri.* There's something more in his
Mean than you may imagine, and he that has let the *French* into
his Country once, may play the same Game again if in his power.
Notable News upon my Faith, the Famous Beau *Fielding*, *alias*
Major General, dies on the 21st for Love of his dear Dutchess,
and buried in every bodies Thoughts before his Herse carries
him to the Grave. The 27th is likewise *nigro signanda Lapillo*, for
the Death of a certain Accomptant-General, that hated *Tom
Double*, till he play'd his Part himself, and was always against
Occasional Conformity till he came to know the Sweets of it.
The 29th a certain Fleet will be in danger in its return from the
Streights, but through the Vigilance of the Admiral shall come

safe into Port, with little or no damage. The *Dragon* points also with her Tail on a *Scabbed* Country Northwards of *England*, and seems to foretel Disturbances on that side, but those that have the direction of publick Affairs soon put a stop to them, and all Things are reduc'd to their first Tranquillity and Order.

DECEMBER. The Duke of *Mantua*'s Negotiations for a Peace having prov'd successless, and the *French* Endeavours been in vain to make a Rupture between the *Germans* and the *Turks*, a great Council is held at *Versails* on the 3d, where, in consideration of the ill Condition of their Affairs, it is determin'd to make Overtures of Evacuating *Spain*, and all the Dominions belonging to it in the Old and New World; and accordingly three Mareschals of *France* (the Stars do not tell me their Names) set out for the *Hague* on the 9th, to Communicate the Proposals of that Court. The 11th brings News of the Submission of the Kingdoms of *Arragon* and *Valentia* with their Capitals, and the Reduction of *Badajos* by the *Portugueze*, in which Siege the Lord *Paston*'s Regiment shall signalize it self by first Storming the Breach, and taking the Marquis *de Bay* Prisoner. The 15th, nine *English* Men of War shall meet with the *Dunkirk* Squadron off of *Ostend*, and after three Hours Engagement sink five and take three, without the loss of one Ship on their side. The 19th proves fatal to the Czar of *Muscovy*, who finding himself strip'd of a great part of his Country by the Victorious *Suedes*, and unable to make a stand against them, falls into a deep Melancholy of which he dies, and is succeeded by his Son, after having been as little lamented by his Subjects as his Enemies. The 24th gives hopes of a Peace between the Young *Czar* and the King of *Sueden*, which succeeds a Truce that commences this day, to the Joy of both their Subjects. The 27th brings us the Arrival of a great Prince, who is highly Caressed by the *British* Court, and dismiss'd with the greatest Satisfaction imaginable to his own Country.

JANUARY. A certain great Lawyer goes as a New-Years Gift to the Grave on the First of this Month. Had he been as honest as he was Learn'd in the Law, it would be better for him at another Tribunal; where he must not appear as Judge, but Criminal. The 12th will bring us News of the Duke of *Vendosme*'s fine House at *Aret* being burn'd down, and sack'd through the Rage of the Populace, who are provok'd against him as the chief Promoter of the War. The 13th the Duke of *Berry* is dangerously hurt in being dismounted from his Horse in the Chase of a Wild Boar. The 18th brings over the Duke of *Mantua* to implore her Majesty of *Great Britain*'s gracious Intercession in his Behalf at the Conclusion of a General Peace, but I am to seek what Answer the Queen gives him, being not let into the Mysteries of the *British* Court. The Month terminates in the going and coming of Couriers to and from the *Hague*. And on the 31st nothing so much talk'd of as a speedy Peace.

FEBRUARY. The 8th of this Month makes us acquainted or threatned with a great Fire, in *Warwickshire, Glocestershire,* or *Worcestershire,* which of them it is not the power of Art to determine, though I visibly foresee it from the Tails of the *Two Dogs* which incline towards those three Counties; therefore it behoves them to be upon their Guard. On the 7th your *Old Friend Dr. Case,* that has been so often in for the Grand P—— departs this Life, after having been suffocated by the Steams of his own Ointments. The 14th the Princess Royal of *Prussia* shall be brought to Bed of another young Prince, to the great Joy of that Court; and King *Charles* the Third's Queen of a Prince of the *Asturia*'s on the 17th. The 19th brings us News of a Glorious Peace, whereby the Confederate Interest is so strengthned, and the Protestant Religion so fix'd upon a strong Bulwark, that the Power of *France,* nor the Gates of Hell, can ever prevail against it. Nothing but Rejoicing for the rest of this Month, all other Occurrences are drown'd in the Satisfaction of seeing that happy Day, when we shall have a Free Trade with *Spain,* and share with them in the Wealth of the *West-Indies*. So God Bless Queen *Anne,* for bringing Matters about as they now stand, and making the course of Nature wear such a promising Face. As for you Reader, I take my leave of you, till I present you with my Calculations for the Year 1709, which will be of equal Certainty with these I have now submitted to your perusal, if my Skill don't fail me.

POSTSCRIPT

HAVING, since the Writing of this, met with a Couple of illiterate Answers to my former *Predictions*, one in *Octavio*, and the other in *Folio*, under the Name of Dr. *Partridge*; this is to acquaint those two unworthy Scoundrels, that I have consulted the Stars for their Names, and find one of them to be *Rich. Ball*, formerly Running Stationer to Mr. *Bradford* the Printer; and the other *Richard Burridge*, a Fellow that drew Drink on the Common-side of *Newgate*. As for the Day of their Death, I find Nature took so little notice of them at their Creation, that as they come by chance into the World, so 'tis ten to one but they go unexpectly, and without notice, out of it. Only this I dare be bold to say, That as the first is just got out of the *Savoy*, after having been Listed for a Vagabond, and at the Expence of Ten Pounds and two able Men to serve in his Place, so the last will be taken up under the same Denomination, and sent on Board the Fleet on the 24th of next *March*, in spight of the Patch he wears over one of his Eyes to counterfeit himself disabled and unfit for Service.

FINIS

'Squire BICKERSTAFF *Detected*:*
OR, THE
Astrological Impostor Convicted.

By JOHN PARTRIGE,
Student in PHYSICK *and* ASTROLOGY.

IT is hard, my dear Countrymen of these united Nations: It is very hard, that a *Briton* born, a Protestant Astrologer, a Man of Revolution Principles, an Asserter of the Liberty and Property of the People, should cry out, in vain, for Justice against a *Frenchman*, a Papist, and an illiterate Pretender to Science; that would blast my Reputation, most inhumanly bury me alive, and defraud my Native Country of those Services, which in my † *double Capacity*, I daily offer the Publick.

WHAT great Provocations I have received, let the impartial Reader judge, and how unwillingly, even in my own Defence, I now enter the Lists against Falshood, Ignorance, and Envy: But I am exasperated at length, to drag out this *Cacus* from the Den of Obscurity where he lurks, detect him by the Light of those Stars he has so impudently traduced, and shew there is not a Monster in the Skies so pernicious and malevolent to Mankind, as an ignorant Pretender to Physick and Astrology. I shall not directly fall on the many gross Errors, nor expose the notorious Absurdities of this prostituted Libeller, till I have let the learned World fairly into the Controversy depending, and then leave the unprejudiced to judge of the Merits and Justice of my Cause.

IT was towards the Conclusion of the Year 1707, when an impudent Pamphlet crept into the World, intituled, *Predictions*,

---

* *The following Piece, under the Name of* John Partrige, *was written by that famous Poet* Nicholas Row, *Esq; and therefore being upon the same Subject, although not by the same Author, we have thought fit to publish it, that the Reader may have the whole Account together.*
† *Physician and Astrologer.*

&c. *by* Isaac Bickerstaff, *Esq*; Among the many arrogant Assertions laid down by that lying Spirit of Divination, he was pleased to pitch on the Cardinal *de Noailles*, and my self, among many other eminent and illustrious Persons, that were to die within the Compass of the ensuing Year; and peremptorily fixes the Month, Day, and Hour of our Deaths: This, I think, is sporting with great Men, and publick Spirits, to the Scandal of Religion, and Reproach of Power; and if sovereign Princes, and Astrologers, must make Diversion for the Vulgar; why then, farewel, say I, to all Governments, Ecclesiastical and Civil. But, I thank my better Stars, I am alive to confront this false and audacious Predictor, and to make him rue the Hour he ever affronted a Man of Science and Resentment. The Cardinal may take what Measures he pleases with him; as his Excellency is a Foreigner, and a Papist, he has no Reason to rely on me for his Justification; I shall only assure the World he is alive; but as he was bred to Letters, and is Master of a Pen, let him use it in his own Defence. In the mean Time, I shall present the Publick with a faithful Narrative of the ungenerous Treatment, and hard Usage, I have received from the virulent Papers, and malicious Practices of this pretended Astrologer.

A true and impartial Account of the Proceedings of *Isaac Bickerstaff*, Esq; against Me *John Partrige*, Student in Physick and Astrology.

THE 28th of *March*, *Anno Dom.* 1708, being the Night this sham Prophet had so impudently fixed for my last, which made little Impression on my self; but I cannot answer for my whole Family; for my Wife, with a Concern more than usual, prevailed on me to take somewhat to sweat for a Cold; and, between the Hours of Eight and Nine, to go to Bed: The Maid, as she was warming my Bed, with a Curiosity natural to young Wenches, runs to the Window, and asks of one passing the Street, who the Bell tolled for? Doctor *Partrige*, says he, the famous Almanack-maker, who died suddenly this Evening:

The poor Girl provoked, told him, he lied like a Rascal; the other very sedately replied, the Sexton had so informed him, and if false, he was to blame for imposing upon a Stranger. She asked a Second, and a Third as they passed; and every one was in the same Tone. Now, I do not say these were Accomplices to a certain Astrological 'Squire, and that one *Bickerstaff* might be sauntring thereabouts; because I will assert nothing here, but what I dare attest, for plain Matter of Fact. My Wife, at this, fell into a violent Disorder; and I must own, I was a little discomposed at the Oddness of the Accident. In the mean Time, one knocks at my Door; *Betty* runs down, and opening, finds a sober, grave Person; who modestly enquires, if this was Dr. *Partrige*'s? She taking him for some cautious City-Patient, that came at that Time for Privacy, shews him into the Dining-Room. As soon as I could compose my self, I went to him, and was surprized to find my Gentleman mounted on a Table, with a Two-foot Rule in his Hand, measuring my Walls, and taking the Dimensions of the Room. Pray, Sir, says I, not to interrupt you, have you any Business with me? Only, Sir, replies he, order the Girl to bring me a better Light, for this is but a very dim one. Sir, says I, my Name is *Partrige*: Oh! the Doctor's Brother, belike, cries he; the Stair-Case, I believe, and these two Apartments hung in close Mourning, will be sufficient, and only a Strip of Bays round the other Rooms. The Doctor must needs die rich, he had great Dealings in his Way for many Years; if he had no Family-Coat, you had as good use the Scutcheons of the Company; they are as showish, and will look as magnificent as if he was descended from the Blood-Royal. With that, I assumed a greater Air of Authority, and demanded who employed him, or how he came there? Why, I was sent, Sir, by the Company of Undertakers, says he, and they were employed by the honest Gentleman, who is Executor to the good Doctor departed; and our rascally Porter, I believe, is fallen fast asleep with the black Cloath, and Sconces; or he had been here, and we might have been tacking up by this Time. Sir, says I, pray be advised by a Friend, and make the best of your Speed out of my Doors, for I hear my Wife's Voice, (which, by the By, is pretty distinguishable) and in that Corner of the Room stands a good Cudgel, which some Body has felt before now; if that light in her Hands, and she know the Business you came about; without consulting the Stars, I can assure you it will be employed very much to the Detriment of your Person. Sir, cries he, bowing with great Civility, I perceive, extream Grief for the Loss of the Doctor disorders you a little at present; but early in the Morning I will wait on you, with all necessary Materials. Now I mention no Mr. *Bickerstaff*; nor do I say, that a certain Star-gazing 'Squire has been a playing my Executor before his Time; but I leave the World to judge, and if it puts Things and Things fairly together, it will not be much wide of the Mark.

WELL, once more I get my Doors closed, and prepare for Bed, in Hopes of a little Repose, after so many ruffling Adventures; just as I was putting out my Light in order to it, another bounces as hard as he can knock; I open the Window, and ask who is there, and what he wants? I am *Ned*, the Sexton, replies he, and come to know whether the Doctor left any Orders for a Funeral Sermon; and where he is to be laid, and whether his Grave is to be plain or bricked? Why, Sirrah, says I, you know me well enough; you know I am not dead, and how dare you affront me after this Manner? Alack-a-day, Sir, replies the Fellow, why it is in Print, and the whole Town knows you are dead; why, there is Mr. *White* the Joiner, is but fitting Screws to your Coffin, he will be here with it in an Instant; he was afraid you would have wanted it before this Time. Sirrah, Sirrah, says I, you shall know To-morrow to your Cost that I am alive, and alive like to be. Why, it is strange, Sir, says he, you should make such a Secret of your Death, to us that are your Neighbours; it looks as if you had a Design to defraud the Church of its Dues; and let me tell you, for one that has lived so long by the Heavens, that it is unhandsomely done. Hist, hist, says another Rogue, that stood by him, away Doctor into your Flanel Gear as fast as you can; for here is a whole Pack of Dismals coming to you, with their black Equipage; and how indecent will it look for you to stand frightening Folks at your Window, when you should have been in your Coffin this three Hours? In short, what with Undertakers, Embalmers, Joiners, Sextons, and your damned Elegy-hawkers, upon a late Practitioner in Physick and Astrology, I got not one Wink of Sleep that Night, nor scarce a Moment's Rest ever since. Now, I doubt not but this villainous 'Squire has the Impudence to assert, that these are entirely Strangers to him; he, good Man, knows nothing of the Matter; and honest *Isaac Bickerstaff*, I warrant you, is more a Man of Honour, than to be an Accomplice with a Pack of Rascals, that walk the Streets on Nights, and disturb good People in their Beds. But he is out, if he thinks the whole World is blind; for there is one *John Partrige* can smell a Knave as far as *Grub-street*; although he lies in the most exalted Garret, and writes himself 'Squire: But I will keep my Temper, and proceed in the Narration.

I COULD not stir out of Doors for the Space of three Months after this, but presently one comes up to me in the Street, Mr. *Partrige*, that Coffin you was last buried in, I have not been yet paid for. Doctor, cries another Dog, how do you think People can live by making of Graves for nothing? Next Time you die, you may even toll out the Bell your self for *Ned*. A third Rogue tips me by the Elbow, and wonders how I have the Conscience to sneak abroad, without paying my Funeral Expences. Lord, says one, I durst have swore that was honest Dr. *Partrige*, my old Friend; but poor Man, he is gone. I beg your Pardon, says another, you look so like my old Acquaintance that I used to consult on some private Occasions; but alack, he is gone the Way of all Flesh. Look, look, look, cries a Third, after a competent Space of staring at me; would not one think our Neighbour the Almanack-maker, was crept out of his Grave, to take another Peep at the Stars in this World, and shew how much he is improved in Fortune-telling by having taken a Journey to the other?

NAY, the very Reader of our Parish, a good, sober, discreet Person, has sent two or three Times for me to come and be buried decently, or send him sufficient Reasons to the contrary; or, if I have been interred in any other Parish, to produce my Certificate as the Act requires. My poor Wife is almost run distracted with being called Widow *Partrige*, when she knows it is false; and once a Term she is cited into the Court, to take out Letters of Administration. But the greatest Grievance is, a paultry Quack, that takes up my Calling just under my Nose, and in his printed Directions with *N. B.* ☞ says he lives in the House of the late ingenious Mr. *Partrige*, an eminent Practitioner in Leather, Physick, and Astrology.

BUT to shew how far the wicked Spirit of Envy, Malice and Resentment can hurry some Men; my nameless old Persecutor had provided me a Monument at the Stone-Cutter's, and would have it erected in the Parish-Church; and this Piece of notorious and expensive Villainy had actually succeeded, if I had not used my utmost Interest with the Vestry, where it was carried at last but by two Voices, that I am still alive. That Stratagem failing, out comes a long sable Elegy, bedecked with Hour-glasses, Mattocks, Sculls, Spades and Skeletons, with an Epitaph as confidently written to abuse me, and my Profession, as if I had been under Ground these twenty Years.

AND after such barbarous Treatment as this, can the World blame me, when I ask, What is become of the Freedom of an *Englishman*? And where is the Liberty and Property, that my *old glorious* Friend came over to assert? We have drove Popery out of the Nation, and sent Slavery to foreign Climes. The Arts only remain in Bondage; when a Man of Science and Character shall be openly insulted in the Midst of the many useful Services he is daily paying the Publick. Was it ever heard, even in *Turky* or *Algiers*, that a State-Astrologer was bantered out of his Life by an ignorant Impostor, or bawled out of the World by a Pack of villainous deep-mouthed Hawkers? Though I print Almanacks, and publish Advertisements; although I produce Certificates under the Ministers and Church-Wardens Hands, I am alive, and attest the same on Oath at Quarter-Sessions; out comes *A full and true Relation of the Death and Interment of* JOHN PARTRIGE; Truth is bore down, Attestations neglected, the Testimony of sober Persons despised, and a Man is looked upon by his Neighbours, as if he had been seven Years dead, and is buried alive in the Midst of his Friends and Acquaintance.

NOW can any Man of common Sense think it consistent with the Honour of my Profession, and not much beneath the Dignity of a Philosopher, to stand bawling before his own Door —— Alive! Alive! Ho! The famous Dr. *Partrige*! No Counterfeit, but all alive! —— As if I had the twelve Celestial Monsters of the *Zodiack* to shew within, or was forced for a Livelihood to turn Retailer to *May* and *Bartholomew* Fairs. Therefore, if Her Majesty would but graciously be pleased to think a Hardship of this Nature worthy Her Royal Consideration; and the next Parliament, in their great Wisdom, cast but an Eye towards the deplorable Case of their old *Philomath*, that annually bestows his poetical good Wishes on them; I am sure there is one *Isaac Bickerstaff*, Esq; would soon be trussed up for his bloody Predictions, and putting good Subjects in Terror of their Lives: And that, henceforward, to murder a Man by Way of Prophecy, and bury him in a printed Letter, either to a Lord or Commoner, shall as legally entitle him to the present Possession of *Tyburn*, as if he robbed on the Highway, or cut your Throat in Bed.

I SHALL demonstrate to the Judicious, that *France* and *Rome*, are at the Bottom of this horrid Conspiracy against me; and that *Culprit* aforesaid, is a *Popish* Emissary, has paid his Visits to St. *Germains*, and is now in the Measures of *Lewis* XIV. That in attempting my Reputation, there is a general Massacre of Learning designed in these Realms: And through my Sides, there is a Wound given to all the Protestant Almanack-makers in the Universe.

Vivat Regina.

Merlinus Liberatus :

BEING AN

ALMANACK

For the Year of our Blessed Saviour's Incarnation
1709

By JOHN PARTRIDGE,

A Lover of Truth.

YOU may remember there was a Paper publish'd predict-
ing my Death on the 29th of *March* at Night, 1708. and
after the day was past, the same Villain told the World I
was dead, and how I died; and that he was with me at the time of
my death. I thank God, by whose Mercy I have my Being, that I
am still alive, and (excepting my Age) as well as ever I was in my
Life; as I was also at that 29th of *March*. And that Paper was said
to be done by one *Bickerstaffe*, Esq; but that was a Sham-Name;
it was done by an *Impudent Lying Fellow*. But his Prediction did
not prove true: What will he say to excuse that? For the Fool had
consider'd the *Star of my Nativity*, as he said. Why the truth is, he
will be hard put to it to find a *Salvo* for his Honor. It was a bold
Touch, and he did not know but it might prove true.*

* This is the paragraph in Partridge's Almanac, 1709, referred to
by Swift in the opening sentences of A Vindication of *Isaac Bickerstaff* Esq; [See above p. 159.]

Title-Page *and* Extract
from one of the later imitations
of

BICKERSTAFF'S
PREDICTIONS

BICKERSTAFF's

ALMANACK:

OR, A

Vindication of the STARS,

From all the False Imputations, and Erroneous Assertions, of the late *JOHN PARTRIDGE*, and all other Mistaken Astrologers whatever.

AS ALSO,

A Brief Account of what Things are Truly Occasioned by the Influence of *Celestial Bodies*: Proving That the Art of Telling Fortunes, is an Imposture upon Innocent Persons by *Mock-Astrologers* and *Gypsies*.

For the YEAR 1710.

Nullum Numen abest, si sit Prudentia ; sed Te Nos facimus, Fortuna, Deam, Cæloq; locamus ! Ju.

While all each other with kind Wishes chear,
And Neighbour-Salutations joy the Year,
Live free (ye *Britons*) from Domestick Strife.
Ask Heav'n all else in one ; ask *ANNA's* Life.

By ISAAC BICKERSTAFF Esq;

Student in Astro'ogy, *Commentator on the* Occult *Sciences, and One of the Eighth Order of* Poets *of the Cities of* London *and* Westminster.

LONDON

Printed for the Company of STATIONERS, *Anno Ære Christiana* 1710.

A
TESTMONIAL
OF THE
Death of Mr. *Partridge*

Cousin Bickerstaff,

HAving observ'd your great Sagacity in Predictions, whereby you have acquir'd perfect Knowledge in the Stars, I cannot but pay you my Compliment of Condolance upon the Death of one of your Fraternity, Mr. Partridge, whom many in the World would not believe to be dead, till I show'd them an undeniable Demonstration of it. For having lately perus'd his Works, Intituled, Merlinus Liberatus, for the Year 1709, I find, that he (contrary to all the Knowledge of the Stars) declares, we shall have a New Moon this present 3d of September. Now I having been abroad last Night, and seeing a pretty large broad-faced Moon, no more like a New Moon than an Owl is like a Partridge, do conclude, that No Man alive cou'd assert a New Moon on Sept. 3. Therefore his Understanding in Predictions must be lost, his Eye-sight totally lost likewise, (as it is certainly in Death) if he can't see that broad-faced Moon; and consequently Mr. Partridge must be dead, let others say what they will. I am,

S I R,

From Staff-Hall *in*
   Staffordshire,
   Sept. 3, 1709.

Your loving Kinsman,
JEREMY WAGSTAFF.

Contributions to
THE TATLER *and*
THE SPECTATOR
Attributed to Swift *or containing hints furnished by him*

The TATLER. [No. 21.

From *Thursd. May* 26. to *Saturd. May* 28. 1709.

From my own Apartment, May 27.

To Isaac Bickerstaff *Esq*;

SIR,   York, May 16. 1709

BEING *convinc'd, as the whole World is, how infallible your Predictions are, and having the Honour to be your near Relation, of
the* Staffian *Family, I was under great Concern at one of your
Predictions relating to your self, wherein you foretold your own Death
would happen on the* 17*th Instant, unless it were prevented by the Assistance of well-disposed People: I have therefore prevail'd on my own
Modesty to send you a Piece of News, which may serve instead of* God-
dard's *Drops, to keep you alive for Two Days, till Nature be able to
recover it self, or till you meet with some better Help from other Hands.
Therefore, without further Ceremony, I will go on to relate a singular
Adventure just happened in the Place where I am writing, wherein it
may be highly useful for the Publick to be inform'd.*

Three young Ladies of our Town were on Saturday *last indicted for
Witchcraft. The Witnesses against the First deposed upon Oath before
Justice* Bindover, *That she kept Spirits locked up in Vessels, which
sometimes appeared in Flames of blue Fire; That she used Magical
Herbs, with some of which she drew in Hundreds of Men daily to her,
who went out from her Presence all inflamed, their Mouths parched, and
a hot Steam issuing from them, attended with a grievous Stench; That
many of the said Men were by the Force of that Herb metamorphos'd
into Swine, and lay wallowing in the Kennels for Twenty-four Hours,
before they could reassume their Shapes or their Senses.*

*It was proved against the Second, That she cut off by Night the
Limbs from dead Bodies that were hang'd, and was seen to dig Holes in
the Ground, to mutter some conjuring Words, and bury Pieces of the
Flesh, after the usual Manner of Witches.*

*The Third was accus'd for a notorious Piece of Sorcery, long practised
by Hags, of moulding up Pieces of Dough into the Shapes of Men,*

Women, and Children; then heating them at a gentle Fire, which had a Sympathetick Power to torment the Bowels of those in the Neighbourhood.

This was the Sum of what was objected against the Three Ladies, who indeed had nothing to say in their own Defence, but downright denying the Facts, which is like to avail very little when they come upon their Tryals.

But the Parson of our Parish, a strange refractory Man, will believe nothing of all this; so that the whole Town cries out Shame! *That one of his Coat should be such an Atheist! And design to complain of him to the Bishop. He goes about very odly to solve the Matter. He supposes, That the First of these Ladies keeping a Brandy and Tobacco Ship, the Fellows went out smoaking, and got drunk towards Evening, and made themselves Beasts. He says, The Second is a Butcher's Daughter, and sometimes brings a Quarter of Mutton from the Slaughter-house over Night against a Market-Day, and once buried a Bit of Beef in the Ground, as a known Receipt to cure Warts on her Hands. The Parson affirms, That the Third sells Gingerbread, which, to please the Children, she is forc'd to stamp with Images before 'tis bak'd; and if it burns their Guts, 'tis because they eat too much, or do not drink after it.*

These are the Answers he gives to solve these wonderful Phænomena; *upon which I shall not animadvert, but leave it among Philosophers: And so wishing you all Success in your Undertakings for the Amendment of the World, I remain,*

Dear Cousin,
    Your most Affectionate Kinsman,
        and Humble Servant,
            Ephraim Bedfast.

P. S. Those who were condemn'd to Death among the *Athenians*, were obliged to take a Dose of Poison, which made them die upwards, seizing first upon their Feet, making them cold and insensible, and so ascending gradually, till it reach'd the Vital Parts. I believe your Death, which you foretold would happen on the 17th Instant, will fall out the same Way, and that your Distemper hath already seiz'd on you, and makes Progress daily. The lower Part of you, that is, the *Advertisements*, is dead; and these have risen for these Ten Days last past, so that they now take up almost a whole Paragraph. Pray, Sir, do your Endeavour to drive this Distemper as much as possible to the extreme Parts, and keep it there, as wise Folks do the Gout; for if it once gets into your Stomach, it will soon fly up into your Head, and you are a dead Man.

*   *   *   *   *   *

The TATLER.   [No. 31.

From *Saturd. June* 18. to *Tuesd. June* 21. 1709.

Dear Cousin,

'I Thought when I left the Town to have raised your Fame here, and helped you to support it by Intelligence from hence; but alas! they had never heard of the *Tatler* 'till I 'brought down a Set. I lent them from House to House; but 'they asked me what they meant. I began to enlighten them, by 'telling who and who were supposed to be intended by the 'Characters drawn. I said for Instance, *Chloe* and *Clarissa* are two 'eminent Toasts. A Gentleman (who keeps his Greyhound and 'Gun, and one would think might know better) told me, he sup-'posed they were Papishes, for their Names were not *English*: 'Then, said he, Why do you call live-People Toasts? I answer'd, 'That was a new Name found out by the Wits, to make a Lady 'have the same Effect as Burridge in the Glass when a Man is 'drinking. But, says I, Sir, I perceive this is to you all bambooz-'ling; why you look as if you were *Don Diego'd* to the Tune of a 'Thousand Pounds. All this good Language was lost upon him: 'He only stared, though he is as good a Scholar as any Layman in 'the Town, except the Barber. Thus, Cousin, you must be con-'tent with *London* for the Center of your Wealth and Fame; we 'have no Relish for you. Wit must describe its proper Circum-'ference, and not go beyond it, lest (like little Boys, when they 'straggle out of their own Parish) it may wander to Places where 'it is not known, and be lost. Since it is so, you must excuse me 'that I am forced, at a Visit to sit silent, and only lay up what 'excellent Things pass at such Conversations.

'This Evening I was with a Couple of young Ladies; one of
'them has the Character of the prettiest Company, yet really I
'thought her but silly; the other, who talked a great deal less, I
'observed to have Understanding. The Lady who is reckoned
'such a Companion among her Acquaintance, has only, with a
'very brisk Air, a Knack of saying the commonest Things: The
'other, with a sly serious one, says home Things enough. The
'first (Mistress *Giddy*) is very quick; but the second (Mrs. *Slim*)
'fell into *Giddy*'s own Style, and was as good Company as she.
'*Giddy* happens to drop her Glove; *Slim* reaches it to her:
'Madam (says *Giddy*) I hope you'll have a better Office. Upon
'which *Slim* immediately repartees, and sits in her Lap, and cries,
'Are you not sorry for my Heaviness? This sly Wench pleased
'me to see how she hit her Height of Understanding so well. We
'sat down to Supper. Says *Giddy*, mighty prettily, Two Hands in
'a Dish, and One in a Purse: Says *Slim*, Ay, Madam, the More the
'Merrier; but the Fewer the Better Chear. I quickly took the
'Hint, and was as witty and talkative as they. Says I,

> '*He that will not when he may,*
> '*When he will he shall have Nay;*

'And so helped my self. *Giddy* turns about, What have you found
'your Tongue? Yes, (says I) 'tis Manners to speak when I am
'spoken to; but your greatest Talkers are the least Doers, and
'the still Sow eats up all the Broth. Ha! Ha! says *Giddy*, One
'would think he had nothing in him, and do you hear how he
'talks when he pleases. I grew immediately roguish and pleasant
'to a Degree in the same Strain. *Slim*, who knew how good Com-
'pany we had been, cries, You'll certainly print this bright Con-
'versation.

*   *   *   *   *   *

The TATLER. [No. 67.

From *Saturday Sept.* 10. to *Tuesday Sept.* 13. 1709.

My Province is much larger than at first Sight Men would
imagine, and I shall lose no Part of my Jurisdiction, which extends not only to Futurity, but also is retrospect to Things past;

and the Behaviour of Persons who have long ago acted their Parts, is as much liable to my Examination, as that of my own Contemporaries.

In order to put the whole Race of Mankind in their proper Distinctions, according to the Opinion their Cohabitants conceived of them, I have with very much Care, and Depth of Meditation, thought fit to erect a Chamber of Fame, and established certain Rules, which are to be observed in admitting Members into this illustrious Society.

In this Chamber of Fame there are to be Three Tables, but of different Lengths; the First is to contain exactly Twelve Persons; the Second, Twenty; the Third, an Hundred. This is reckoned to be the full Number of those who have any competent Share of Fame. At the First of these Tables are to be placed in their Order, the Twelve most famous Persons in the World, not with Regard to the Things they are famous for, but according to the Degree of their Fame, whether in Valour, Wit, or Learning. Thus, if a Scholar be more famous than a Soldier, he is to sit above him. Neither must any Preference be given to Virtue, if the Person be not equally famous.

When the first Table is filled, the next in Renown must be seated at the Second, and so on in like Manner to the Number of Twenty; as also in the same Order at the Third, which is to hold an Hundred. At these Tables no Regard is to be had to Seniority: For if *Julius Cæsar* shall be judged more famous than *Romulus* and *Scipio*, he must have the Precedence. No Person who has not been dead an Hundred Years, must be offered to a Place at any of these Tables: And because this is altogether a Lay-Society, and that sacred Persons move upon greater Motives than that of Fame, no Persons celebrated in holy Writ, or any Ecclesiastical Men whatsoever, are to be introduced here.

At the lower End of the Room is to be a Side-Table for Persons of great Fame, but dubious Existence, such as *Hercules*, *Theseus*, *Æneas*, *Achilles*, *Hector*, and others. But because it is apprehended, that there may be great Contention about Precedence, the Proposer humbly desires the Opinion of the Learned towards his Assistance in placing every Person according to his Rank, that none may have just Occasion of Offence.

The Merits of the Cause shall be judged by Plurality of Voices.

For the more impartial Execution of this important Affair, it is desired, That no Man will offer his Favourite Hero, Scholar, or Poet; and that the Learned will be pleased to send to Mr. *Bickerstaff*, at Mr. *Morphew*'s near *Stationers-Hall*, their several Lists for the First Table only, and in the Order they would have them placed; after which the Composer will compare the several Lists, and make another for the Publick, wherein every Name shall be ranked according to the Voices it has had. Under this Chamber is to be a dark Vault for the same Number of Persons of evil Fame.

It is humbly submitted to Consideration, Whether the Project would not be better, if the Persons of true Fame meet in a middle Room, those of dubious Existence in an upper Room, and those of evil Fame in a lower dark Room.

It is to be noted, That no Historians are to be admitted at any of these Tables, because they are appointed to conduct the several Persons to their Seats, and are to be made Use of as Ushers to the Assemblies.

I call upon the learned World to send me their Assistance towards this Design, it being a Matter of too great Moment for any one Person to determine. But I do assure them, their Lists shall be examined with great Fidelity, and those that are exposed to the Publick, made with all the Caution imaginable.

*   *   *   *   *   *

The TATLER.   [No. 68.

From *Tuesday Sept.* 13. to *Thursday Sept.* 15. 1709.

From my own Apartment, September 14.

THE Progress of our Endeavours will of Necessity be very much interrupted, except the learned World will please to send their Lists to the Chamber of Fame with all Expedition. There is nothing can so much contribute to create a noble Emulation in our Youth, as the honourable Mention of such whose Actions have outlived the Injuries of Time, and recommended themselves so far to the World, that it is become Learning to know the least Circumstance of their Affairs. It is a great Incentive to see, that some Men have raised themselves so highly above their Fellow Creatures; that the Lives of ordinary Men are spent in Inquiries after the particular Actions of the most Illustrious. True it is, that without this Impulse to Fame and Reputation, our Industry would stagnate, and that lively Desire of pleasing each other die away. This Opinion was so established in the Heathen World, that their Sense of Living appeared insipid, except their Being was enlivened with a Consciousness, that they were esteemed by the rest of the World.

Upon examining the Proportion of Men's Fame for my Table of Twelve, I thought it no ill Way, since I had laid it down for a Rule, That they were to be ranked simply as they were famous, without Regard to their Virtue, to ask my Sister *Jenny*'s Advice, and particularly mentioned to her the Name of *Aristotle*. She immediately told me, he was a very great Scholar, and that she had read him at the Boarding-School. She certainly means a Trifle sold by the Hawkers, called, *Aristotle*'s *Problems*. But this raised a great Scruple in me, Whether a Fame increased by Imposition of others is to be added to his Account, or that these Excrescencies, which grow out of his real Reputation, and give Encouragement to others to pass Things under the Covert of his Name, should be considered in giving him his Seat in the Chamber? This Punctilio is referred to the Learned. In the mean Time, so ill-natured are Mankind, that I believe I have Names already sent me sufficient to fill up my Lists for the dark Room, and every one is apt enough to send in their Accounts of ill Deservers. This Malevolence does not proceed from a real Dislike of Virtue, but a diabolical Prejudice against it, which makes Men willing to destroy what they care not to imitate. Thus you see the greatest Characters among your Acquaintance, and those you live with, are traduced by all below them in Virtue, who never mention them but with an Exception. However, I believe I shall not give the World much Trouble about filling my Tables for those of Evil Fame, for I have some Thoughts of clapping up the *Sharpers* there as fast as I can lay hold of them.

At present, I am employed in looking over the several Notices which I have received of their Manner of Dexterity, and the Way at Dice of making all Rugg, as the Cant is. The whole Art of securing a Die, has lately been sent me by a Person who was of the Fraternity, but is disabled by the Loss of a Finger, by which Means he cannot practise that Trick as he used to do. But I am very much at a Loss how to call some of the Fair Sex, who are Accomplices with the *Knights of Industry*; for my Metaphorical Dogs are easily enough understood; but the Feminine Gender of Dogs has so harsh a Sound, that we know not how to name it. But I am credibly informed, that there are Female Dogs as voracious as the Males, and make Advances to young Fellows, without any other Design but coming to a Familiarity with their Purses. I have also long Lists of Persons of Condition, who are certainly of the same Regimen with these *Banditti*, and instrumental to their Cheats upon undiscerning Men of their own Rank. These add their good Reputation to carry on the Impostures of others, whose very Names would else be Defence enough against falling into their Hands. But for the Honour of our Nation, these shall be unmentioned, provided we hear no more of such Practices, and that they shall not from henceforward suffer the Society of such, as they know to be the common Enemies of Order, Discipline, and Virtue. If it appear that they go on in encouraging them, they must be proceeded against according to severest Rules of History, where all is to be laid before the World with Impartiality, and without Respect to Persons.

So let the stricken Deer go weep.

Per varios Casus, per tot Discrimina Rerum,
Tendimus. ——— Virg.

From *Thursd. Nov.* 9. to *Saturd. Nov.* 11. 1710.

From my own Apartment, November 10.

I WAS last Night visited by a Friend of mine who has an inexhaustible Fund of Discourse, and never fails to entertain his Company with a Variety of Thoughts and Hints that are altogether new and uncommon. Whether it were in Complaisance to my Way of Living, or his real Opinion, he advanced the following Paradox, That it required much greater Talents to fill up and become a retired Life, than a Life of Business. Upon this Occasion he rallied very agreeably the busie Men of the Age, who only valued themselves for being in Motion, and passing through a Series of trifling and insignificant Actions. In the Heat of his Discourse, seeing a Piece of Money lying on my Table, I I defie (says he) any of these active Persons to produce half the Adventures that this Twelvepenny-Piece has been engaged in, were it possible for him to give us an Account of his Life.

My Friend's Talk made so odd an Impression upon my Mind, that soon after I was a-Bed I fell insensibly into a most unaccountable *Resverie*, that had neither Moral nor Design in it, and cannot be so properly called a Dream as a Delirium.

Methoughts the Shilling that lay upon the Table reared it self upon its Edge, and turning the Face towards me, opened its Mouth, and in a soft Silver Sound gave me the following Account of his Life and Adventures:

I was born, says he, on the Side of a Mountain, near a little Village of *Peru*, and made a Voyage to *England* in a Ingot, under the Convoy of Sir *Francis Drake*. I was, soon after my Arrival, taken out of my *Indian* Habit, refined, naturalized, and put into the *British* Mode, with the Face of Queen *Elizabeth* on one Side, and the Arms of the Country on the other. Being thus equipped,

I found in me a wonderful Inclination to ramble, and visit all the Parts of the new World into which I was brought. The People very much favoured my natural Disposition, and shifted me so fast from Hand to Hand, that before I was Five Years old, I had travelled into almost every Corner of the Nation. But in the Beginning of my Sixth Year, to my unspeakable Grief, I fell into the Hands of a miserable old Fellow, who clapped me into an Iron Chest, where I found Five Hundred more of my own Quality who lay under the same Confinement. The only Relief we had, was to be taken out and counted over in the fresh Air every Morning and Evening. After an Imprisonment of several Years, we heard some Body knocking at our Chest, and breaking it open with an Hammer. This we found was the old Man's Heir, who, as his Father lay a dying, was so good as to come to our Release: He separated us that very Day. What was the Fate of my Companions I know not: As for my self, I was sent to the Apothecary's Shop for a Pint of Sack. The Apothecary gave me to an Herb-Woman, the Herb-Woman to a Butcher, the Butcher to a Brewer, and the Brewer to his Wife, who made a Present of me to a Nonconformist Preacher. After this Manner I made my Way merrily through the World; for, as I told you before, we Shillings love nothing so much as travelling. I sometimes fetched in a Shoulder of Mutton, sometimes a Play-Book, and often had the Satisfaction to treat a Templer at a Twelve-penny Ordinary, or carry him with Three Friends to *Westminster-Hall*.

In the Midst of this pleasant Progress which I made from Place to Place, I was arrested by a superstitious old Woman, who shut me up in a greazy Purse, in Pursuance of a foolish Saying, That while she kept a Queen *Elizabeth*'s Shilling about her, she should never be without Money. I continued here a close Prisoner for many Months, till at last I was exchanged for Eight and Forty Farthings.

I thus rambled from Pocket to Pocket till the Beginning of the Civil Wars, when, to my Shame be it spoken, I was employed in raising Soldiers against the King: For being of a very tempting Breadth, a Serjeant made Use of me to inveigle Country Fellows, and list them in the Service of the Parliament.

As soon as he had made one Man sure, his Way was to oblige

him to take a Shilling of a more homely Figure, and then practise the same Trick upon another. Thus I continued doing great Mischief to the Crown, till my Officer chancing one Morning to walk Abroad earlier than ordinary, sacrificed me to his Pleasures, and made Use of me to seduce a Milk-Maid. This Wench bent me, and gave me to her Sweetheart, applying more properly than she intended the usual Form of, *To my Love and from my Love*. This ungenerous Gallant marrying her within few Days after, pawned me for a Dram of Brandy, and drinking me out next Day, I was beaten flat with an Hammer, and again set a running.

After many Adventures, which it would be tedious to relate, I was sent to a young Spendthrift, in Company with the Will of his deceased Father. The young Fellow, who I found was very extravagant, gave great Demonstrations of Joy at the receiving the Will; but opening it, he found himself disinherited and cut off from the Possession of a fair Estate, by Vertue of my being made a Present to him. This put him into such a Passion, that after having taken me in his Hand, and cursed me, he squirred me away from him as far as he could fling me. I chanced to light in an unfrequented Place under a dead Wall, where I lay undiscovered and useless, during the Usurpation of *Oliver Cromwell*.

About a Year after the King's Return, a poor Cavalier that was walking there about Dinner-time fortunately cast his Eye upon me, and, to the great Joy of us both, carried me to a Cook's Shop, where he dined upon me, and drank the King's Health. When I came again into the World, I found that I had been happier in my Retirement than I thought, having probably by that Means escaped wearing a monstrous Pair of Breeches.

Being now of great Credit and Antiquity, I was rather looked upon as a Medal than an ordinary Coin; for which Reason a Gamester laid hold of me, and converted me to a Counter, having got together some Dozens of us for that Use. We led a melancholy Life in his Possession, being busy at those Hours wherein Current Coin is at rest, and partaking the Fate of our Master, being in a few Moments valued at a Crown, a Pound, or a Sixpence, according to the Situation in which the Fortune of the Cards placed us. I had at length the good Luck to see my

Master break, by which Means I was again sent Abroad under my primitive Denomination of a Shilling.

I shall pass over many other Accidents of less Moment, and hasten to that fatal Catastrophe when I fell into the Hands of an Artist who conveyed me under Ground, and with an unmerciful Pair of Sheers cut off my Titles, clipped my Brims, retrenched my Shape, rubbed me to my inmost Ring, and, in short, so spoiled and pillaged me, that he did not leave me worth a Groat. You may think what a Confusion I was in to see my self thus curtailed and disfigured. I should have been ashamed to have shown my Head, had not all my old Acquaintance been reduced to the same shameful Figure, excepting some few that were punched through the Belly. In the midst of this general Calamity, when every Body thought our Misfortune irretrievable, and our Case desperate, we were thrown into the Furnace together, and (as it often happens with Cities rising out of a Fire) appeared with greater Beauty and Lustre than we could ever boast of before. What has happened to me since this Change of Sex which you now see, I shall take some other Opportunity to relate. In the mean Time I shall only repeat Two Adventures, as being very extraordinary, and neither of them having ever happened to me above once in my Life. The First was, my being in a Poet's Pocket, who was so taken with the Brightness and Novelty of my Appearance, that it gave Occasion to the finest Burlesque Poem in the *British* Language, entituled from me, *The Splendid Shilling*. The Second Adventure, which I must not omit, happened to me in the Year 1703, when I was given away in Charity to a blind Man; but indeed this was by a Mistake, the Person who gave me having heedlesly thrown me into the Hat among a Pennyworth of Farthings.

*   *   *   *   *   *

The TATLER. [No. 258.

From *Thursd. Nov.* 30. to *Saturd. Dec.* 2. 1710.

To Isaac Bickerstaff *Esq*;

S I R,   *Nov.* 22. 1710.

'DINING Yesterday with Mr. *South-British* and Mr.
William North-Briton, Two Gentlemen, who, before you
ordered it otherwise, were known by the Names of Mr.
'*English* and Mr. *William Scott.* Among other Things, the Maid
'of the House (who in her Time I believe may have been a *North-*
'*British* Warming-Pan) brought us up a Dish of *North-British*
'Collops. We liked our Entertainment very well, only we ob-
'served the Table-Cloth, being not so fine as we could have
'wished, was *North-British* Cloth: But the worst of it was, we
'were disturbed all Dinner-Time by the Noise of the Children,
'who were playing in the paved Court at *North-British* Hoppers;
'so we paid our *North-Briton* sooner than we designed, and took
'Coach to *North-Briton* Yard, about which Place most of us live.
'We had indeed gone a-foot, only we were under some Appre-
'hensions lest a *North-British* Mist should wet a *South-British*
'Man to the Skin.

'We think this Matter properly expressed, according to the
'Accuracy of the new Style settled by you in one of your late
'Papers. You will please to give your Opinion upon it to,

S I R,

Your most humble Servants,

J. S.
M. P.
N. R.

Harrison's TATLER.   [No. 1.

Quis ego sum Saltem, si non sum Sosia? Te interrogo.
                        PLAUT. AMPHITRUO.

Saturday, January 13. 1710-11.

IT is impossible perhaps for the best and wisest amongst us, to keep so constant a Guard upon our Temper, but that we may at one Time or other lie open to the Strokes of Fortune, and such Incidents as we cannot foresee. With Sentiments of this Kind I came Home to my Lodgings last Night, much fatigued with a long and sudden Journey from the Country, and full of the ungrateful Occasion of it. It was natural for me to have immediate Recourse to my Pen and Ink; but before I would offer to make Use of them, I resolved deliberately to tell over a Hundred, and when I came to the End of that Sum, I found it more advisable to defer drawing up my intended Remonstrance, till I had slept soundly on my Resentments. Without any other Preface than this, I shall give the World a fair Account of the Treatment I have lately met with, and leave them to judge, whether the Uneasiness I have suffered be inconsistent with the Character I have generally pretended to. About three Weeks since, I received an Invitation from a Kinsman in *Staffordshire*, to spend my *Christmas* in those Parts. Upon taking Leave of Mr. *Morphew*, I put as many Papers into his Hands as would serve till my Return, and charged him at parting, to be very punctual with the Town. In what Manner he and Mr. *Lillie* have been tampered with since, I cannot say; they have given me my Revenge, if I desired any, by allowing their Names to an idle Paper, that in all human Probability cannot live a Fortnight to an End. My self, and the Family I was with, were in the midst of Gaiety, and a plentiful Entertainment, when I received a Letter from my Sister *Jenny*, who, after mentioning some little Affairs I had intrusted to her, goes on thus: 'The inclosed, I believe,

'will give you some Surprise, as it has already astonished every
'body here: Who Mr. *Steele* is, that subscribes it, I don't know,
'any more than I can comprehend what could induce him to it.
'*Morphew* and *Lillie*, I am told, are both in the Secret. I shall not
'presume to instruct you, but hope you will use some Means to
'disappoint the ill Nature of those who are taking Pains to de-
'prive the World of one of its most reasonable Entertainments.
'I am, *&c.*

I am to thank my Sister for her Compliment; but be that as it
will, I shall not easily be discouraged from my former Undertaking. In Pursuance of it, I was obliged upon this Notice to
take Places in the Coach for my self and my Maid with the utmost
Expedition, lest I should, in a short Time, be rallied out of my
Existence, as some People will needs fancy Mr. *Partridge* has
been, and the real *Isaac Bickerstaff* have passed for a Creature of
Mr. *Steele*'s Imagination. This Illusion might have hoped for
some tolerable Success, if I had not more than once produced
my Person in a crowded Theatre; and such a Person as Mr.
Steele, if I am not misinformed in the Gentleman, would hardly
think it an Advantage to own, though I should throw him in all
the little Honour I have gained by my *Lucubrations*. I may be
allowed, perhaps, to understand Pleasantry as well as other Men,
and can (in the usual Phrase) take a Jest without being angry; but
I appeal to the World, whether the Gentleman has not carried it
too far, and whether he ought not to make a publick Recanta-
tion, if the Credulity of some unthinking People should force
me to insist upon it. The following Letter is just come to Hand,
and I think it not improper to be inserted in this Paper.

To Isaac Bickerstaff *Esq*;

SIR,

'I AM extreamly glad to hear you are come to Town, for in
'your Absence we were all mightily surprised with an un-
'accountable Paper, Signed *Richard Steele*, who is esteemed
'by those that know him, to be a Man of Wit and Honour; and
'therefore we took it either to be a Counterfeit, or a perfect
'*Christmas* Frolick of that ingenious Gentleman. But then, your
'Paper ceasing immediately after, we were at a Loss what to

'think: If you were weary of the Work you had so long carried
'on, and had given this Mr. *Steele* Orders to signify so to the
'Publick, he should have said it in plain Terms; but as that Paper
'is worded, one would be apt to judge, that he had a Mind to
'perswade the Town that there was some Analogy between *Isaac*
'*Bickerstaff* and him. Possibly there may be a Secret in this which
'I cannot enter into; but I flatter my self that you never had any
'Thoughts of giving over your Labours for the Benefit of Man-
'kind, when you cannot but know how many Subjects are yet
'unexhausted, and how many others, as being less obvious, are
'wholly untouched. I dare promise, not only for my self, but
'many other abler Friends, that we shall still continue to furnish
'you with Hints on all proper Occasions, which is all your
'Genius requires. I think, by the Way, you cannot in Honour
'have any more to do with *Morphew* and *Lillie*, who have gone
'beyond the ordinary Pitch of Assurance, and transgressed the
'very letter of the Proverb, by endeavouring to cheat you of
'your Christian and Surname too. Wishing you, Sir, long to live
'for our Instruction and Diversion, and to the defeating of all
'Impostors, I remain

> '*Your most obedient humble Servant*,
> '*and affectionate Kinsman*,
> > '*Humphry Wagstaff*.

*Alios Viri Reverentia, vultusque ad continendum populum mire for-
matus: Alios etiam, quibus ipse interesse non potuit, Vis scri-
bendi tamen, & Magni Nominis autoritas pervicere.*

Tull. Epist.

From *Saturd. Jan.* 13 to *Tuesd. Jan.* 16. 1710.

I Remember *Menage* tells a Story of Monsieur *Racan*, who had
appointed a Day and Hour to meet a certain Lady of great
Wit whom he had never seen, in order to make an Acquaintance between them. 'Two of *Racan*'s Friends, who had heard
'of the Appointment, resolved to play him a Trick. The first
'went to the Lady two Hours before the Time, said his Name
'was *Racan*, and talked with her an Hour; they were both mightily
'pleased, began a great Friendship, and parted with much Satis-
'faction. A few Minutes after comes the Second, and sends up the
'same Name; the Lady wonders at the Meaning, and tells him
'Mr. *Racan* had just left her. The Gentleman says it was some
'rascally Impostor, and that he had been frequently used in that
'Manner. The Lady is convinced, and they laugh at the Oddness
'of the Adventure. She now calls to mind several Passages, which
'confirm her that the former was a Cheat. He appoints a second
'Meeting, and takes his Leave. He was no sooner gone, but the
'true *Racan* comes to the Door, and desires, under that Name, to
'see the Lady. She was out of all Patience, sends for him up, rates
'him for an Impostor, and, after a Thousand Injuries, flings a
'Slipper at his Head. It was impossible to pacify or disabuse her;
'he was forced to retire, and it was not without some Time, and
'the Intervention of Friends, that they could come to an Eclair-
'cisement.' This, as I take it, is exactly the Case with Mr. S——*le*, the
pretended TATLER from *Morphew*, and myself, only (I presume)
the World will be sooner undeceived than the Lady in *Menage*.
The very Day my last Paper came out, my Printer brought me

another of the same Date, called the TATLER, by *Isaac Bicker-staff* Esq; and, which was still more pleasant, with an Advertise-ment at the End, calling me the *Female* TATLER: It is not enough to rob me of my Name, but now they impose a Sex on me, when my Years have long since determined me to be of none at all. There is only one Thing wanting in the Operation, that they would renew my Age, and then I will heartily forgive them all the rest. In the mean Time, whatever Uneasiness I have suf-fered from the little Malice of these Men, and my Retirement in the Country, the Pleasures I have received from the same Oc-casion, will fairly ballance the Account. On the one Hand I have been highly delighted to see my Name and Character assumed by the Scribblers of the Age, in order to recommend themselves to it; and on the other, to observe the good Taste of the Town, in distinguishing and exploding them through every Disguise, and sacrificing their Trifles to the supposed *Manes* of *Isaac Bicker-staff* Esquire. But the greatest Merit of my Journey into *Staf-fordshire*, is, that it has opened to me a new Fund of unreproved Follies and Errors that have hitherto lain out of my View, and, by their Situation, escaped my Censure. For, as I have lived generally in Town, the Images I had of the Country were such only as my Senses received very early, and my Memory has since preserved with all the Advantages they first appeared in.

HENCE it was that I thought our Parish-Church the noblest Structure in *England*, and the Squire's Place-House, as we called it, a most magnificent Palace. I had the same Opinion of the Alms-House in the Church-Yard, and of a Bridge over the Brook that parts our Parish from the next. It was the common Vogue of our School, That the Master was the best Scholar in *Europe*, and the Usher the second. Not happening to correct these No-tions by comparing them with what I saw when I came into the World, upon returning back, I began to resume my former Imaginations, and expected all Things should appear in the same View as I left them when I was a Boy: But to my utter Dis-appointment I found them wonderfully shrunk, and lessened almost out of my Knowledge. I looked with Contempt on the Tribes painted on the Church-Walls, which I once so much ad-mired, and on the carved Chimney-Piece in the Squire's Hall. I found my old Master to be a poor ignorant Pedant; and, in short, the whole Scene to be extreamly changed for the worse. This I could not help mentioning, because though it be of no Consequence in it self, yet it is certain, that most Prejudices are contracted and retained by this narrow Way of Thinking, which in Matters of the greatest Moment are hardly shook off: and which we only think true, because we were made to believe so, before we were capable to distinguish between Truth and Falshood. But there was one Prepossession which I confess to have parted with, much to my Regret: I mean the Opinion of that native Honesty and Simplicity of Manners, which I had always imagined to be inherent in Country-People. I soon observed it was with them and us, as they say of Animals; That every Species at Land has one to resemble it at Sea; for it was easy to discover the Seeds and Principles of every Vice and Folly that one meets with in the more known World, though shooting up in different Forms. I took a Fancy out of the several Inhabitants round, to furnish the Camp, the Bar, and the Exchange, and some certain Chocolate and Coffee-Houses, with exact Parallels to what, in many Instances, they already produce. There was a drunken quarrelsome *Smith*, whom I have a hundred Times fancied at the Head of a Troop of Dragoons. A Weaver, within two Doors of my Kinsman, was perpetually setting Neighbours together by the Ears. I lamented to see how his Talents were misplaced, and imagined what a Figure he might make in *Westminster-Hall*. Goodman *Crop* of *Compton-Farm*, wants nothing but a Plumb and a Gold Chain to qualify him for the Government of the City. My Kinsman's Stable-Boy was a gibing Companion that would always have his Jest. He would often put Cow-itch in the Maids Beds, pull Stools from under Folks, and lay a Coal upon their Shoes when they were asleep. He was at last turned off for some notable Piece of Roguery, and when I came away, was loitering among the Ale-houses. Bless me, thought I, what a prodigious Wit would this have been with us! I could have matched all the Sharpers between St. *James*'s and *Covent Garden*, with a notable Fellow in the same Neighbourhood, (since hanged for picking Pockets at Fairs) could he have had the Advantages of their Education. So nearly are the Corruptions of the Country ally'd to those of the Town, with no further Difference than what is made by another Turn of Thought and Method of Living.

Many more Grievances, though not of equal Importance, have been laid before me from several Parts of this Kingdom, which, as they fall not under any ones Cognizance so properly as my own, oblige me to a speedy and effectual Regulation of them. When I was prevailed upon to act as Censor of *Great Britain*, I did not enough consider the Extent of that Province, nor how difficult it would be to make my Authority understood in the remoter Parts of this Island; for most of the Natives being Strangers to Literature, I cannot hope my Lucubrations should meet with a general Reception amongst them; and therefore I have now resolved on an Expedient, which I shall explain by the following Order.

Saturday, January 13. 1710.

To all and every one of the Church-wardens and Sidesmen, in their re-spective Parishes, throughout the Kingdom of Great Britain, Isaac Bickerstaff *Esq; Censor of the said Kingdom, wishes Health, and many happy New Years.*

Gentlemen,

Whereas I have from many Parts of the Kingdom, as well Villages as Country Towns, received credible Information of several Innovations, Abuses, and Offences, lately crept into them, much derogating from their Honour, nor less pernicious to the Quiet of Society, and at the same Time not punishable by any Law, Common or Municipal, as yet in Force; and whereas my Age, growing Infirmities, and necessary Residence in this Place, will not give me Leave to come in Person, and put a Stop to these Evils: I do hereby charge and require you, and every one of you, within Five Days after Receipt of this, to repair forthwith to the Vestry, or what other Place shall to your Wisdom seem most proper; there to chuse, elect, and nominate, some candid, sober, and understanding Person, being not above the Dignity of a Squire, nor under that of Clerk of the Parish, aged Fifty Years at least; whom so chosen, elected, and nominated, I do hereby authorize and depute, under the Title of a Rural Censor, to remark, examine, and take Cognizance of all such Offences;

provided always that he does not presume to pronounce Sentence, or make any final Determination, not having first communicated to me, by Letter, the Persons, Quality, Circumstances, *etc.* or not having received my Instructions therein.

In Witness whereof, I have Set my Hand the Day and Date above:
                                                   Isaac Bickerstaff.

Signed KIDNEY, Clerk of the Court, during the Incapacity of *Charles Lillie*, whose Petition relating to his Suspension, is referred to the next Court-day. In the mean Time, all Letters and Advices are to be directed to Mrs. *Baldwins*.

This Day the Case of *John Morphew* came on: He was indicted for having made many scandalous Reflections on the Censor, as likewise for Breach of Trust; and being found guilty of the same, was sentenced to continue printing Sham-Tatlers, and one or two more such Papers. Six other Causes were heard afterwards, which it is not thought proper to make publick, many noble Persons, yet alive, being concerned therein.

O Lycida, vivi pervenimus, Advena nostri
(Quod nunquam veriti sumus) ut Possessor Agelli
Diceret, Hæc mea sunt, veteres migrare Coloni. **Virg.**

From *Tuesd. Mar.* 13. to *Thursd. Mar.* 15. 1710.

From my own Apartment in Channel-Row, *March* 14.

THE Dignity and Distinction of Men of Wit is seldom enough considered, either by themselves or others; their own Behaviour, and the Usage they meet with, being generally very much of a Piece. I have at this Time in my Hands an Alphabetical List of the *Beaux Esprits* about this Town, Four or Five of whom have made the proper Use of their Genius, by gaining the Esteem of the best and greatest Men, and by turning it to their own Advantage in some Establishment of their Fortunes, however unequal to their Merit; others satisfying themselves with the Honour of having Access to great Tables, and of being subject to the Call of every Man of Quality, who upon Occasion wants one to say witty Things for the Diversion of the Company. This Treatment never moves my Indignation so much as when it is practised by a Person who, though he owes his own Rise purely to the Reputation of his Parts, yet appears to be as much ashamed of it, as a rich City Knight to be denominated from the Trade he was first apprenticed to, and affects the Air of a Man born to his Titles, and consequently above the Character of a Wit, or a Scholar. If those who possess great Endowments of the Mind would set a just Value upon themselves, they would think no Man's Acquaintance whatsoever a Condescension, nor accept it from the greatest upon unworthy or ignominious Terms. I know a certain Lord that has often invited a Set of People, and proposed for their Diversion a Buffoon Player, and an eminent Poet, to be of the Party; and which was yet worse, thought them both sufficiently recompenced by the Dinner, and

II S

the Honour of his Company. This Kind of Insolence is risen to such a Height, that I my self was the other Day sent to by a Man with a Title, whom I had never seen, desiring the Favour that I would dine with him and half a Dozen of his select Friends. I found afterwards, the Footman had told my Maid below Stairs, that my Lord having a Mind to be merry, had resolved right or wrong to send for honest *Isaac*. I was sufficiently provoked with the Message; however I gave the Fellow no other Answer, than that *I believed he had mistaken the Person, for I did not remember that his Lord had ever been introduced to me*. I have Reason to apprehend that this Abuse hath been owing rather to a Meanness of Spirit in Men of Parts, than to the natural Pride or Ignorance of their Patrons. Young Students coming up to Town from the Places of their Education, are dazzled with the Grandeur they every where meet, and making too much Haste to distinguish their Parts, instead of waiting to be desired and caressed, are ready to pay their Court at any Rate to a great Man, whose Name they have seen in a publick Paper, or the Frontispiece of a Dedication. It has not always been thus; Wit in polite Ages has ever begot either Esteem or Fear: The Hopes of being celebrated, or the Dread of being stigmatized, procured an universal Respect and Awe for the Persons of such as were allowed to have the Power of distributing Fame or Infamy where they pleased. *Aretine* had all the Princes of *Europe* his Tributaries, and when any of them had committed a Folly that laid them open to his Censure, they were forced by some Present extraordinary to compound for his Silence; of which there is a famous Instance on Record. When *Charles* the Fifth had miscarried in his *African* Expedition, which was looked upon as the weakest Undertaking of that great Emperor, he sent *Aretine* a Gold Chain, who made some Difficulty of accepting it, saying, *It was too small a Present in all Reason for so great a Folly*. For my own Part, in this Point I differ from Him, and never could be prevailed upon, by any valuable Consideration, to conceal a Fault or a Folly since I first took the Censorship upon me.

Having long considered with my self the ill Application that some make of their Talents, I have this Day erected a Court of *Alienation*, by the Statutes of which the next a Kin is impowered to *beg* the Parts and Understanding of any such Person as can be proved, either by imbezelling, making a wrong Use, or no Use at all of the said Parts and Understanding, not to know the true Value thereof: Who shall immediately be put out of Possession, and disqualified for ever; the said Kinsman giving sufficient Security that he will employ them as the Court shall direct. I have set down under certain Heads the several Ways by which Men prostitute and abuse their Parts, and from thence have framed a Table of Rules, whereby the Plaintiff may be informed when he has a good Title to eject the Defendant. I may in a following Paper give the World some Account of the Proceedings of this Court. I have already got Two able Criticks for my Assessors upon the Bench, who, though they have always exercised their Pens in taking off from the Wit of others, have never pretended to challenge any themselves, and consequently are in no Danger of being engaged in making Claims, or of having any Suits commence against them. Every Writer shall be tried by his Peers, throughly versed in that Point wherein he pretends to excel; for which Reason the Jury can never consist of above half the ordinary Number, I shall in general be very tender how I put any Person out of his Wits; but as the Management of such Possessions is of great Consequence to the World, I shall hold my self obliged to vest the Right in such Hands as will answer the great Purposes they were intended for, and leave the former Proprietors to seek their Fortune in some other Way.

Morte carent Animæ; semperque priore relicta
Sede, novis Domibus vivunt habitantque receptæ.
Ipse ego (nam memini) Trojani Tempore Belli
Panthoides Euphorbus eram —— Ovid. Met.

From *Thursd. Mar.* 22. to *Saturd. Mar.* 24. 1710–11.

From my own Apartment, March 22.

MY other Correspondents will excuse me, if I give the Precedency to a Lady, whose Letter, amongst many more, is just come to Hand.

'*Dear* Isaac,

'I Burn with Impatience to know what and who you are. The 'Curiosity of my whole Sex is fallen upon me, and has kept me 'waking these Three Nights. I have dreamed often of you within 'this Fortnight, and every Time you appeared in a different 'Form. As you value my repose, tell me in which of them I am 'to be

Your Admirer,
SYLVIA.

I T is natural for a Man who receives a Favour of this Kind from an unknown Fair, to frame immediately some Idea of her Person, which being suited to the Opinion we have of our own Merit, is commonly as beautiful and perfect as the most lavish Imagination can furnish out. Strongly possessed with these Notions, I have read over *Silvia*'s billet; and notwithstanding the Reserve I have had upon this Matter, am resolved to go a much greater Length than I yet ever did in making my self known to the World, and in particular to my charming Correspondent. In order to it I must premise, That the Person produced as mine in the Play-house last Winter did in no wise appertain to me. It wa such a one however as agreed well with the Impression my Writings had made, and served the Purpose I intended it for; which was to continue the Awe and Reverence due to the Character I was vested with, and at the same Time to let my Enemies see how much I was the Delight and Favourite of this Town. This innocent Imposture, which I have all along taken Care to carry on, as it then was of some Use, has since been of singular Service to me, and by being mentioned in one of my Papers, effectually recovered my *Egoiety* out of the Hands of some Gentlemen who endeavoured to wrest it from me. This is saying, in short, what I am not: What I am, and have been for many Years, is next to be explained. Here it will not be improper to remind *Sylvia*, that there was formerly such a Philosopher as *Pythagoras*, who, amongst other Doctrines, taught the Transmigration of Souls, which, if she sincerely believes, she will not be much startled at the following Relation:

I WILL not trouble her, nor my other Readers, with the Particulars of all the Lives I have successively passed through since my first Entrance into mortal Being, which is now many Centuries ago. It is enough that I have in every one of them opposed my self with the utmost Resolution to the Follies and Vices of the several Ages I have been acquainted with, that I have often rallied the World into good Manners, and kept the greatest Princes in Awe of my Satyr. There is one Circumstance which I shall not omit, though it may seem to reflect on my Character, I mean that infinite Love of Change which has ever appeared in the Disposal of my Existence. Since the Days of the Emperor *Trajan* I have not been confined to the same Person for Twenty Years together; but have passed from one Abode to another much quicker than the *Pythagorean* System generally allows. By this Means I have seldom had a Body to my self, but have lodged up and down wherever I found a Genius suitable to my own. In this Manner I continued, some Time with the Top Wit of *France*, at another with That of *Italy*, who had a Statue erected to his Memory in *Rome*. Towards the End of the 17th Century I set out for *England*; but the Gentleman I came over in dying as soon as he got to Shore, I was obliged to look out again for a new Habitation. It was not long before I met with one to my Mind, for having mixed my self invisibly with the *Literati* of this Kingdom, I found it was unanimously agreed amongst them, That no Body was indowed with greater Talents than *Hiereus*; or, consequently, would be better pleased with my Company. I slipped down his Throat one Night as he was fast asleep, and the next Morning, as soon as he awaked, he fell to writing a Treatise that was received with great Applause, though he had the Modesty not to set his Name to that nor to any other of our Productions. Some Time after he published a Paper of Predictions, which were translated into several Languages, and alarmed some of the greatest Princes in *Europe*. To these he prefixed the Name of *Isaac Bickerstaff* Esq; which I have been extremely fond of ever since, and have taken Care that most of the Writings I have been concerned in should be distinguished by it; though I must observe, that there have been many Counterfeits imposed upon the Publick by this Means. This extraordinary Man being called out of the Kingdom by Affairs of his own, I resolved however to continue somewhat longer in a Country where my Works had been so well received, and accordingly bestowed my self with *Hilario*. His natural Wit, his lively Turn of Humour, and great Penetration into humane Nature, easily determined me to this Choice, the Effects of which were soon after produced in this Paper, called, *The Tatler*. I know not how it happened, but in less than Two Years Time *Hilario* grew weary of my Company, and gave me Warning to be gone. In the Height of my Resentment I cast my Eyes on a young Fellow, of no extraordinary Qualifications, whom for that very Reason I had the more Pride in taking under my Direction, and enabling him by some Means or other to carry on the Work I was before engaged in. Lest he should grow too vain upon this Encouragement, I to this Day keep him under due Mortification. I seldom reside with him when any of his Friends are at Leisure to receive me, by whose Hands however he is duly supplied. As I have passed through many Scenes of Life, and a long Series of Years, I choose to be considered in the Character of an old Fellow, and take Care that those under my Influence should speak consonantly to it. This Account, I presume, will give no small Consolation to *Sylvia*, who may rest assured, That *Isaac Bickerstaff* is to be seen in more

Forms that she dreamt of; out of which Variety she may choose what is most agreeable to her Fancy. On *Tuesdays* he is sometimes a black proper young Gentleman, with a Mole on his left Cheek. On *Thursdays*, a decent well looking Man, of a middle Stature, long flaxen Hair, and a florid Complexion. On *Saturdays*, he is somewhat of the shortest, and may be known from others of that Size by Talking in a low Voice, and passing through the Streets without much Precipitation.

The SPECTATOR. [No. 50.

Friday, April 27. 1711.

Nunquam aliud Natura, aliud Sapientia dixit.
Juv.

WHEN the four *Indian* Kings were in this Country about a Twelve-month ago, I often mixed with the Rabble, and followed them a whole Day together, being wonderfully struck with the Sight of every thing that is new or uncommon. I have, since their Departure, employed a Friend to make many Enquiries of their Landlord the Upholsterer, relating to their Manners and Conversation, as also concerning the Remarks which they made in this Country: For, next to the forming a right Notion of such Strangers, I should be desirous of learning what Ideas they have conceived of us.

THE Upholsterer finding my Friend very inquisitive about these his Lodgers, brought him some time since a little Bundle of Papers, which he assured him were written by King *Sa Ga Yean Qua Rash Tow*, and, as he supposes, left behind by some mistake. These Papers are now translated, and contain abundance of very odd Observations, which I find this little Fraternity of Kings made during their Stay in the Isle of *Great Britain*. I shall present my Reader with a short Specimen of them in this Paper, and may, perhaps, communicate more to him hereafter. In the Article of *London* are the following Words, which without doubt are meant of the Church of St. *Paul*.

'ON the most rising Part of the Town there stands a huge 'House, big enough to contain the whole Nation of which I am 'King. Our good Brother *E Tow O Koam*, King of the *Rivers*, is 'of Opinion it was made by the Hands of that great God to 'whom it is consecrated. The Kings of *Granajah* and of the *Six* '*Nations* believe that it was created with the Earth, and produced 'on the same Day with the Sun and Moon. But for my own Part, 'by the best Information that I could get of this Matter, I am apt 'to think that this prodigious Pile was fashioned into the Shape

'it now bears by several Tools and Instruments, of which they
'have a wonderful Variety in this Country. It was probably at
'first an huge mis-shapen Rock that grew upon the Top of the
'Hill, which the Natives of the Country (after having cut it into
'a kind of regular Figure) bored and hollowed with incredible
'Pains and Industry, till they had wrought in it all those beautiful
'Vaults and Caverns into which it is divided at this Day. As soon
'as this Rock was thus curiously scooped to their Liking, a pro-
'digious Number of Hands must have been employed in chip-
'ping the Outside of it, which is now as smooth as the Surface of
'a Pebble; and is in several Places hewn out into Pillars that
'stand like the Trunks of so many Trees bound about the Top
'with Garlands of Leaves. It is probable that when this great
'Work was begun, which must have been many Hundred Years
'ago, there was some Religion among this People; for they give
'it the Name of a Temple, and have a Tradition that it was de-
'signed for Men to pay their Devotions in. And indeed, there
'are several Reasons which make us think, that the Natives of
'this Country had formerly among them some sort of Worship;
'for they set apart every seventh Day as sacred: But upon my
'going into one of these holy Houses on that Day, I could not
'observe any Circumstance of Devotion in their Behaviour:
'There was indeed a Man in Black who was mounted above the
'rest, and seemed to utter something with a great deal of Vehe-
'mence; but as for those underneath him, instead of paying their
'Worship to the Deity of the Place, they were most of them
'bowing and curtisying to one another, and a considerable Num-
'ber of them fast asleep.

'THE Queen of the Country appointed two Men to attend us,
'that had enough of our Language to make themselves under-
'stood in some few Particulars. But we soon perceived these two
'were great Enemies to one another, and did not always agree in
'the same Story. We could make a Shift to gather out of one of
'them, that this Island was very much infested with a monstrous
'Kind of Animals, in the Shape of Men, called *Whigs*; and he
'often told us, that he hoped we should meet with none of them
'in our Way, for that if we did, they would be apt to knock us
'down for being Kings.

'Our other Interpreter used to talk very much of a kind of
'Animal called a *Tory*, that was as great a Monster as the *Whig*,
'and would treat us as ill for being Foreigners. These two Crea-
'tures, it seems, are born with a secret Antipathy to one another,
'and engage when they meet as naturally as the Elephant and the
'Rhinoceros. But as we saw none of either of these Species, we
'are apt to think that our Guides deceived us with Misrepresen-
'tations and Fictions, and amused us with an Account of such
'Monsters as are not really in their Country.

'These Particulars we made a Shift to pick out from the
'Discourse of our Interpreters; which we put together as well as
'we could, being able to understand but here and there a Word
'of what they said, and afterwards making up the Meaning of it
'among ourselves. The Men of the Country are very cunning
'and ingenious in handicraft Works; but withal so very idle, that
'we often saw young lusty raw-boned Fellows carried up and
'down the Streets in little covered Rooms by a Couple of Porters,
'who are hired for that Service. Their Dress is likewise very bar-
'barous, for they almost strangle themselves about the Neck, and
'bind their Bodies with many Ligatures, that we are apt to think
'are the Occasion of several Distempers among them which our
'Country is entirely free from. Instead of those beautiful Feathers
'with which we adorn our Heads, they often buy up a monstrous
'Bush of Hair, which covers their Heads, and falls down in a
'large Fleece below the Middle of their Backs; with which they
'walk up and down the Streets, and are as proud of it as if it was
'of their own Growth.

'We were invited to one of their publick Diversions, where
'we hoped to have seen the great Men of their Country running
'down a Stag or pitching a Bar, that we might have discovered
'who were the Persons of the greatest Abilities among them; but
'instead of that, they conveyed us into an huge Room lighted up
'with abundance of Candles, where this lazy People sate still
'above three Hours to see several Feats of Ingenuity performed
'by others, who it seems were paid for it.

'As for the Women of the Country, not being able to talk
'with them, we could only make our Remarks upon them at a
'Distance. They let the Hair of their Heads grow to a great

'Length; but as the Men make a great Show with Heads of Hair
'that are none of their own, the Women, who they say have very
'fine Heads of Hair, tie it up in a Knot, and cover it from being
'seen. The Women look like Angels, and would be more beauti-
'ful than the Sun, were it not for little black Spots that are apt to
'break out in their Faces, and sometimes rise in very odd Figures.
'I have observed that those little Blemishes wear off very soon;
'but when they disappear in one Part of the Face, they are very
'apt to break out in another, insomuch that I have seen a Spot
'upon the Forehead in the Afternoon, which was upon the Chin
'in the Morning.

THE Author then proceeds to shew the Absurdity of Breeches
and Petticoats, with many other curious Observations, which I
shall reserve for another Occasion. I cannot however conclude
this Paper without taking Notice, That amidst these wild Remarks there now and then appears something very reasonable.
I cannot likewise forbear observing, That we are all guilty in
some Measure of the same narrow way of Thinking, which we
meet with in this Abstract of the *Indian* Journal; when we fancy
the Customs, Dresses, and Manners of other Countries are ridiculous and extravagant, if they do not resemble those of our
own.

The SPECTATOR [No. 575.

Monday, August 2. 1714.

THE following Question is started by one of the Schoolmen. Supposing the whole Body of the Earth were a great Ball or Mass of the finest Sand, and that a single Grain or Particle of this Sand should be annihilated every thousand Years. Supposing then that you had it in your Choice to be happy all the while this prodigious Mass of Sand was consuming by this slow Method till there was not a Grain of it left, on Condition you were to be miserable for ever after; or, supposing that you might be happy for ever after, on Condition you would be miserable till the whole Mass of Sand were thus annihilated at the Rate of one Sand in a thousand Years: Which of these two Cases would you make your Choice?*

*This paragraph has been usually attributed to Swift.

Bickerstaffe's

PREDICTION

Confirm'd

In the DEATH of *Partridge,* the Almanack-Maker, the 29th Day of this Instant *March,* at 13 minutes past 11 at Night.

With farther Predictions for the Months of *October, November,* and *December,* 1708.

With an Invitation of the whole Astrologick Tribe, and others, of both Sexes, that are pleas'd to come to my House at *Chelsea,* where I will resolve all their lawful Questions *gratis.*

I Need say no more to convince the World of the Ignorance and Insufficiency of the common Pretenders to Astrology, and their Rules, than what I have done in my former Paper; especially since my first Prediction of *Partridge's* Death,(that happen'd last Night) was but 13 Minutes after the Time; tho' doubtless there are some that have Confidence enough to affirm him to be alive as they have done of many others, that are actually as dead as he is.

And as this plainly demonstrates the Certainty and Validity of my Rules, so I shall require no other Belief from my Readers, for the Future, than as they find the Truth of this.

I am sensible it will here be objected, Why I was silent in something else that has happen'd in this Month more material? I answer, That besides the Rule I have prescrib'd to my Self, for my own Safety, not to meddle with Home-Affairs, I plainly foresaw that Expedition would, in Conclusion, be in a manner as insignificant to the Publick, as the Loss of a poor Almanack-maker. All which I hinted to the very same Friends, that I had predicted the Miscarriage at *Thoulon*, the Loss of Admiral *Shovel*, and the Battel of *Almanza*, as they may readily testify.

I think it necessary to forewarn my Readers, That there will be several spurious Papers and Predictions publish'd in my Name; but except my six Months Predictions, and this Paper, they are all false; nor do I intend to publish any Thing more this Year.

As I begun my former Predictions but with a Trifle, so I do these. And it relates to *Les——y*, the *Rehearser*: And I must needs say I have been concern'd at nothing more, than to see so many Parsons, that for their Bulk and Figure, might be Bishops, to lie poring Hours together on the *Rehearsal*, to find out all the intricate Mazes of the *Jure Divino* Doctrine, and the Defence of the Church of *England*, by a Champion that dares not profess himself of that Communion, no more than he durst own his Name at the *Bath*, when he went by the Name of *S——th*, and so plentifully drank Healths to the little Gentleman of *St. Germains*. But I ask my Reader's Pardon for this Digression, and to the Matter. I have consulted the ruling Star of his Nativity, and his *Aphæta*, by my own Rules, and find he will infallibly be hang'd upon the 8th Day of *October*, between 11 and 1 Afternoon; but I cannot certainly determine yet, whether by his own Hands, or not.

The 13th Day of this Month will be very remarkable for the Exit of several Eminent *Perkinites*, *A-la-mode de Lesley*.

The 21st, an eminent Fortress in *Spain*, by Stratagem, will fall into the Hands of the Allies.

The 23d, the *Hungarian* Malecontents commit great Spoil in the Emperor's Hereditary Country.

The 26th, a smart Rencounter in *Flanders*, to the Advantage of the Allies, on the *French* breaking up their Camp.

The 30th, the young King of *France* will be in great Danger of Death, occasion'd by a Fall from his Horse some Time before; but will recover again.

The Duke of *Savoy* very successful at this Time.

November, altho' not a Month of Action, will yet produce many surprizing Occurrences.

On the 4th of this Month, there will happen a very great Breach between the *French* King and the Elector of *Bavaria*; even to the Banishment from his Dominions, on Suspicion of Bribery.

The 5th, there will be great Damage done at *Dunkirk*, by the blowing up a Magazine of Powder.

The 16th, a Marshal of *France*, and the Elector of *Cullen*, in Disgrace at the *French* Court, and under Arrest.

The 17th, six large *French* Privateers taken and brought into the *Downs*, by a *Dutch* Admiral.

The 24th, a great Consultation held at *Marli*, in order to pave the Way to a general Peace. But I dont find, 'twill be after the same Scheme or Model, that was laid in *March* last.

But that which will make this Month memorable to Posterity, is, the Death of the pretended Prince of *Wales*, on St. *Andrew*'s Day, after inconsolable Melancholy, together with a violent Looseness and Vomiting, contracted in his Voyage to *North Britain*.

December the 5th, great Damage done by Storm, to Shipping on the *French* and *Spanish* Coast.

The 14th, the Duke of *Anjou*, after a short Sickness of a putrid Fever, either dies, or in great Danger.

The 25th, the Duke of *Berwick*, by a Great Man, makes Overtures to reconcile himself to the Protestant Religion, and the *British* Court.

The 29th, methinks I see an Ambassador from *France*, with a Project of Peace; but his Terms will be rejected.

This is the farthest I have proceeded in my Calculations for this present Year. I do not pretend, that these are all the Great Events which will happen in this Period, or all that I could lay; but that those I have set down, will as infallibly come to pass, as any Thing I have predicted in my former Paper.

I have purposely omitted any Predictions for the Months of *January* and *February* next, least the common Tribe of annual Scriblers, should steal from me, to stuff into their bombastical Almanacks: But to oblige their whole Clan, and others, of both Sexes, I fairly invite as many as are pleas'd to come to my House, at *Chelsea*, next *Thursday*, with this Paper, and I promise to answer all their Questions *Gratis*, (if they relate not to publick

Affairs) and for that Purpose I shall give Attendance from Six in the Morning 'till Twelve; and from Two in the Afternoon until Eight; that the whole Tribe of Astrologers may confess their own Ignorance in the Art they profess; and that they cannot reach to the Certainty and Excellency of my Rules, so far above those of vulgar Pretenders.

Isaac Bickerstaffe Esq;

From my House in Church-Street,
   next the Coffee-house in Chelsea, March 30. 1708.

L O N D O N Printed: And Sold by *J. Morphew*, near *Stationers-Hall*. 1708. Price 1*d*.

That Part of the

Laſt Will

AND

TESTAMENT

OF

Iſaac Bickerſtaff, Eſq; deceas'd ;

Which relates to the PUBLICK:

Together with his

Strange and Wonderful *Prophecies*; all
to be fulfill'd in the YEAR, 1725.

To which is Added,

An Important Meditation on a STAFF.

A Fragment.

Publiſh'd in Purſuance of the ſaid Will,
By *GABRIEL BICKERSTAFF*, Eſq;
His Nephew and Executor.

---

*Sed ſi ſumma petat, Capitiſq; invaſerit Arcem,
Progenies Cœli eſt, et conſcia Flamma Futuri.*

LONDON,
Printed, and Sold *by* A. MOOR, near St.
Paul's. MDCCXXV.
Price Six Pence.

II t

TEXTUAL NOTES

Notes on the Text of the 'Miscellanies'

The volume of *Miscellanies in Prose and Verse*, published in 1711, was printed by Tooke with considerable care, partly from Swift's manuscripts and partly from earlier printed copies. The second edition, issued in 1713, shows no sign of revision; it introduces certain errors. The *Miscellanies in Prose and Verse*, published in 1727, reproduces some of these errors, and must therefore have been set from the second edition. The text of this volume was corrected by Swift himself in preparation for the edition of his collected *Works*, published by Faulkner at Dublin in 1735. The copy of the *Miscellanies*, 1727, containing Swift's manuscript corrections, both in ink and pencil, now in the possession of Lord Rothschild, indicates definitely Swift's interest in the text of the new edition and shows that he cared about details of style and usage. For there are not only corrections which improve the sense, but constant changes in punctuation. He removes also abbreviations and elisions: for example, *'tis* becomes *it is*; *tho'* becomes *though* or *although*; and the ending *-eth* is frequently introduced. Such changes have been incorporated in Faulkner's text and are therefore not separately noted in the following collations. More important changes made by Swift himself are indicated below by an S. It is true, that these corrections were not made consistently throughout the volumes, but were probably intended by Swift as a sample of what he desired. They prove that he was interested in the minute details of the collected edition of 1735. Faulkner's text, however, contains further alterations which must have been made later in proof. The character of these further changes is, in some cases, sufficient evidence to prove that they were made by Swift himself; but in others it is just as likely that they may have been due, as Swift himself claimed, to the proof-reading of his friends.

There is, however, no reason to believe that anything was included in the early volumes of the collected edition published in 1735 of which Swift would not approve.

THE SENTIMENTS OF A CHURCH OF ENGLAND MAN, WITH RESPECT TO RELIGION AND GOVERNMENT

Miscellanies in Prose and Verse, 1711, p. 95. Second edition, 1713, p. 93.
Miscellanies in Prose and Verse, The First Volume, 1727, p. 87.
The Works of J.S.D.D.D.S.P.D., Dublin, 1735. Vol. I, p. 56.
The present text is taken from the *Works*, 1735, collated with copies of the *Miscellanies*. Readings in the second edition, 1713, are only indicated where they differ from the edition of 1711.

Page	Line	PRESENT TEXT	VARIANTS
1	*b*	a Play	at Play 11, 27
		N.B. 'Play' is used here in the sense of 'Gaming'; the earlier reading therefore may well be the correct one.	
2	3	then, that we	then we 11, 27
	5	*real* 11, 27	real 35
	10	one of the two Sides	a Side 11, 27
	18	do his S	do in his 11, 27
3	11	it is 11, S	is it 27
	7 *f.b.*	Aversion from S	Aversion to 11, 27

Page	Line	PRESENT TEXT	VARIANTS
5	6	its present 11, S	his present 13, 27
	27	there must never be an End 11, S	they must never be at an End 13, 27
	30	everyone who S	everyone that 11, 27
6	2	an Evil	any Evil 11
	8	whatever S	what 11, 27
	11	about for some 11, 27	about some 35
7	37	*Fault*; and I wish may not be	Fault, and I hope is not 11, 27
9	19	that Prince's S	the Prince's 11, 27
11	29	I leave it among *Divines*	I shall leave it among the *Divines* 11, 27
12	8	the Instruments	instrumental 11, 27
	23	Hatred against	Hatred to 11, 27
13	5	Parties; I mean	Parties, and that is 11, 27
14	8	in Religion	of Religion 11, 27
	13	their mutual Aversions	their aversions for each other 11, 27 ... against each other S
	30	the best Institution is no long Security S	the Institution is no longer Security 11, 27
15	17	is in a	is a 11, 27
	20-21	Thing, which ... But this	Thing which ... which however 11, 27 Thing that ... which however S
	24	some Experience	small Experience 11, 27
16	22	learned Men	Learned 11
	8f.b.	often fall	fall 11, 27
17	3	horrid	unhappy 11, 27
	18	the Government	that 11, 27
18	26	less	little 11, 27
19	3	consent	consents 11, 27
	8	but little S	little 11, 27
	20-21	for these he is *answerable* ... be, who	for those he is to *answer* ... do, that 11, 27
20	2	in whose	with whose 11, 27
	5	Example	Examples 11, 27
	37	the Nation	they 11, 27
21	19	was an S	was then an 11, 27
	b	[Footnote]	Mr Nelson S
22	24	Tie but Conscience 11, 27	Tie of Conscience 35
23	18	it	it was 11, 27
	26	Point be	Point is
	27	other Professions	others, 11, 27
	27-31	(N.B. This passage is marked by a line in the margin of Swift's copy.)	
24	9	Nobles, or those who represent the People.	Legislature. 11, 27
	25-6	with	in with 11, 27
	26	Nature 27	Natures 11
	2f.b.	wise and good 27	wise and a good 11
25	3	Church 11, 27	the Church 35
	14	may not	is not 11, 27

AN ARGUMENT AGAINST ABOLISHING
CHRISTIANITY

Miscellanies in Prose and Verse, 1711, p. 152. Second edition, 1713, p. 150.
Miscellanies in Prose and Verse, The First Volume, 1727, p. 140.
The Works of J.S.D.D.D.S.P.D., Dublin, 1735. VOL. I, p. 91.

The present text is taken from the *Works*, 1735, collated with the earlier editions, and the following variants noted. N.B. A number of passages in the *Argument* have been italicized for emphasis in the text of 1735; some of these were marked by Swift himself and the others may possibly have been added under his direction in the proofs. As they have the effect of emphasizing the irony, it seemed well to indicate these changes in the following collations.

Page	Line	PRESENT TEXT	VARIANTS
26	15	Severe S	several 11, 27
	16	*Union* S	—— 11, 27
	23	appear	seem 11, 27
27	14	Abolishing of 11, 27	Abolishing 35
	28	between	betwixt 11, 27
	9f.b.	*real*	Real 11, 27
	5f.b.	*all . . . half*	all . . . half 11, 27
28	3	of Cure	of a Cure 11, 27
	8	*nominal*	Nominal 11, 27
	10	our	all our 11, 27
	17	System	Systems 11, 27
		Protestant	Protestant 11, 27
		Priest-craft	Priest-craft 11, 27
		Gentlemen	Gentlemen soldiers S
	10f.b.	great Hopes S	real Hopes 11, 27
	3f.b.	*obsolete*	obsolete 11, 27
		only for *Blasphemy* S	for Blasphemy 11, 27
29	2	*nominal*	Nominal 11, 27
	4	*God*	God 11, 27
	5	*speak Evil of Dignities*	speak Evil of Dignities 11, 27
	13	*great Company*	great Company 11, 27
	14		
	18	I know	we know 11, 27
	28	shaken	shook 11, 27
	2f.b.	confirmed S	to be confirmed 11, 27
30	3	*Nominal* S	Nominal 11, 27
	8	Execution? S	Execution. 11, 27
	21	*one*	one 11, 27
	27	*easy* S	Easy 11, 27
	7f.b.	Productions	Production 11, 27
31	8	Theatres	Play-houses, 11, 27
	5f.b.	grievous	mutual 11, 27
	4f.b.	dispose Men	are apt 11, 27
32	16	*Potshaws*	Patshaws 11, 27
	17–18	*would be in* it *if they could?*	would be in it if they could? 11, 27
	29–30	would serve	serve 11, 27
	5f.b.	Therefore	And therefore 11, 27
33	9	Taste	Test 11, 27; Tast S

Page	Line	PRESENT TEXT	VARIANTS
	28	several	some 11, 27
	8 *f.b.*	are	were 11, 27
35	3	Modes	Forms and Modes 11, 27
	16	that	which 11, 27
	25–6	refusing to enter	not coming in 11, 27
	4 *f.b.*	choqued S	choaked 27
	3 *f.b.*	who	that 11, 27
36	5	*Danger to their Persons*	Danger to their Persons 11, 27
	7	would 11	could 27, 35
37	2	this S	they 11, 27
38	8 *f.b.*	Because, the Turks	For they 11, 27
39	3	*Preservation*	Preservation 11, 27
	4	*destroying*	destroying 11, 27

A PROJECT FOR THE ADVANCEMENT OF RELIGION, etc.

First published in 1709. For facsimile of the title-page, see above, p. 41.
Another edition printed by H. Hills, 1709.
Miscellanies in Prose and Verse, 1711, p. 182. Second edition, 1713, p. 180.
Miscellanies in Prose and Verse, The First Volume, 1727, p. 169.
The Works of J.S.D.D.D.S.P.D., Dublin, 1735. Vol. I, p. 110.
The present text is from the *Works*, 1735, collated with the earlier editions and the following variants noted.

Page	Line	PRESENT TEXT	VARIANTS
43	9	BERKELEY 9, 11	BERKLEY 9, 27, 35
44	23	meerly	properly 9, 11, 27
45	7	Fear	Pain 9, 11, 27
	10	short	small 9
	b	Wench	Whore 9, 11, 27
46	4	be	is 9, 11, 27
	6	any	absolute 9, 11, 27
	23	an ill S	ill 13, 27
	24	answer	answer for S
	5 *f.b.*	Interest	Interests 9, 11, 27
47	7	these Corruptions	these 9, 11, 27
	12	Employments	Employment 9
	18	will not S	will 13, 27
	27	Probability	all Probability 9
	27	till more	till some more 9, 11, 27
	8 *f.b.*	the Example	That 9, 11, 27
	4	a year	in the year 9, 11, 27
48	13	whether	if 9, 11, 27
	21	a mighty	mighty 9, 11, 27
	25	they might	it might 9, 11, 27
	27	necessary to	necessary for 9, 11, 27
49	6	recommended to, . . . gener-ally	recommended, . . . very often 9, 11, 27
50	6	Princess	Prince 9, 11
51	17	was	were 9, 11, 27

Page	Line	PRESENT TEXT	VARIANTS
	23	that Vice	Vice 9, 11, 27
	28	enacted	made 9, 11, 27
52	13	Drinking	Drink 9, 11, 27
	21	nine in ten 8, S	nine or ten 13, 27
54	12	*one* among them; who 9,	*one* among them of great Merit and Distinction, who 11, 27
	16	this mistaken S	the mistaken 11, 27
	24	choqued S	chocqued 9, 11, choaked 27
55	6	Contempt?	Contempt? Though in my opinion it were infinitely better if all the Clergy (except the Bishops) were permitted [allowed, 9] to appear like other Men of the graver Sort, unless at those Seasons when they are doing the Business of their Function. 9, 11, 27
	8	when	that 9, 11, 27
	20	Goaler's	Jaylors 9, 11; Gaolor's 27
	30	would	will 9, 11, 27
	2f.b.	been often	by others been 9
56	25	Man 9, 11	Men 13, 27, 35
	31	a Scandal ... of	the Scandal ... to 9, 11; a Scanda ... to 27
57	11	as it is with	as with 11, 27
	27	*imperas.*	*imperas.* Hor. 9, 11, 27
	29–31	A ... Because	Because a ... For 9, 11, 27
58	2	good	great 9, 11, 27
	5	Point	Thing 9, 11, 27
	11	who	as 9, 11, 27
	20	Use	Uses 9
59	4	than	but 9, 11, 27
	4f.b.	only in a	only a 9, 11, 27
60	24	malignant Disease	one Disease in the Bill of Mortality 9
	27	Banquier	Goldsmith 9, 11, 27
	9f.b.	thither	there 9, 11, 27
	3f.b.	pretends	pretend 9, 11, 27
61	3	that neither Party avow	neither Party will avow 9, 11 neither Party avow 27
	16	mention	therefore mention 9, 11, 27
		a Parliament	the Parliament 9, 11, 27
	5f.b.	the due	a due 9, 11, 27
	4f.b.	return therefore	therefore return 9, 11, 27
62	4	I may possibly	Perhaps I may 9
	3f.b.	*attained*	attainted 27
	2f.b.	at least	at last 13, 27
63	1	one principal	the principal 9, 11, 27
	4	more often	oftner 9, 11, 27

REMARKS upon a Book, intitled, the RIGHTS of the CHRISTIAN CHURCH, &c.

Begun in 1707, and left unfinished. Swift possessed a copy of the third edition of Tindal's book, which came out in 1707, two editions having appeared in 1706. In the *Sale Catalogue* (ed. Harold Williams, 1932, see page 11) it is not marked as being annotated. I assume therefore that Faulkner printed from a manuscript, in which Swift had jotted down references and phrases from Tindal, with his comments. Hawkesworth simply remarks in the Advertisement to vol. 7 of his 4to editions: 'So soon as these were printed in *Dublin*, in a new edition of the Dean's works, it was a justice due to them to select them thence, to complete the *London* edition.' He edits them considerably, enlarging the quotations from Tindal, and eliminating certain difficulties in the text, which were due either to the carelessness of Faulkner's editing or to the imperfections of Swift's uncorrected first draft.

Works 1763 (Faulkner), VOL. X, p. 91.
Works 1764 (Hawkesworth), 4to, VOL. VII, p. 43.
The present text is printed from the Faulkner edition.

Page	Line	PRESENT TEXT	VARIANTS
65	3	1708	1708, but left unfinished. H
66	8	sowered	soured H
	13	find is H	find it F
	8 f.b.	. . .	Thread of F, Train of H
	7 f.b.	. . .	Thread of F, H; Sir W. Scott *omits*
71	28	Fl(e)ame	Flame F; phlegm H
72	21	misrepresentations	misinterpretations H
75	26	receive it, H	receive, it F
76	16	believe, that	believe, H
	28	breathe	breathed F; breath H
	30	Cases	causes H
77	24	refusing	refuse F, H
79	22	*relinques*	*relinquas* H
80	7 f.b.	that	who H
81	7	case H	Cause F
82	5	*pertractandum*	*pertrectentur* H;

(The passage quoted from Tacitus, *Germania*, c. 11, has the reading per- *or* praetractentur, but Swift was probably quoting as usual from memory.)

86	16	he	who H
87	14	83. Ibid.	83 H
92	26	*Rules* H, [as in Tindal's text]	*Rule* F
	31	not be	not to be H
93	b	when	whilst H
94	22	that Some	those some H
	22	*as* H, [as in Tindal's text]	*of* F
95	17	that	which H
96	12	the fewer and poorer the better, and the contrary among the Clergy	the fewer and poorer the clergy the better, and the contrary among the laity H

(The text in Faulkner is obviously corrupt, but I doubt whether the emendation in Hawkesworth is what Swift wrote. It is clear that Swift is simply jotting down a reference to the following sentence of Tindal's: '. . . the more they (the clergy) have in any Nation abounded in Number, Power and Riches, the more Religion has been depraved; and on the contrary, the less Power and Riches they have had, and the fewer their Numbers have been, the more it has been preserv'd pure and intire:' see *Rights of the Christian Church*, sect. 27, p. 211.)

97	17	People are H	People who are F
98	2	*France* famous	*France* is H
	19	you say	as you say H
99	18	his Scheme	this scheme H
	21	Speculations	speculation H
	25	after	when H
	4*f.b.*	meant	means F; is meant H
100	29	misrepresenting	between misrepresenting H
	3*f.b.*	make	which makes H
102	1	loosely put	closely put H
	8	before	to be preferable to H
103	6*f.b.*	Lay	laity H
104	10	strongest	strangest F
105	2	*Ecclesiastical*	ecclesiasticals H
	3	*compose*	composes H
	10	College	colleges H
	14	Laws	law H
	18	were [not] H	were F
106	28	and the latter is	the latter it is H

A LETTER FROM A MEMBER OF THE HOUSE OF COMMONS OF IRELAND etc., CONCERNING THE SACRAMENTAL TEST

First printed in 1709. For facsimile of the title-page, see above, p. 109.
Miscellanies in Prose and Verse, 1711, p. 315.
Miscellanies in Prose and Verse, The First Volume, 1727, p. 215.
The Works of J.S.D.D.D.S.P.D., Dublin, 1735, Vol. IV, p. 1.
The present text is taken from the *Works*, 1735, collated with the *Miscellanies*. Certain errors remained which have been corrected by restoring readings from the first edition, 1709, as shown below. The large omissions which Swift made himself for the *Miscellanies*, 1711, are also printed here.

Page	Line	PRESENT TEXT	VARIANTS
110		Publisher's Advertisement *here printed from* 35	ADVERTISEMENT II
111	7, 8	*Half-title*: OF IRELAND, &c.	in *Ireland*, to a Member of the House of Commons in *England*, concerning the SACRAMENTAL TEST. Written in the Year, 1708. 09, 11, 27
112	5	which Abuse, although	which, tho' 09, 11, 27
	6	was	it was 09, 11, 27
	18	pretend	undertake 09, 11, 27
	19	But sufficient Care hath been taken to explain it.	but Care has been taken to give it sufficient Explanation. 09, 11, 27
113	15	*Presbyterian* Brother.	

Here all earlier editions have the following passage; it was marked for omission in Swift's own copy of the 1727 *Miscellanies*, from which volume it is here printed with certain minor corrections marked by Swift, pp. 219–222.

'The Reason why I mention him, is to have an Occasion of letting you know, that you have not dealt so gallantly with us, as we did with you in a parallel Case: Last Year, a Paper was brought here from *England*, called, *A Dialogue between the Archbishop of* Canterbury *and Mr* Higgins, which we ordered to be burnt by the Common Hangman, as it well deserved, though we have no more to do with his Grace of *Canterbury* than· you have with the Archbishop of *Dublin*; nor can you love and reverence your Prelate more than we do ours, whom you tamely suffer to be abused openly, and by Name, by that Paultry Rascal of an *Observator*; and lately upon an Affair wherein he had no Concern; I mean the Business of the *Missionary* of *Droghedah*, wherein our excellent *Primate* was engaged, and did nothing but according to Law and Discretion. But, because the Lord Archbishop of *Dublin* hath been upon several Occasions of late Years misrepresented in *England*, I would willingly set you right in his Character. For his great Sufferings and eminent Services, he was by the late King promoted to the See of *Derry*. About the same Time he wrote a Book to justify the Revolution, wherein was an Account of King *James's* Proceedings in *Ireland*, and the late Archbishop *Tillotson* recommended it to the King as the most serviceable Treatise that could have been published at such a Juncture. And as his Grace set out upon those[1] Principles, he has proceeded so ever since, as a loyal Subject to the Queen, entirely for the Succession in the Protestant Line, and for ever excluding the *Pretender*; and though a firm Friend to the Church, yet with Indulgence towards Dissenters, as appears from his Conduct at *Derry*, where he was settled for many Years among the most virulent Sect; yet upon his Removal to *Dublin*, they parted from him with Tears in their Eyes, and universal Acknowledgments of his Wisdom and Goodness. For the rest, it must be own'd, he does not busy himself by entering deep into any Party; but rather spends his Time in Acts of Hospitality and Charity, in building of Churches, repairing his Palace; in introducing and preferring the worthiest Persons he can find, without other Regards: In short, in the Practice of all Virtues that can become a publick or private Life. This and more, if possible, is due to so excellent a Person, who may be justly reckoned among the greatest and most learned Prelates of his Age, however his Character may be defiled by such mean and dirty Hands as those of the *Observator*, or such[2] as employ him.'

Page	Line	Present Text	Variants
113	28	attempted to	attempt to 09
	2f.b.	a Step	one Step 09, 11, 27
114	17	*Town* 09	*Towns* 11, 27, 35
	7f.b.	if they had thought they were	had they thought they had been 09, 11, 27
115	5	these two	those two 09, 11, 27
	10-11	the Expression includes a Falsehood; for when King *James* was *Prince*, 09, 11, 27	[line omitted in error in 35]

[1]those Principles   Revolution Principles 09

[2]or such as employ him   { or such as employ him, who ought not to have forgot that in the late Prosecution of *Forbes* for Reflecting on K. *William*, the A.Bp. did so distinguish himself, that the City gave him their publick Thanks. 09

Page	Line	PRESENT TEXT	VARIANTS
	27	it is the same	'tis that 09, 11, 27
	5 f.b.	which equally	that equally 09, 11, 27
116	5	them, who shall S	them shall 09, 11, 27
	15	an industrious	a Brave, industrious 09, 11, 27
117	8	gives 09	give 11, 27, 35
	9	County S	Country 09, 11, 27
		Offices S	Officers 09, 11, 27
	26	that 27	what 11, 35
	9 f.b.	some years ago, in Parliament Time,	in Parliament time (I think it was last Year) 09
	5 f.b.	*the Kingdom.*	*the Kingdom.* Now, because that Gentleman is ambitious to be thought one of our Patriots, I can put him upon a much better way of serving his Countrey, which is to take some Course that himself and his *whole worthy Family* may be *Hang'd* tomorrow Morning; and if this had been done (How long is it since my Lord *Capel's* Government?) about Fifteen Years ago, our miserable *Betrayed* Kingdom had been some Millions the better. 09
118	5–6	any Attempt	an attempt 11, 27
	16	stanch and thorough-paced	stranch and thorow-pace 09
	20	Parliament.	Parliament. I remember when I was last in *England,* I told the King, that the highest Tories we had with us, would make tolerable Whigs there; this was certainly right, and still in the general continues so, unless you have since admitted new Characteristicks, which did not come within our Definition. 09, 11, 27
	27	with an *Indulgence* for scrupulous Consciences;	with a Toleration for Dissenters 09
	28	right Principles	*Revolution* Principles 09
	5 f.b.	a *Conventicle*	*Conventicle* 27
	b	will not	will hardly 09, 11, 27
119	8	our	the *Revolution* 09
	13	rest, with	rest of 27
	15	intire Body . . . is	whole Body . . . are 09, 11, 27
	19	*Refinement*	*Refinements* 09, 11, 27
	20	(N.B. Swift has written in his copy of the *Miscellanies* (1727) in the margin here: *Quantum mutati*)	
	22	Opinions	Opinions 09, 11, 27
	24	Affair	Affairs 09, 11, 27
	8 f.b.	Preacher	Parson 09, 11, 27
120	3	his *Interest.*	

(N.B. In the Advertisement prefixed to this Letter in the *Miscellanies*, 1711, p. 314, Swift wrote: 'I have taken leave to omit about a Page which was purely Personal, and of no use to the Subject.' This refers to the following passage which occurred in the first edition at this point.

'You indeed hint something to me about *Two Divines* of this Kingdom now in *London*, which seems to differ from what I said of the rest. I have not the Honour to be acquainted with either, and I think they have not been much among us; but by what I have heard of them, I do not believe they are one degree greater Whigs than Five Hundred of their Brethren, and I have heard, that *one of them* (who is they say made chief Chaplain to our new Governour) has always declared against Repealing the *Test*; He is reckoned a worthy Person, and I know not how it can be consistent with that Character to employ his Pen either in a Publick or Private manner against his Opinion, neither do I think he designs it. As for the *other Divine*, we all expected here that he was to be the Person his Excellency would bring over his Chaplain: But since that hath otherwise happened, it may not be altogether improbable that his great Friends have dropp'd him, which Disappointment, if he be a right C[our]t[ie]r may chance to cool his Zeal that way, if he had any before, of which I cannot accuse him. However that be, he will find it a difficult matter, with his Skill in Politicks, or Talent at Ridicule, backed by all the Wit he is said to be Master of, to Reason or Laugh us out of the *Sacramental Test*; and will find by the event that my P R E D I C T I O N S are truer than *His*.

But if I am mistaken in my Sentiments of those Two Divines, there is a *Third* now among you, of as much Consideration as either, and as good a Whig in all the necessary Fundamentals, from whose Opinions you may form a truer Judgment of his Brethren here; and I dare engage he will not be reserved in owning them, and besides he has reason to know as much as our House of Commons as any of its Members, his *Office* giving him free Access there at all times.'

Page	Line	PRESENT TEXT	VARIANTS
120	5	Necessity	the Necessity 09, 11, 27
	13	as not to be	not to be 09, 11, 27
	2 f.b.	all	all the 09, 11, 27
121	16	satisfied in	satisfied 09
	3 f.b.	called	call 09, 11, 27
122	14	repine at	grudge us 09, 11, 27
	19	who offered S	that offered 09, 11, 27
124	11	by Law	by a Law 09
	21	who argues S	that argues 09, 11, 27
	2 f.b.	Law	Laws 09, 11, 27
125	20	please.	please. For the other Part of your Letter I can only tell you, that I have Obey'd your Commands as far as it was in my Power, and I hope well enough to encourage you to honour me with more. I am with great Respect, Sir, Dublin, December Yours &c. 09; the 4th, 1708. please. *I am with great Respect, Sir, Your*, &c. 11, 27 Dublin, December *the* 4th, 1708.

A LETTER TO A MEMBER OF PARLIAMENT
IN IRELAND UPON CHOOSING A NEW SPEAKER
THERE

Autograph MS. in Forster Collection, written on 8 quarto pages, with numerous corrections, in Swift's hand, made in part probably at a later date. The letter appears to be unfinished. The manuscript has been folded and endorsed on the back by Swift:

> 'Writt in Ireland
> upon the chusing a
> new Speaker there
> 1708 (as I rememb.)

Works, 1765, (Hawkesworth) (4to ed.) VIII, 128.
Works, 1765, (Faulkner) XII, 203.

The present text gives the readings of the MS., and its spelling and capitalization; but abbreviations and elisions are removed, and punctuation of Faulkner's text adopted. The only variants worth recording seemed to be the earlier readings of the MS.

Page	Line	PRESENT TEXT	UNREVISED READINGS OF MS.
129	12	strange	odd
	14	the two following Circumstances are of great Advantage	there are two Circumstances of great Advantage
	18	zealous	and zealous
	19	Favour	Power
	2 f.b.	Merits	Regularity
130	4	Persons ready to go any	such who would refuse to go no
	5	with onely . . . among	after onely . . . by
	8	Language	Style
	9	affecting	that affected
	12	was still	will still be
	13	Side to be	Side was
	2 f.b.	will, I hope, ever	can possibly
131	14	the onely Hedge	a Hedge
	20	must go	go
	25	prefer a man to a Bishoprick, who denyes revealed Religion.	(1) promote a professed Atheist. (2) promote a man who doubts revealed Religion to a Bishoprick.
	26	possibly be	be
	29	Sollicitor	promoter
132	1–2	I should hardly chuse, even among my Footmen,	you would hardly chuse among yr Footmen
	9	thought	always thought
	18	Side	Party
	24	Importance. Yet	Importance. However this is of such (1) moment (2) a nature as concerns the very Life and Being of that Cause. Yet
	26–27	upon one . . . versed	on one . . . apt
133	7	many	some

Page	Line	Present Text	Variants
	8	dangerous	weighty
	16	seem most reasonable	be more convenient
	23	succeeded but ill	mett but little Success
	25ff.	I have forgot which; but as much I remember, that his Conduct (Behavior) was such as they soon grew weary of him.	whom they soon had Reason to grow weary of.
	8f.b.	that Test	it
	5 f.b.	a sort of Contravention to	in fact to repeal
134	18	Lenity	Gentleness
	21	new	further
	25	hyperbolicall way of reckoning, when it came to be	Hyperbole, when
	8f.b.	Swarm	number
	5f.b.	joyning with	uniting to
	4f.b.	by their Agents placed a good Sum of money to engage	by a good Sum of money engaged
135	1	any	the least
	2	Whereupon	upon which
	3–4	as I remember to about	to
	6	took the other handle	altered his Language
	11	would onely serve to	might

BICKERSTAFF PAPERS

Note: All the genuine Bickerstaff papers were reprinted in the following collections.

Miscellanies, 1711, p. 259. (2nd Edition, 1713, p. 259.)

Miscellanies, 1727, i, 261. *Works*, 1735, i, 148.

The present text of these papers is printed from the *Works*, 1735, collated with the *Miscellanies* and the original editions.

1. PREDICTIONS FOR THE YEAR 1708.

First printed by John Morphew as a small 8vo of 8 pages. See facsimile of title-page, p. 139 above. A number of pirated editions immediately followed, printed by T. Wise, John Stiles, and by W.B., and another without any imprint. An Irish reprint, and German and Dutch translations appeared also in the same year.

Page	Line	Present Text	Variants
141	9	Having long	I having long 11; I have long 08
	10	upon S	and upon 08, 11, 27
	18	this noble	that noble 08, 11, 27
142	15	But I rather	but rather 08, 11, 27
	25	Grammar	common Grammar 08, 11, 27
	27	to write	correct 08; write 11
143	11	fell out 08, 11, 27	unluckily fell out 35
	14	*Drinks* 08, 11	*Drink* 27, 35
	25	two last	last two 08

Page	Line	PRESENT TEXT	VARIANTS
	4 f.b.	at such	in such 08, 11
144	2	upon	on 08, 11, 27
		found	find 08, 11, 27
	14	Point	Thing 08, 11, 27
	16	might	would 08, 11, 27
	17	such as	that 08, 11, 27
	28	learned Persons	Learned 08, 11, 27
	32	assure that	assure 08, 11, 27
	37	evil	bad 08, 11, 27
	38	depending S	depend 08, 11, 27
145	18	those	these 08, 11
	20	Star S	Stars 11, 27
	31	such Events	it is 08, 11, 27
	4 f.b.	in some 08, 11, 27	some 35
146	27	which many . . . were to	that many . . . should 08, 11, 27
	6 f.b.	talk 08, S	walk 11, 27
147	12	Intention	Intentions 08, 11
148	5	the Break	Break 08, 11, 27
149	2	It may	It will 08, 11, 27
	22	Cast 11, 27	Last 08
	23	Scribbles 08, S	Scribblers 11, 27
	24	writing	Scribbling 08, 11, 27
	29	it is no 11, 27	it no 08

2. THE ACCOMPLISHMENT OF THE FIRST OF MR BICKERSTAFF'S PREDICTIONS.

First printed in a small 4to of 4 pages with a half-title (facsimile, see p. 151) and the imprint *London*: Printed in the Year 1708. [This is extremely rare. The copy which was in the Armagh Library can no longer be found. President W. A. Eddy kindly lent me his photograph of the copy in Yale University Library.]

Page	Line	PRESENT TEXT	VARIANTS
154	9	Hours 08, 11	Time 13, 27, 35
	12	I was sorry	how sorry I was 08, 11, 27
	14	ingenuously	ingeniously 08
	30	judge	know 08, 11, 27
155	14	Discourse	Discourses 08, 11, 27
	19	almost stifled	half stifled 08, 11, 27

3. A VINDICATION OF ISAAC BICKERSTAFF ESQ.

First printed in a small 8vo of 8 pages in 1709. For facsimile of title-page, see p. 157.

Page	Line	PRESENT TEXT	VARIANTS
159	b.	ingenuous 09, 11	ingenious 27, 35
160		(These footnotes clearly added by Swift himself.)	
161	1	*magnum illud Angliae sidus.* —Another great Professor writing of me, has these words: *Bickerstaffius,* 09, 11, 27	(By the printer's error omitted in 35)
	11	these Examples	this Example

Page	Line	PRESENT TEXT	VARIANTS
	14	Errors 09, 11, 27	Error 35
	27	first is	first was 09, 11, 27
	8 f.b.	Cause	Case 09, 11, 27
162	13	Almanacks	Almanack 09
	19	But now, 11, 27, 35	Secondly, Death is defined by all Philosophers, a Separation of the Soul and Body. Now it is certain, that the poor Woman who has best Reason to know, has gone about for some time to every Alley in the Neighbourhood, and swore to the Gossips, that *Her Husband had neither Life nor Soul in him.* Therefore 09
	22	Boy 11, S	Body 13, 27
	25	Secondly	Thirdly 09
	30	Thirdly	Fourthly 09
	2 f.b.	the 29th	that 29th 11, 27
163	2	he be	he is 11, 27
	5	Fourthly	Fifthly 09
	8	is an	in an 09, 11, 27
	17	*four*	*two* 09
	20	was 09, 11, 27	were 35
164	3	become	became 09
	5	Death.	Death: Or, perhaps a Name can *make* an Almanack, as well as it can *sell* one. And to strengthen this Conjecture, I have heard the Booksellers affirm, That they have desired Mr *Partridge* to spare himself further Trouble, and only lend them his Name, which could make Almanacks much better than himself. 09
	10	these	those 11, 27
	13	Hawkers	Hawkers of Grubstreet. 09
	17	*will shew*	*would shew* 11, 27
	25	but that . . . For	that . . . But 11, 27
	27-28	foretold; and not four Hours sooner . . . so gross a Mistake.	foretold. 09

A FAMOUS PREDICTION OF MERLIN

First printed as a Half-sheet with the imprint *London: Printed and Sold by H. Baldwin,* . . . *MDCCIX.*

For facsimile, see p. 165.

Another edition printed by H. Hills, 1708.

Another printed in Edinburgh by James Wilson, 1709.

Miscellanies, 1711, p. 305 (2nd ed., 1713, p. 303).

Miscellanies, 1727, ii, 253.
Works, 1735, i, 238.

Page	Line	PRESENT TEXT	VARIANTS
167	15	learnedly vindicated	vindicated 09, 11, 27
	17	farther Defence	further Vindication 09
			farther Vindication 11, 27
168	14	Ripe 09, 11, 27	Rife 35
	23	make	makes 09, 11, 27
	b	could	would 09, 11, 27
169	6	*Dauphin*	Dolphin 09, 11
	7	the Kings	their Kings 09, 11, 27
	11	should	shall 09, 11
	b	[note added in 35]	
170	4	overturning	Overcoming 09, 11

PAPERS CONTRIBUTED TO THE TATLER

The three papers included in the *Works*, 1735, and therefore presumed to be acknowledged by Swift as wholly his work, are here printed from Faulkner's text collated with the text of the original *Tatler* and that of the first collected edition, and the following variants noted.

1. *TATLER* No. 230, Sept. 28, 1710.

Page	Line	PRESENT TEXT	VARIANTS
175	9	of it	in it 10, 11
	3 *f.b.*	of words	our Words 10, 11
176	1	*Plenipo's*	*Plenipo* 10, 11
	3	had made	has made 10, 11
	25	Arguments	Argument 10, 11
	4 *f.b.*	sparing of	sparing in 10, 11
	3 *f.b.*	On this Head	And upon this Head 10, 11
177	1	fraught	fraight 10, 11
	10	*a great Noise*	*most Noise* 10, 11
	16	human Life	Life 10, 11

2. *TATLER* (Harrison's Continuation No. 5, January 27, 1710–11.)
Collated with Vol. V of collected editions (1) 1712 and (2) 1720.

Page	Line	PRESENT TEXT	VARIANTS
178	12	Nature	Natures 12, 20
	17	might	should 12, 20
	25	could	would 12, 20
179	9	adapted to please	to please 12
	13	Impertinence	Impertinences 12
	14	who	that 12
	15	*Serving-Men of low Degree*	Serving-Men of low Degree 12
180	7	her Bones	the Bones 12, 20
	26	came	has been 12, 20
181	10–11	after the Company should be gone	when the Company F was gone 12, 20
182	8 *f.b.*	who	that 12
	2 *f.b.*	a male Animal	an Animal of that Sex 12, 20
183	13	*five Months*	Four Months 12

II   u

3. *TATLER* (Harrison's Continuation No. 20, March 6, 1710–11.)
Collated with original paper (10) and with VOL. V of collected editions (1)
1712 and (2) 1720.

Page	Line	PRESENT TEXT	VARIANTS
184	10	*les petites Morales* 20	*les petite Morale* 10, 12
	4 f.b.	put	forced 12, 20
185	3	The Girl	she 12, 20
	11	were	was 10, 12, 20
	25	Apologies	Apology 10, 12, 20
186	7	desired 20	had desired 10, 12
	21	in the Rules	of the Rules 10, 12, 20
	27	every Occasion	all Occasions 10, 12, 20
	4 f.b.	who are not of	that are not 10, 12, 20
	2 f.b.	some among	some of 10, 12, 20
187	1	Religion and Morality, except	Morality, or Religion but, 10, 12, 20
	7	may serve	serves 10, 12, 20
	10	likely	like 10, 12, 20
	12	but converseth	that he converses 10, 12, 20
	15	may perhaps a little excuse him	makes some Amends for it, 10, 12, 20

APPENDICES

A. The text of *The Presentment of the Grand Jury etc.* is taken from Swift's *Works* 1763 (Faulkner) Vol. X, pp. 86–90.

B. The text of *An Answer to Bickerstaff* is taken from Swift's *Works* 1765 (Hawkesworth) 4to, Vol. VIII, pp. 232–7.

The text of *Mr Partridge's Answer to Bickerstaff's Predictions* is taken from a photostat of the copy in the Bodleian Library (Ashmole, 1819 (27)). Corrections of obvious misprints have been made.

The text of *A Continuation of the Predictions for the Remaining Part of 1708* is taken from a photostat of a copy in the Library of Emmanuel College, Cambridge, which was very kindly brought to my notice by Mr Bennett.

The text of *'Squire Bickerstaff Detected* is taken from Swift's *Works* 1735 (Faulkner) Vol. I, pp. 167–76.

The text of the extract from Partridge's *Merlinus Liberatus for 1709* is taken from the copy in the Bodleian Library.

The title-page and extract from *Bickerstaff's Almanack for 1710* is taken from a photostat of the copy in the Yale College Library, kindly lent to me by President William A. Eddy.

C. The contributions to *The Tatler* and *The Spectator* included here are reprinted from copies of the first collected editions.

Addendum to Appendix B. The text of *Bickerstaff's Prediction confirmed . . . with farther Predictions for October to December, 1708* is taken from a photostat of the copy in the possession of Professor D. Nichol Smith, who very kindly drew my attention to it, and allowed me to reproduce it here. It would seem to be very rare.

THE INDEX